12·75₂

WITHDRAWN

# The Sociology of Urban Education

# The Sociology of Urban Education

**Desegregation and Integration**

**Charles Vert Willie**
Harvard University

**Lexington Books**
D.C. Heath and Company
Lexington, Massachusetts
Toronto

**Library of Congress Cataloging in Publication Data**

Willie, Charles V.
    The sociology of urban education.

    Includes index.
    1. School integration—United States.  2. Education, Urban—United
States.  I. Title.
LC214.2.W54                    370.19'348'0973                    78-4403
ISBN 0-669-02348-5

Published simultaneously in Canada

Printed in the United States of America

International Standard Book Number:  0-669-02348-5

Library of Congress Catalog Card Number:  78-4403

# Contents

# List of Tables

# Preface

Education in a nation most of which is urban essentially is urban education. Because cities and metropolitan areas are places to which all sorts and conditions of people have come, pluralism is a central concern for urban education. Pluralism is at once a liability or an opportunity. Whether it is one or the other depends largely on how well cultural and racial desegregation and integration are handled. Sooner or later desegregation and integration will affect all. Pluralism is the essence of urban society.

In the United States, local educational authorities are creatures of the state. And state educational authorities must uphold the federal Constitution which guarantees equal protection of the laws to all citizens. As long as education remains a compulsory experience for children and is supported by public funds, educational opportunities provided must be equitable and fair. The Supreme Court of the United States has determined that segregated education is inherently unequal education. Thus, desegregation and integration are the challenges confronting urban education in the cities and suburbs of this nation.

In the past, communities adapted to segregated educational systems by denying their culpability. Such systems, said community leaders, were the unanticipated consequences of voluntary action in a free society. By denying that they were the problem, few communities accepted responsibility for providing solutions to segregated education. Thus plans and procedures to achieve desegregation and integration were seldom proposed. Communities that denied that people of specific racial and cultural groups had been deliberately excluded were not about to develop plans that used racial and cultural characteristics of people as the basis for determining whom to include in their educational system. Most cities and metropolitan areas, therefore, face court orders to desegregate with little, if any, advance preparation. Consequently, their integration plans frequently were faulty, seldom profited from past experiences, were *ad hoc*, and were not based on theory.

The material presented in this book should enable parents, pupils, educational policymakers, planners, and public officials who oversee public education to develop a conceptual approach to desegregation and integration and replace the trial-and-error action of the past. The discussion is both theoretical and operational, philosophical and pragmatic. Desegregation and integration in elementary and secondary public schools are emphasized. The college scene, however, is not omitted as so often is the case in most discussions on this topic. A full and frank analysis is presented on the meaning of racial and cultural differences and the implications of these for a constitutional democracy based on laws enacted by representatives of the people. Minorities are cast in the role of creative dissenters who contribute to social change and educational reform by refusing to go along with custom and tradition.

This book then serves as a manual in educational politics, a treatise on race relations, an operational guide for school desegregation, and as a resource in urban education and the sociology of education. The perspective essentially is sociological but draws additionally upon the disciplines of social psychology, anthropology, and population genetics. Social change, human development, and interdependence are endemic themes that link all chapters.

The author is grateful to Praeger Publishers for granting permission to republish the chapters that have to do with integration in elementary and secondary schools and the role of the principal and teachers that first appeared in *Race Mixing in the Public Schools.*

I am indebted to my editorial consultant Dorothy Judd Sickels, who was both cheerleader and copyeditor, dispensing advice and encouragement as this project unfolded; to Ann Craig, formerly administrative assistant for the Black College Project at Harvard, who prepared this manuscript in typescript; the Maurice Falk Medical Fund and its president, Philip Hallen, supported the writing of this book with a generous grant. Despite these supports, this book would have remained unwritten without the tender loving care of my wife, Mary Sue, and the affection of our children, Sarah Susannah, Martin Charles, and James Theodore. On them I bestow all glory and honor. Their courage, commitment, and compassion make desegregation and integration a living and loving reality.

# Introduction: Testimony about the Past, Present, and Possible

**Mr. Howard A. Glickstein:** The next witness is Dr. Charles Willie.

**Chairman Eugene Patterson:** Dr. Willie, would you raise your right hand, please? Do you swear that the testimony you are about to give is the truth, the whole truth and nothing but the truth, so help you God?

**Dr. Willie:** I do.

**Chairman Patterson:** Please be seated. Will counsel proceed.

**Mr. Glickstein:** What is your academic background, Dr. Willie?

**Dr. Willie:** I am an urban sociologist. I have conducted several studies in community organization. Specifically, I have conducted a study on the assimilation of youngsters who were bused from inner-city schools to predominantly white schools in Centralia. And this study was conducted over a two-year period: the report on the study is just being concluded. The study was conducted in cooperation with Dr. Jerome Beker, who was the principal investigator.

**Mr. Glickstein:** Can you give the commissioners, please, some idea of what these studies of the integration efforts in Centralia revealed?

**Dr. Willie:** Yes, some of our studies dealt with achievement, but other studies with adjustment, accommodation, or assimilation. The assimilation studies were concerned with the acceptance of students—that is, whether the students who were bused felt that they were part of the schools and accepted by the students in the schools to which they were bused, as well as whether they accepted other students. Most of the material which I have to report has to do with the assimilation of the students rather than their achievement. We found that black students who were bused from the inner-city assimilated into the middle-class schools about as well as middle-class white children who also were new to those schools. A unique aspect of our study was that it was not limited to an investigation of black children who were bused from the inner city only;

---

In accordance with an agreement with the superintendent of the school district studied, a fictitious name is used. The testimony was given at a public hearing of the United States Civil Rights Commission in Rochester, New York. The city and school names are pseudonyms. Chapters 9, 10, and 11 cover in great detail the schools mentioned in this introduction, and the same pseudonyms are used. It was the research discussed in this hearing that has guided my proposals for school desegregation in Boston and elsewhere.

the idea occurred to us that maybe the problems black inner-city youngsters experience in schools in which they are new may be problems that any new youngsters would experience. So we investigated youngsters who were new to the schools because their parents had recently moved into the neighborhood, and we investigated youngsters who were new to the schools because they were bused from the inner-city schools. We found that there was no difference in the self-perceived adjustment of youngsters who came from the inner city and middle-class youngsters who lived in the neighborhood but were new to these schools.

**Mr. Glickstein**: Were your studies at the Simpson School?

**Dr. Willie**: Yes, my studies include the Simpson School, the Lincoln School, the Monroe School, and the Highland School, two elementary schools and two junior high schools.

**Mr. Glickstein**: I think the superintendent of schools suggested that because the children in the Simpson School were studied so much, it might have interfered with their performance. Did you think there was any validity to that?

**Dr. Willie**: Well, this is a matter of opinion. My opinion would differ.

**Mr. Glickstein**: Were there a lot of people studying the children in the school when you were there?

**Dr. Willie**: At the Simpson School we had one participant-observer who stayed in the school the entire year and observed the school about ten hours per week. I don't think it was the researching that was the problem at Simpson, if there was a problem. I think that the problem at Simpson was the school atmosphere. You see, much of our discussion of what happens to children is focused upon the individual child without recognizing that the school provides a system within which the child functions. Simpson School in Centralia has a reputation of being the most enlightened school. It is the school where many of the college faculty send their children. Its teachers, its principal, and its parents, many of its parents, were very much concerned that the busing of fifty to sixty black youngsters from the inner city would lower that school's overall achievement rating. Therefore, they were very tense and not very accepting of the children in the beginning. I might add that toward the end of the year the faculty and staff at Simpson did relax. In spite of the fact that the teachers were tense in the beginning, the children liked Simpson; so I think that in terms of social adjustment, attendance at Simpson was not a negative experience for the black youngsters who were bused there. But in terms of the school personnel themselves, they were a little jittery, and they didn't "sit easy in the saddle."

**Mr. Glickstein:** What is the effect on children of busing them out of their neighborhoods? Do you have an opinion on that?

**Dr. Willie:** Well, of course, busing is not unique in the cities. It's been going on for a long time in the suburban schools, and I've said in one published paper that some of the Presidents of our country came from schools that were not neighborhood schools. As a matter of fact, they were private schools distant from their home setting. So I can't see any negative effect of going to a school outside one's neighborhood. Going to school within one's neighborhood may be a convenience, but I don't know of any evidence which indicates a correlation between what one learns and the convenience one experiences in learning it. As a matter of fact, some forms of convenience are contrary to our American ideal of ruggedness, such as walking miles to school like Abraham Lincoln and other famous people. So I can't see any correlation at all between learning and the nearby location of a school. I think the important thing is the kind of school one attends; and I would say most important is the attitude of the school superintendent. Second to that would be the attitude of the principal, and after that the teachers. They provide the atmosphere. And I mean this very candidly because the parents don't have an opportunity to do very much about what goes on in a school. It's the school system (dominated by the principal and the teachers) that determines what kind of education the children get.

**Mr. Glickstein:** Dr. Willie, do you believe that a compensatory education program such as the Monroe Area Project, carried out in a segregated or predominantly black school, can improve the performance of the students?

**Dr. Willie:** My reaction to that is not a direct answer. I never have seen a real compensatory program, and I don't think that there ever will be a compensatory program as long as there are segregated schools. The reason for separating people in the first place is so they can be treated differently. In Centralia, for example, the so-called compensatory program in Monroe School paid differential salaries to teachers. You know, the inner city is supposed to be a hardship area. As soon as the money from the federal government and the Ford Foundation—well, I don't know if the federal government contributed—but I will say this: as soon as the money from the Ford Foundation ran out, the compensatory salaries were reduced.

**Mr. Glickstein:** Teachers in Monroe were paid more money?

**Dr. Willie:** That is right; but the increased salaries for teachers were reduced as soon as the Foundation grant ran out, which means to me that there was not a commitment on the part of the Centralia community to make the Monroe inner-city school a better school. So the compensatory programs that have been suggested, I have never really seen in operation and to the fullest extent.

**Mr. Glickstein:** Are compensatory programs in your judgment generally regarded as black programs?

**Dr. Willie:** Yes, I think so. The only way you get a good school system is the entire city has to be behind it. And we will never get good schools until all people throughout the city have some investment in all of the schools; this is why I'm very much in favor of integrated education rather than attempts at compensatory segregated education. I've lived a long time as a black person and I know myself that it's very seldom that people are concerned about me unless there is some other investment they have in me other than just my own well-being.

**Mr. Glickstein:** Do you think then that black children will experience an increase in learning when they are placed in an integrated classroom?

**Dr. Willie:** I think it isn't the integrated schoolroom alone that contributes to increased learning; I think an integrated classroom means that the school system will spend more money on all of its schools. Our Centralia school board president indicated that he had a misconception about what compensatory education would bring before it was tried in Centralia without much success. I think his misconception was based on the fact that he never had any children who had gone to school in a slum-area or inner-city school. So, to the extent that white children go to school in a slum-area school, they and their parents will have some understanding of what goes on in that kind of school. To the extent that black children go to school in a nonslum-area school, they and their parents will have some understanding of what goes on in that school. What I'm saying is this: in the pluralistic society in which we live people have to get all mixed up to understand each other and, I would add, to trust each other. I would think that all of our schools, in order to provide the best education for knowledge as well as character, have got to start mixing up our children as a matter of policy.

**Mr. Glickstein:** Dr. Willie, what steps do you see as necessary to achieve a successful integration of the schools?

**Dr. Willie:** Well, I personally favor centralized campus school programs, (also known as educational parks) rather than neighborhood schools because I think that this is one way of operating fewer buildings but providing more resources to do the kind of educational job that we ought to do for our black and white children. I think white children are being shortchanged in the educational situation as well as black children; so I favor centralized campus schools appropriately placed throughout the city, because I think they offer a possibility of responding to changing neighborhood patterns better and of providing the kinds of resources that we need to offer the best kind of education for all children. My only concern about campus schools as a way of successfully integrating the schools is that I don't really see any commitment on the part of our city governments to moving ahead with them fast. And if I understand the feeling in many of the ghettos, the people are saying that they are not going to wait. So this is the thing that really bothers me. But if we could go ahead with campus plans immediately as a replacement for the neighborhood school concept, I think that we would be in a position to solve many of the problems pertaining to quality education as well as racial integration.

**Mr. Glickstein:** As an urban sociologist, knowing the difficulties in many urban areas of getting around the city, do you think that campus-type schools are practical?

**Dr. Willie:** Oh, of course I think campus-type schools are practical. I think they are practical beyond the fact of achieving integration. They are really in accord with a trend in the urban community; I mean they are in accord with the trend of locating facilities in places where they can perform at their highest level. We have moved factories out of the center of the city to places where we could establish horizontal production lines. Many people go past many churches in order to go to a particular style of church they are interested in. So I think the development of campus-type schools is in keeping with a trend not only in education, but a trend found in other segments of our urban society. This is why I think the movement toward campus-type schools is the best movement to get the quality education we need. We certainly found in the suburban and rural areas that the one-room schoolhouse in the neighborhood could not provide the quality education we needed; by centralizing schools, suburban and rural areas provided a better quality of education. I think within cities, also, we will have to do this.

**Mr. Glickstein:** Thank you. I have no further questions, Mr. Chairman.

**Part I:**
**Urban Education Issues**

# 1 Urbanization, Diversification, and Education

This discussion of education, urban problems, and the pluralistic populations of the city sets the stage for a more detailed analysis in later chapters. The issue of universal education is examined, the role of subdominant and dominant people of power in educational decision-making, how some schools adapt to desegregation, and the consequences of their adaptation for integration.

Several years ago, sociologist Louis Wirth wrote an essay which has become a classic and which is entitled "Urbanism as a Way of Life." In that essay, he pointed out the simple but profound fact that "increasing the number of inhabitants in a settlement beyond a certain limit will affect the relationships between them and the character of the city."[1] Wirth indicated a dimension of the urbanized industrial society to which our attention should be turned today; and that dimension is the nature of the interaction among large heterogeneous masses of people who occupy a limited geographic area. In urban communities there is intense interaction among people of diversified interests and backgrounds who are uncontrolled by the "bonds of kinship, of neighborliness, and the sentiments arising out of living together for generations under a common folk tradition."[2]

If our educational system is to be in line with the needs of the contemporary situation — that is, if we are to help young people fulfill themselves in the urbanized industrial society — we must educate them for life in a pluralistic community. They must learn how to develop a sense of community among heterogeneous and diversified people. This requires cosmopolitan skills of indirect communication, coordination and negotiation as well as the more traditional skills of face-to-face interaction in the folk community. Thus far, our schools have been slow to respond to the pressing need to teach people how to create a sense of community among pluralistic populations.

The phrases "poor motivation" and "poor attitude" are but camouflaging verbiage that cover up the poor effort at creating community in school and elsewhere by the adult and affluent members of society. They will not reach out to deprive, disadvantaged, or alientated youth to provide opportunities for them in the mainstream of society. We tend to attribute to others the problems which are our own. Thus, youths who are pushed out of school because schools are not flexible enough and sufficiently creative to accommodate their special needs are labeled "dropouts." This label places the onus on the child and not on the school. Poor, fearful, lower-class families who have been rejected by welfare agencies are classified as "unccoperative clients." This label places the

3

responsibility on the family and not on the agency. We have used these techniques to rationalize the inadequacies of a society that cares but does not care enough for the poor, oppressed, and afflicted. When outreach is in good faith, alienated young people tend to respond and a sense of community is experienced.

Georgetown University proved that youth from inner-city areas of Washington respond well when opportunities to participate in the educational mainstream of community life are offered. Fifty-one high-school seniors were invited to the campus during a summer session to participate in an eight-week college orientation program consisting of English, chemistry, and mathematics courses and field trips. Ninety-eight percent of the young people remained in the program the entire period. They had a full day of classes but did not receive high-school or college credit. One-fourth of the students with averages below B for the spring semester in high school performed at B or A levels during the summer at Georgetown. Chemistry and English were the courses in which the most dramatic improvement occurred. For example, more than half of the youths with below-B averages for the spring semester in high school worked at B or A levels in chemistry during the summer. Moreover, the university faculty members who taught these high-school seniors felt that they could recommend three out of every four for college on the basis of their summer's performance.

We know that low-income black families are acquainted with the good life and want it for their children. We surveyed a randomly selected sample of 1,000 households in a deprived and predominantly black neighborhood in Washington, D.C. Respondents were asked to tell what they hoped each of their children would do when he or she grew up. About half replied that job preference is for the child to decide. Of the remaining number who had specific occupational preferences, 90 percent wanted their child to be a professional worker such as a doctor, lawyer, engineer, minister, teacher, nurse, or social worker. Moreover, these low-income, unskilled, or unemployed workers in our sample were aware of the educational requirements for professional work. These families had dreamed no small dreams. Their aspirations were high. But their means of fulfilling them were small. Their encounter with racial discrimination had been real. In summary, they experienced a blocked opportunity system.

After facing up to the problem as it actually is, the next task is to devise an appropriate methodology for solving it. In general, two alternatives lie before us − one, change the individual, and the other, change the system and its institutional procedures. Attempts to change the individual are easier because a person is vulnerable and defenseless. Attempts to change the system are more difficult because institutions are structured, regularized, and time-honored. But change the institutional system we must, if school people are to be more than a Band-Aid brigade.

Helping deprived, disadvantaged, and alienated youth is necessary and essential. However, these efforts must be viewed in proper perspective as acts of rehabilitation. Changing the system that generates alienation and deprivation is an act of prevention. While tackling the backlog of past misdeeds requires much time and may appear to be overwhelming, we must also assign part of our energy to prevention activities if the same problems we are working so hard to overcome today will not be visited upon future generations.

Leslie Wilkins has reminded us of the limitation of our approach to crime control, which focuses largely on individuals. Wilkins pointed out that it is easy to say of the criminal, "He did it—deal with him." He also said that "crime has *not* been considered as a failure of social controls but has been simplified to the wrong doing of single persons or gangs." "It should be clear," he concluded, "that dealing with him has not solved the problem of crime and seems unlikely to do so . . . ." According to Wilkins, there are social as well as personal control mechanisms, and to operate on only half of the problem (that is, the personal mechanism) may not solve even half of it, let alone the whole.[3]

The same may be said of problems of deprivation and alienation of individuals in the school. To focus only on the deprived or alienated child without considering also the social system which limits the child's opportunity and blocks his or her progress may not solve even half of the problem and certainly not the whole.

One of the major institutional changes school systems must make if they desire to overcome the alienating effects of racial and socio-economic segregation is to renounce commitment to the concept of the neighborhood school. The neighborhood schools are likely to be unequal and therefore contribute to a dual school system within a single school district; on this basis, they cannot be justified in a free society that guarantees equal protection of the laws for black, brown, and white people.

No one argued about the virtues of the neighborhood high school in Dallas, Texas, before the 1950s when I attended Lincoln High School for blacks in that city. Although my family lived in the western sector of Dallas, in a neighborhood called Oak Cliff, my brothers and sister and all of our playmates traveled by bus several miles to the southern sector of Dallas to attend high school; and we paid our own bus fare. The only other high school for blacks was in the northern sector. There were high schools in the Oak Cliff neighborhood; but they were for whites only. This was during the era of segregation. Then, the neighborhood school was not exalted when blacks were bused elsewhere. The concept of the neighborhood school, therefore, was not relevant in the city of my youth. Had the little Willie boys and girl attended the neighborhood high school in Dallas in the 1930s, 1940s, or 1950s there would have been unmistakable racial integration.

As the black population in cities has increased during the second half of the twentieth century and as this increase has been limited largely to ghettolike neighborhoods in the central city, the concept of the neighborhood school has assumed greater relevance in education. One suspects that the concept of the neighborhood school has been assuming increasing importance since the Supreme Court's decision against segregated school systems.

Boarding schools have been attended by the children of the affluent for years. They certainly are not neighborhood schools; yet, they graduate many persons of good character and sound mind. Can it be that neighborhood schools are recommended as a way of containing blacks, other minorities, and the poor? The concept of the neighborhood school should remain an open issue in public education. It needs more study and analysis, particularly from the point of view of its possible association with segregation, alienation, and deprivation, and the denial of equal protection of the laws for children of all races who are compelled to attend school to receive an education.

Another institutional change that would enhance the capacity of schools to educate pluralistic urban populations would be deliberate diversification of administrative and teaching personnel. The racial composition of the teaching staff of many big-city schools tends to reflect the racial composition of the neighborhoods in which these schools are located. There are school principals who are black, but few of them are principals of schools in predominantly white neighborhoods. Moreover, the schools in predominantly black neighborhoods tend to have many black faculty members and the schools in predominantly white neighborhoods tend to have predominantly white faculties. The argument is made frequently that teachers prefer to teach in schools that are near their homes. This reasoning suggests that one of the primary variables in a quality educational experience is the residential location of the instructor. I disagree. No study of which I am aware has found any correlation between the teaching talents of an instructor and his or her residential address. Furthermore, a diversified teaching staff provides a distinct educational experience for the student and is beneficial beyond the fact that an affirmative action employment requirement is fulfilled.

Every school in a city system could have an integrated teaching staff of men and women teachers. What better way to teach students that people of different racial and ethnic groups can live together peacefully than to show them daily that black, brown, and white people can work together as teaching colleagues?

We must make these and other institutional changes in the school system to overcome the festering problems of deprivation and alienation which are contributed to by segregation. Changes in an individual's behavior may or may not affect the community's institutional systems. But changes in the institutional system usually produce changes in individual behavior. This kind of change tends to be more enduring because it is sanctioned and supported. The time has come not only to redeem the fallen individual but to modify the system that contributed to his or her downfall.

We still concentrate out efforts on changing the individual, although after two world wars and several other lesser wars, we know that good individuals do not automatically give rise to good societies. There were many good individuals in Nazi Germany when millions of Jews were murdered by the state. There were many good individuals in the United States in the early 1940s when loyal Japanese-Americans were uprooted from their West Coast homes and detained in relocation camps, like prisoners, by the state. We cannot create a sense of community by limiting our educational concerns to the development of intellectual gifts and occupational skills of individuals only. The record of the past is against this approach in education.

Consider the purpose of Harvard as stated in the 1650 Charter: "The advancement of all good literature, arts, and science." Skills in the development and understanding of knowledge in these fields were necessary for the learned leaders: clergymen and statesmen.[4] Unlike the past, however, our learned leaders of today are not limited to the clergy and public administrators; neither are they members of the middle and upper social classes only. Our colleges and universities are still places for training and educating leaders. But the demand today placed upon educational institutions is to seek out and educate all sorts of leaders—those in the upper, middle, and lower classes—for the public good.

If the school is a place where we search for truth, it is a distinct advantage to have a diversified student body, because truth often emerges out of the clashing of ideas. Plato believed that philosophers should rule the state because of the union of qualities they possessed, the most important of which was their love for truth. But Plato erred in thinking that truth is an inherent quality of any single category of people. It is not that anyone intentionally caters to falsehood. Rather, each person's version of truth is conditioned by his or her station in life, self-image, experiences in the past, and aspirations for the future. Thus a student body that consisted only of persons who aspired to be clergy or members of any single occupational category is likely to find itself in a dull educational environment. And the truth which it discovers is likely to be deficient.

An issue in the Syracuse, New York, public school system during the 1960s demonstrates how one's assessment of success or failure is associated with one's station in life and the perspective from which he or she evaluates life circumstances. The board of education transferred fifty to sixty black children from an inner-city elementary school with a predominantly black student body to a predominantly white elementary school in a middle-class neighborhood. The president of the school board, who was white, Protestant, and a captain of industry said that he was in favor of busing programs because he had become convinced that programs of compensatory education are not very effective in schools in the slums. Obviously, the president of the school board valued high achievement and believed that white children who experience education in privileged settings had a responsibility to share these experiences with persons who have experienced more disadvantaged circumstances.

The president of the Syracuse Board of Education, however, opposed the busing of white children into predominantly black inner-city schools. But when sufficient pressure was brought upon the school board to equalize the burden of busing through an integration plan for whites to attend an inner-city school with a predominantly black student body, the school board agreed to bus white children into a predominantly black inner-city school and to provide extra services in that school only if enough white children volunteered so that they would become a majority. The plan was adopted without enthusiasm and the public campaign to recruit white students to transfer voluntarily was not launched until three weeks before the opening of school. The board of education recommended that 700 white students should be recruited for the inner-city school, which had a capacity for 1,000 students. Had this number been reached, the school no longer would have had a predominantly black student body. Because of the circumstance under which the project was launched, only sixty-eight white children signed up to transfer to the inner-city school. These children would have been a minority in that school.

The president of the school board stated that the effort was a failure because of the small number of whites who volunteered, and the plan to bus white children into the inner-city school was canceled. My assessment of the program was quite different. My own background has been that of a minority person who was educated in ghetto public schools. While the circumstances of life for members of a minority population may be disadvantaged from one perspective, they are advantaged from another. To persevere in the face of great adversity, the members of a minority must develop courage. Not only that, the members of a minority know the humility of receiving because they have to trust others on whom their safety depends. The development of courage, humility, and trust are but a few advantages that flow from being a member of the minority. These characteristics might well benefit members of the majority who in some circumstances may become the minority. Courage, humility, and trust are good qualities to cultivate and they should be cultivated by all. Sixty-eight white children who volunteered to become minority members of an inner-city, predominantly black school could have begun learning about these. But the board of education canceled the opportunity for a new kind of learning by whites because the board did not understand the many benefits that result from being a member of a minority population.

When fifty to sixty black inner-city children volunteered to attend a predominantly white school in a middle-class neighborhood a year earlier, the president of the school board considered that program to be successful. But when sixty to seventy white children volunteered to attend a predominantly black school, he considered that program to be a failure. The numbers involved in the two programs were about the same, but the perspective of the board president varied according to the situation, his values, and his position in life. A black student who was a minority in a white setting was acceptable; but a white student who would be a minority in a black setting was not acceptable.

In terms of the station in life which I have occupied and the perspective that I bring, there are advantages in living the life of a minority. And so I would have considered the program to be successful which would have exposed sixty-eight white children to these advantages. I am not suggesting, however, that my assessment of the situation is right and that the assessment of the president of the school board was wrong. Each of us possessed partial truth, based upon a limited view of reality and the perspective of a particular set of circumstances. The truth emerges only when differing assessments have an opportunity to encounter each other in open competition.

No one—saint or sinner, philosopher or fool—can fully know the truth because the knowledge which anyone possesses is always partial and is conditioned by the uniqueness of the being who possesses it and limited by his or her perspective. Thus a school which actively searches for truth should be actively seeking to attract all kinds of persons into its student body, faculty, and administrative staff.

If an educational institution is in the business of educating leaders, it must deliberately include among its students leaders from the slums and leaders from the suburbs. It is necessary to recruit a diversified student body because we know that students learn from each other as well as from their teachers and that the truth which they learn will emerge out of the competition of ideas, images, and aspirations of the multitude. Each leader partially defines truth in terms of his or her present and past experiences. Schools that specialize in teaching whites and the upper class or the middle class only, and schools that specialize in teaching blacks and the working class or the lower class only, have thus specialized in imparting a truth which is partial.

We have strongly asserted that the education of leaders of all socioeconomic status levels is a major responsibility of schools because truth and justice, which are essential in community life, tend to emerge from adversary arrangements in which all categories of people can effectively confront each other. We cannot expect one sector of society to be continuously concerned about the interests of other sectors. Even the most understanding and compassionate people view the needs of others from their own vantage point. It is a limitation imposed by our finite human condition.

Specialization and the division of labor, which characterize the urban setting, mean that one person must do for another what the other cannot do for himself or herself. People of the urban community are truly interdependent. In the past, the poor and some race, sex, and age categories have been cut off from the mainstream of community life. This has limited their opportunity for personal fulfillment and has eliminated from the social life of the total community the enriching contribution of their full participation. Educational institutions must deliberately develop programs in leadership training for all categories of people, including the high and the mighty and the meek and the lowly. No longer can efforts be limited to training leaders for the Establishment only. A sense of community is present only when there is full and effective participation of all. Adversaries should be adequately equipped with the knowledge and skills necessary for honest deliberation. It is out of such deliberations that the truth may emerge.

A former president of Massachusetts Institute of Technology once said that "the historic roles of the university—to educate youth, to preserve knowledge, and to create new knowledge—remain the same; but the emphasis on them becomes greater in a more demanding society, and the greatest emphasis will be on developing leadership." He spoke of leaders who will be concerned with service to society, service in the cause of society, and the well-being of others. He further said that students would come closer to understanding humanity's purpose on this earth by seeking to serve others. The president of this school stated his belief that "the general range of problems attacked by M.I.T. in the future will shift more and more to those that understandably affect the ways in which our society lives." He said that while science would remain a central concern, "it would be inadequate for the basic education of the M.I.T. [person] to stop at science and engineering." Howard Johnson went on to say that M.I.T. would "increasingly exert its power towards problems of human significance."[5] I have quoted a president of the Massachusetts Institute of Technology because this is an educational center that has become famous worldwide for teaching students how to deal effectively with things but which acknowledges in the words of its president the need to teach students how to deal effectively with people.

The experience of University College, the adult-education division of Syracuse University, should be mentioned as an illustration of the initial turbulence that accompanies diversification in education. It represents the kind of reaction that may be anticipated as schools move in earnest into the business of educating community leaders of all races and at all levels of the social class hierarchy. Of the several programs pertaining to community leadership development at the school, two are reviewed: (1) the Thursday Breakfast Roundtable and (2) the Community Action Training Center. These two programs were initiated during the same school year. The first program continued to operate for several years; the second program was dropped soon after it began.

The Thursday Breakfast Roundtable was limited to community leaders, including business people, prominent lawyers, high governmental officers, executives of major community associations such as the United Way and the Chamber of Commerce, a few professors, some outstanding clergy, and others. The Thursday Breakfast Roundtable was a public service provided by University College as a continuing channel of communication for civic leaders in the metropolitan area. These weekly informal meetings represented an opportunity to exchange ideas and opinions on important public issues and problems.

In effect, the Thursday Breakfast Roundtable brought together the local Establishment for the purpose of sharing and exchanging views, for the benefit of the total community. At the end of the school year in which the Roundtable was initiated one local daily newspaper published an editorial declaring that the enterprise was a success and expressing the hope that it would continue. And so the Roundtable continued, reaching out to top community leaders and involving them in a public-affairs educational venture.

Also, it was during the same school year that University College established the Community Action Training Center. A publication, describing the program, stated the following:

We are seeking candidates who, on the basis of existing knowledge, are likely to enter long careers of organization of low income populations. They should be young, responsible, committed to hard work for seven days a week, including evenings, in the field. They should, if possible, be from low income areas themselves and able to identify with and be accepted by most people in neighborhoods of poverty, and not be perceived as deviant by the general population.

Applicants should have a controlled, but intense anger about continued injustice and should be committed to hard work for people who are grappling with apparently overwhelming problems. They should be able to plan and act over a long period of time in the development of democratic organizations with enough power to alter the corrosive condition of living in poverty.

They will need to put neighborhood issues ahead of personal concerns and to be enablers to the development of organizations, instead of themselves assuming leadership roles in the organization which is created . . . .

In practice, trainees will have varying levels of education ranging from those with relatively few years of school to students in the Graduate School of Social Work . . . .

There will be no academic prerequisites. A certificate will be issued to each graduate by University College, the adult education division of Syracuse University.[6]

From the descriptive material presented, it is clear that the university's adult-education division was serious in its attempt to develop leadership programs for the high and mighty, the meek and lowly, for people of all races and at all levels of the socioeconomic status hierarchy including the poor and affluent. While one local daily newspaper praised the Roundtable, another damned the Training Center. It called the federal grant which financed the Center "a strange misuse of public funds"! The project was strange to the editorial writers (1) because the field work unit of the Community Action Training Center was organizing "beneficiaries of public housing to protest because they are not getting more assistance," and (2) because of the kinds of students recruited and their "lack of academic prerequisites."[7] The Community Action Training Center upset the local Establishment.

A local business leader wrote a letter to the President of the United States signifying his alarm over the involvement of the federal government in a program which, he said, was designed to train "agitators" for the poor. Some business-men canceled their pledges to the university's fund drive, although they later were reinstated. Several local citizens, including the mayor, waited upon the chancellor of the university and made known their complaints. Finally, the grant ended and federal support was not renewed for the Community Action Training Center at Syracuse University.

This first major effort by a major university in leadership development among the poor should not be viewed as a failure. The brief existence of the Community Action Training Center confronted institutions of higher learning with their responsibility to educate leaders of the poor as well as the affluent, and to educate leaders who live in the slums as well as in the suburbs. In due time, I predict they and other institutions of teaching and learning will find ways of fulfilling this responsibility on a continuing basis as a new educational service in an urban society consisting of pluralistic populations.

## Notes

1. Louis Wirth, "Urbanism as a Way of Life," in Paul K. Hatt and Albert J. Reiss, eds., *Reader in Urban Sociology* (New York: The Free Press, 1951), pp. 38-39.

2. Ibid., p. 39.

3. Leslie T. Wilkins, "Criminology: An Operational Research Approach," in A.T. Welford et al., eds., *Society Problems and Methods of Study* (London: Routledge and Kegan Paul, Ltd., no date), p. 329.

4. The President and Fellows of Harvard College, *The Story of Harvard, A Short History* (Cambridge: The University Information Center, 1966), p. 3.

5. *Boston Evening Globe,* Friday, October 7, 1966, p. 1.

6. Published with permission of Clifford L. Winters, Jr., Vice Chancellor of Syracuse University and Former Dean of University College.

7. Editorial, "Wanted: Angry Young Agitators," *Post Standard Newspaper*, April 21, 1965.

# 2

## Racial Balance and Quality Education: The Boston Experience

In the process of accommodating the educational concerns, interests, and needs of students of different social classes who identify with the different racial and cultural groups, the school is confronted with the problem of maintaining quality. The achievement of equity at the expense of quality is of value, but of limited value. How to achieve both in a unitary school system that meets desegregation requirements of the Constitution is a mission that was assigned to a panel of masters by the United States District Court in Boston. This chapter indicates how the issue and proposals for resolving it were conceptualized. The desegregation plan proposed was for the city of Boston but could be modified for use in other communities.

Racial segregation prohibits exchange and learning among black, brown, and white students and therefore was declared to be unlawful, so far as public education is concerned, by the United States Supreme Court in *Brown* v. *Board of Education.* Children are compelled by law to attend school but cannot be fully educated under racially segregated conditions. Thus a school segregated by actions of public authorities is a denial of equal protection of the laws for those who must attend it.

Because of the complexity of the various plans filed to desegregate the Boston public schools and the need for speed in the adoption of a plan to go into effect immediately, Judge W. Arthur Garrity, Jr., of the United States District Court in Boston appointed a panel of four masters in 1975 and gave the panel the authority to conduct hearings and make recommendations to the court.

I served as one member of this panel. The panel of masters was a diversified group in terms of race, religion, and ethnicity. Professionally, two were lawyers and two were educators. The judge believed that truth had a better chance of emerging from a diversified group of masters than from a single expert or a homogeneous body. A small panel of masters and experts to assist the court is one technique used in Boston that can be recommended to others. Sometimes a single expert or master is retained by the court to assist in the evaluation or development of a desegregation plan. Usually this person is white, middle class, middle-aged, and male. He is expected to recommend or to oversee the development of a plan of remedy for the grievances of the plaintiffs who, in most school desegregation cases, are children and parents of black and brown racial minorities. Since truth is not entirely a function of intellectual power and the capacity to think, as mentioned in Chapter 1, the possibility of error is increased when the advice of only one expert is sought. The whole truth about school desegregation and education can be told only in part by anyone who is middle class, middle-aged, male, and white, or who is of any other category. Whom one is willing to believe always has been a hindrance to the full discovery of truth and is a problem in the sociology of knowledge worthy of further study. Some people are more inclined to believe that the ideas, plans, and proposals advanced by others who exhibit racial, ethnic, or social class characteristics that are similar to their own are more authentic. Judge Garrity departed from this practice in the appointment of persons to advise the court.

The main matter before the panel of masters was to evaluate plans submitted and eventually to develop a plan that would meet the constitutional requirement for a unitary public school system and, at the same time, enhance the quality of education in the Boston public schools. The masters kept this two-fold goal in focus. But the community did not. Liberals as well as conservatives insisted that the scope of the masters' work should deal only with devising a method to desegregate the Boston public schools. The conservatives thought that the desegregation plan should be limited and the liberals said it should be comprehensive. In both instances, their concern was with race mixing. Commenting on the appropriate standard for the total school system, John W. Roberts of the Civil Liberties Union of Massachusetts, in a letter to the editor of the *Boston Globe*, said the judge must evaluate plans placed before him "not on the basis of the educational quality of the plans, but rather on the basis of whether or not they meet the standards for school desegregation. . . ." The Boston Home and School Association, a voluntary organization of parents, claimed that the desegregation remedy should be applied only to about fifty of the 162 schools in Boston in which the court "found specific evidence of segregative School Committee action" and that the court order should not require any child to be bused "beyond the next nearest school." These were among the contentions set forth by attorneys in the association's petition of appeal to the Supreme Court, which was rejected. The attorneys for the plaintiffs criticized the plan developed by the court-appointed masters as not providing the "greatest practicable actual desegregation." The central concern of individuals associated with these and other groups was the extent of desegregation—some wanting more and others wanting less.

The masters explained that their plan, which had many innovative features including the pairing of colleges, universities, and local businesses with individual schools, was concerned with "equality and excellence." Their dual concern had only a limited impact and did not appeal to many. On the basis of the Boston school desegregation experience, I learned that it is difficult to get the attention of the public and to conduct useful discussions of means for achieving quality education in the heat of a legal battle. The reason for desegregation is to enhance the quality of education; so stated the Supreme Court in its landmark

1954 decision. If "separate educational facilities are inherently unequal," as
stated by the Court, white as well as black children are harmed. Most Bostonians did not see it this way. They viewed desegregation as helpful to black
and brown children and harmful or of neutral benefit to whites. The criterion
of benefit for many Bostonians was achievement in communication and calculation skills as reflected by scores on standardized tests.

The masters' plan was described by some observers as offering a quality
educational program for the city of Boston. But this aspect of the school
desegregation plan seemed to be less important to some than the ratio of white,
black, and other minority students in each school. In his initial comment upon
Judge Garrity's final school desegregation order, the president of the Boston
chapter of the National Association for the Advancement of Colored People
(NAACP) said the order, in general, was a good one, but that he would examine
it carefully to determine whether it desegregated all segregated schools. He
said he would examine the order to determine "whether there are any schools
left which are predominantly black." He implied that there should not be any
such schools and stated that this was the requirement that must be met.[1] The
initial NAACP response to the judge's final order focused on the method rather
than the purpose of desegregation.

Purpose and method complement each other and always ought to be considered together. Yet the analysts of contemporary social issues tend to focus
on purpose or method, and in most instances on method at the exclusion of
concern for the purpose of social action. This is to say that some activists and
analysts often violate the principle of complementarity by not considering the
two together, how they function and support each other.

An illustration of this violation is the call for law and order without expressing concern for the presence of love and justice. Love and justice have to
do with the purpose of social organization; law and order are methods of achieving this purpose. Thus, law and order without love and justice are demonic and
oppressive. The Age of Watergate and the oppressive tactics of the government
at that time against citizens in the United States clearly demonstrated these facts.
The method as well as the purpose of social organization should not be separated,
should always be considered together—particularly the method and purpose of
school desegregation.

The focus of the NAACP and the plaintiff parents in the Boston school
desegregation case on the racial ratio of each school was in accord with the state
action taken ten years earlier. The Massachusetts legislature passed the State
Racial Imbalance Act, which declared that any school with more than 50 percent
nonwhite students was racially imbalanced. The state law itself could be classified as racist because it declared illegal and, therefore, not in the public interest,
any school that had a majority black student body. A principle deduced from
the above is that it is not in the public interest for whites to be a minority in
any school, an idea similar to that expressed by the president of the Syracuse

Board of Education that was mentioned in Chapter 1. Neither of these principles, of course, is true according to sociological and learning theory.

Social psychologist Thomas Pettigrew has reminded us that "many relatively unprejudiced Whites engage in [racial discrimination] virtually every day of their lives," and that one need not be a racist to contribute to and perpetuate institutional racism.[2] Judge Garrity found that the Boston School Committee "intentionally and purposefully caused or maintained racial segregation in meaningful or significant segments of the public school system in violation of the Fourteenth Amendment." He concluded that such segregation "need not have been inspired by any particular racial attitude in order to be unconstitutional." The State Racial Imbalance Act may be racist, although many who supported the act also supported school desegregation. The intent of the person acting may be the ultimate test, legally; but the consequence of personal or public action is the ultimate test, morally. The consequence of the Racial Imbalance Act was to restrict the opportunity of black and brown racial groups to be the majority in a public school, and to experience the responsibilities associated therewith.

The lawmakers probably were not governed by any racist attitudes. But the effect of their action in the State Racial Imbalance Act was to declare that the public good is least served when blacks and other racial groups are more than half of a public school's student body. That principle was institutionalized as public law and became normative for the Commonwealth of Massachusetts.

Because laws are statements of social norms, they affect the behavior of minority as well as majority members of society. Indeed, the Supreme Court decision *Plessy* v. *Ferguson*, delivered at the close of the nineteenth century, declared that state law may sanction separate facilities for black and white citizens if the facilities are equal. That interpretation of the law also became the norm for race relations in our nation and influenced the actions of Americans for decades until the "separate but equal" doctrine was knocked down by the *Brown* v. *Board of Education* decision at mid-twentieth century.

With the concern of such powerful opinion molders as state legislators focusing on the method rather than the purpose of school desegregation, it is hard to overcome a preoccupation with racial ratios. Concern with quality education tends to get sidetracked.

The court-appointed masters in Boston tried to link school desegregation with quality education. Many but not all of their proposals were included in the final court order to desegregate the city public schools. Some of the highlights of their proposals are presented here as a guide to the future—to a new approach to school desegregation which focuses on purpose as well as method.

While busing is a powerful symbol that fans the passions of persons in favor of and opposed to desegregation, the masters determined that it was a phony and fake issue. Their conclusion, in part, was based on information provided by the Massachusetts Commissioner of Education. He said, "Thirty thousand

kids were being bused in Boston before there was any desegregation plan."[3]
This number was about one-third of the students enrolled in Boston public
schools at that time and was less than the number of students who would be
required to use transportation in the plan proposed by the masters. The number
of students to be bused in their plan was half the number being transported to
school even before court-ordered desegregation. The estimated number of
students to be bused in the final court order was 21,000 to 24,000—still less
than the number that used transportation before court-ordered desegregation.

The organization of the school system into large geographic districts
encompassing one or two natural and contiguous areas and the drawing of
district boundaries to achieve this goal could promote a sense of community
and minimize concern about busing: so believed the masters. Their effort to
refocus public attention from transportation to education was deliberate. The
enlarged district of one or two natural areas that consisted of diversified students
and schools with different grade levels so that students in lower levels feed into
schools of higher grades is a variant of the educational park idea without a common campus.

Before the draft plan of the masters was issued, the Superintendent of
Schools for the City of Boston said, "It is the issue of busing . . . , which, whether
correctly or not, has assumed major importance to a considerable segment of
Greater Boston's population."[4]  The masters wanted the citizens of Boston to
examine the issue of how children go to school in relationship to why they go
to school. Their assumption was that children attend school for the purpose of
obtaining an education.

The masters invited colleges and universities in the Boston metropolitan
area to cooperate with the City School Department for the purpose of improving
educational quality and promoting excellence in the public schools. Judge
Garrity's order took note of the fact that these institutions (approximately
twenty-one in cities and suburbs of the Boston metropolitan area) had "committed themselves to support, assist and participate in the development of educational excellence" in the public schools. In the court order, the members of the
Boston School Committee were directed "to use their best efforts to negotiate
a contract" with each of the colleges and universities. The contract would set
forth scope of authority of the parties and the role to be played by each.

Colleges and universities were expected to do more than to provide tutoring
assistance and develop research projects, which had been traditional ways of involvement. The institutions of higher education were paired with specific schools.
They and the schools as partners were expected to work out appropriate cooperative relationships that would be mutually beneficial.

The idea which encouraged the masters to attempt to foster a cooperative
relationship between colleges and universities, on the one hand, and public
schools, on the other, was contained in the plan for school desegregation prepared
by the Boston School Committee. The total plan of the School Committee was

rejected by the masters as inadequate; but a portion was retained that proposed that some schools should be "magnetized"—that is, assisted in providing extraordinary educational opportunities. The School Committee's plan indicated that the presence of magnet schools would make desegregation more acceptable. The masters were intrigued by this idea and also impressed by the array of excellent colleges and universities in the Boston metropolitan area. They believed that if linkages between the educational institutions could be effected, the Boston public schools could truly become magnets of educational excellence. Thus, the idea of magnet schools (institutions that provided special and extraordinary opportunities) was advanced by the School Committee. The masters merely proposed a way of actually magnetizing the schools. Chapter 7 discusses these schools in greater detail.

While the colleges and universities were asked to come forth and serve as good corporate citizens of the metropolitan area, the masters determined that it was in the self-interest of most institutions of higher education to promote domestic tranquility in the Boston area. Student enrollment has become a significant component in the stability and even viability of some private colleges and universities. Potential students might be disinclined to come to a burning Boston. So it was in the self-interest of most private schools to help defuse the desegregation issue and keep Boston cool and calm.

The colleges and universities were not expected to serve as altruistic lords or benevolent despots, determining unilaterally what ought to be done to and for the public schools. The turbulence at Columbia University in the 1960s was due, in part, to the absence of a good-neighbor policy toward Harlem, and has lingered in the corporate memory of colleges and universities.

Since some members of the panel of masters had had many years of experience working with faculty and administrative personnel of colleges and universities, they knew that appeal to these institutions during these troubled times for their assistance on the basis of altruism might only obtain a short-term involvement but no long-term commitment or follow-through. A clue to the masters that there was a self-interest component in the involvement of the colleges and universities in defusing the desegregation issue in Boston was revealed in the activities of several local businesses.

Even before the court began to formulate its final school desegregation order, several businesses through the National Alliance of Businessmen and the Greater Boston Chamber of Commerce banded together and formed with the Boston School Department the Tri-Lateral Task Force, through which specific businesses were linked in partnership with specific public schools in Boston. The business organizations hoped their involvement would contribute to peaceful desegregation.

Several of the business organizations participating in the partnership program were in retail sales, mortgage banking, insurance, and public services. These enterprises would suffer greatly were Boston to go up in smoke. Thus they

recognized their self-interest in maintaining a cool and calm Boston and volunteered to do whatever they could. Their participation gave the masters the idea
that others might also have a self-interest in peaceful school desegregation.
Thus the colleges and universities were approached. Their participation could
be a double victory—a victory for themselves as well as for the Boston community and its schools. Some business organizations already had arrived at
this conclusion.

What made the masters enthusiastic about the arrangement between colleges
and universities and elementary and secondary public schools within the context
of a court order was that it provided the possibility of uniting school desegregation, a method, with quality education, which is the purpose. Moreover, this
arrangement could be replicated in major metropolitan areas throughout this
nation. Such an arrangement is not new in Boston or elsewhere. But a unique
feature of the pairing of public schools with colleges and universities in Boston
is that there were so many involved.

In the past, local communities such as Roxbury, a black community in
Boston, worked with more colleges and universities than it wanted or needed,
while Italian or Irish sections, such as East Boston or Charlestown, were more
or less ignored. The masters' plan recommended the pairing of a college or
university with all high schools and several middle and elementary schools. For
many of these public schools, this cooperative relationship with an institution
of higher education was a first-time experience.

Mentioned earlier was the fact that a desegregation plan which followed
the guidelines of the 1965 State Racial Imbalance Act was legal but racist. It
is important to bear in mind both assertions. A decade ago school desegregation
was thought to be basically for the benefit of blacks. Seldom has public law
been analyzed to determine its racist content, especially public law thought to
be beneficial for minorities.

The thought patterns which contributed to the enactment of the racial
imbalance law in Massachusetts were similar to the beliefs of many in the nation
who interpreted the data that were derived from the survey of educational
opportunity that was mandated by Congress in 1964. James Coleman, the
senior researcher involved in that study, said that ". . . there is evident, even
in the short run, an effect of school integration on the reading and mathematics
achievement of Negro pupils" and that "in the long run, integration should be
expected to have a positive effect on Negro achievement. . . ." Further discussing
the contributory factors to high and low educational performance, Coleman
concluded that "the achievement of minority pupils depends more on the schools
they attend than does the achievement of majority pupils."[5] Thus, the push
toward integrating blacks with whites in predominantly white schools was
accelerated because of the higher achievement level recorded by whites on various
paper-and-pencil tests. This was the wisdom of the mid-1960s out of which the
Massachusetts Racial Imbalance Act emerged. The racist character of that law,

which inferred that predominantly black schools were not in the public interest, was benign, not necessarily exhibiting malice aforethought on the part of legislators and citizens who supported it. The basic motive for integrating blacks with whites in predominantly white schools was for the purpose of improving the achievement level of blacks; so believed the social engineers during the early years of the second half of the twentieth century.

The Coleman Report had other findings, however, such as the following: (1) "minority pupils . . . have far less conviction than whites that they can affect their own environments and futures"; (2) "when minority students have a belief that they can affect their own environments and futures, . . . their achievement is higher than that of whites who lack that conviction"; and (3) "those blacks in schools with a higher proportion of whites have a greater sense of control."[6] A sense of control over environment was linked with achievements. Elaborating upon the latter point, Coleman said, "Black children in an integrated school come to gain a greater sense of their efficacy to control their destiny. It is very likely due to the fact that they see that they can do some things better than whites . . . a knowledge which they never had so long as they were isolated in all-black school."[7] These findings tend to be ignored by the developers of school desegregation plans.

Apparently an important condition to which more attention should be given is the sense of control which school desegregation might generate among blacks and other minorities. According to the Coleman survey, this may be more significantly related to educational excellence, which is one purpose of race mixing in the public schools.

In the light of these little-mentioned findings of the Coleman Report, the masters veered from the requirement of a similar ratio of black, white, and other children in each school and proposed that the student bodies of Boston schools be diversified rather than strictly balanced. Whites need not always be the majority in good schools, according to the masters' proposal. If a sense of control is significant educationally, some schools should have a majority of whites in the student body with a sufficient minority of blacks and students of other races to have educational impact upon the total system. Other schools should have a majority of blacks or browns with a sufficient minority of whites to have a meaningful influence.

The concept, sufficient minority, is relative and could vary from 49 percent to 20 percent for any specific racial or ethnic group. My own studies of community organizations have indicated that the participation of less than one-fifth for a specific group in a democratic and free organization is tokenism and tends to have little effect upon its decision-making structure. The important point to remember is that the population size of a specific group that can influence the affairs of an institution or organization is a phenomenon that may be larger than the size of that group within the total community. While 20 percent is the lower limit in terms of critical mass for a particular group, it is possible that the actual proportion of minority representation within a total school, including several different minority groups, should be larger.

The masters' concept of diversity in the composition of student populations in specific schools and districts did not adhere to a strict racial ratio. This concept introduced another idea which seldom has been discussed in litigation for school desegregation. The idea was that there is educational benefit in being a member of the minority, as we mentioned in Chapter 1. Being in control is something of value. But learning how to depend upon others, to trust others, or to receive and accept assistance when needed, is something of value too. Some racial groups have learned these things and have been strengthened by enduring their minority status, persevering, and transcending adversity. The recent studies of self-concept by Gloria Johnson Powell[8] and Morris Rosenberg and Roberta G. Simmons[9] indicate that minority children have developed positive concepts of themselves, sometimes more positive than the self-concept that majority children have of themselves. By recommending the creation of student bodies and school districts in which black and brown populations would be a majority, the masters were creating an opportunity for some whites to experience the beneficial effects of being a minority.

In a pluralistic and cosmopolitan society, all are members of a minority in one context or another at some period in time. It is well that in school whites should learn not to fear the consequences of minority status; and blacks should learn to be comfortable with the responsibilities and requirements of majority status. Such would be effective education for life in a pluralistic society.

Some parents insisted through a legal representative retained by the Home and School Association that desegregation would be more acceptable if students and their parents could have a choice regarding school of enrollment. The masters knew that "freedom of choice" plans had been used in the past as a way of circumventing desegregation rather than promoting it. Yet the desire for choice in a free society is compelling and should be accommodated if it can be done in a way that is consistent with the requirements for desegregation. In the masters' plan, students could choose magnet schools but would be assigned to district schools.

Magnet schools with extraordinary educational opportunities had citywide attendance zones and would be guaranteed a desegregation experience with a student body at a fixed racial ratio similar to that of the total city. In the community district, students could not choose particular schools. Students were assigned for the purpose of achieving desegregation; and the ratio of whites, blacks, and other minorities in each school was similar to the racial ratio of the community district; variations were permitted within a range of 25 percent. Most districts within Boston had a majority of white students, but some had a majority of blacks, according to the masters' plan.

According to folklore, whites will not attend schools in neighborhoods that are predominantly black. The masters examined the facts and determined that this folklore had an empirical base that both affirmed and contradicted it. A few Boston schools with extraordinary programs that were located in areas densely populated by blacks were attended by whites who came from all sectors of the city. Examples were the Trotter Elementary School and Boston Technical High School. Moreover, the masters were told of similar experiences in other communities such as the Martin Luther King, Jr., Elementary School in Syracuse, New York, when it was under the principalship of William Wayson.

In fact, the masters determined that the most appropriate locations for magnet schools were in neighborhoods to which persons might not be attracted unless the educational programs were extraordinary. Schools in such locations truly could become magnets for desegregation as well as quality education. One idea discussed among the masters but not included in their final report was a proposal to magnetize Roxbury High, East Boston High, Charlestown High, and South Boston High Schools. These schools were located in predominantly black, Italian, and Irish areas. Their educational programs would become extraordinary by linking them with Harvard University, Massachusetts Institute of Technology, Bunker Hill Community College, the University of Massachusetts in Boston, and several major businesses in the city. The ethnic and racial communities surrounding these high schools were relatively isolated.

White students already had demonstrated that they would go into neighborhoods in which the racial population was different from their own if the quality of education at the school was outstanding. The masters believed that black and brown students also would go into ethnic neighborhoods in which the population was unlike that of their own if the education was extraordinary. Magnetizing schools in the major racial and ethnic communities of the city would overcome their isolation and at the same time provide a unique cultural context within which to achieve desegregation, while upgrading the quality of education.

To guarantee space in the four high schools for outsiders—that is, students not resident in the black, Italian, or Irish communities, the masters proposed an experimental Freshman Studies Program for ninth graders in Roxbury, East Boston, Charlestown, and South Boston. These first-year high-school students who probably had had only limited interracial and interethnic contact in the past were to be educated together in a neutral location outside their home community and away from the negative prejudice of friends who may have become accustomed to their isolation and who justified it with many rationalizations.

Even if the magnet-school concept failed to attract outsiders to the more or less closed and isolated racial and ethnic communities, the experimental Freshman Studies Program guaranteed that a desegregation experience would begin for some of the students in these communities. The two-fold process of recruiting students to the high schools in the racial and ethnic communities because of the extraordinary quality of their educational programs and also sending out the freshmen class to a neutral territory where an interracial and interethnic experience was guaranteed was a custom-tailored approach designed by the masters to achieve racial desegregation as well as defuse potential violence. The masters attempted to design a special approach for the special racial and ethnic areas in Boston which would recognize this principle of the court while stimulating the least amount of resistance and violence. The approach was tailor-made for Boston; but it could be used in other major cities that have relatively isolated racial and ethnic communities that nevertheless must desegregate.

Because of the need to limit the number of magnet schools so as to maintain their unique attractiveness, the number was cut back and the final report of the masters recommended that East Boston and Charlestown High Schools only should be part of the citywide magnet system. These, however, were not included in the final court order, and the experimental Freshman Studies Program was eliminated too because of the unavailability of a facility in downtown Boston where students from the four communities could be educated together. Nevertheless, this particular proposal of the masters has been fully discussed for the benefit of education and desegregation planners in other communities.

As the masters analyzed the testimony received in public hearings and took counsel with official and community leaders, two themes for recommended action emerged—one, a populist theme which proclaimed value involving people at the grass roots in planning programs of educational excellence, and the other, an elitist theme. These two would appear to be contradictory, yet both often were expressed by the same person. Careful analysis of these two themes—one supporting inclusive and the other advocating exclusive educational arrangements—reveals the intersection of social-class interests with racial desegregation concerns.

Populist advocates encouraged the masters to get the people involved, especially parents. They supported the masters' recommendation that a citywide committee of leading citizens monitor the desegregation process. Also they were enthusiastic about the proposed community councils for each of the subdistricts into which the Boston citywide school system was organized. Some even felt that they would be representative of the people. The masters hesitated about recommending an election, fearing that such might become one more issue over which to wrangle and divide the community and fearing further that the energy consumed in the electoral process might leave the winners spent and unable to mobilize sufficiently to deal with the real issue of desegregated quality education. Notwithstanding these doubts, the final plan of the masters recommended community district councils to which parents could be elected to serve with teachers, students, public officials, and others. Thus the masters embraced the populist view of getting the people involved.

The populist orientation of the parties to this school desegregation case, however, was limited largely to citizen participation in an advisory capacity to the school administration. The masters proposed that the populist view of getting everyone involved also should extend to the involvement of poor white students in the Metropolitan Council for Educational Opportunity Program (METCO), sponsored by the State Board of Education. This program each day bused nearly 3,000 black students from Boston to relatively affluent suburban communities. The suburban schools participated in the program on a voluntary basis but received state aid that varied with the number of students accepted. The masters wanted to extend the beneficial effects of METCO for overcoming racial isolation to poor whites for the purpose of overcoming social class isolation, particularly for whites enrolled in Title I schools. The response in general was unsympathetic. It seemed that the community wanted to keep poor whites as invisible as all blacks. There was little desire to expand the program for blacks or provide extraordinary opportunities for whites who were poor. Thus the proposal to make Title I poor whites eligible for the METCO program was not included in the final court order. In short, the populist desire to get everyone involved in the mainstream did not include poor whites.

With reference to the examination schools, including the two Latin schools and the technical high school, the goal of the masters was to maintain their excellence, indicated by the high rate of students from these schools who enroll in college, and at the same time open these schools to a broader range of students of different racial and ethnic backgrounds. Students had been admitted to these schools on the basis of their performance on standardized examination. The masters proposed that previous performance, such as rank in class, might be a fairer criterion for admission than performance on a specific test given on a particular day, although examination scores might be used to provide the lower limit for an eligible pool of applicants.

All of the proposals for the examination schools were received as unwelcomed news. "Don't tamper with the examination schools" was the prevailing statement made by leaders in the Boston community. The masters discovered that those who were populists with respect to other matters were elitists regarding the examination schools and wished to eliminate any influences which might change the exclusive character of these extraordinary schools. In general, populism was acceptable as long as it did not require a rearrangement of the educational opportunity system with reference to the affluent social classes who were disproportionately represented in the student body of the examination schools.

The concept of diversity, with neither whites nor blacks always dominating, was abandoned in the final court order. Some parties to the Boston school desegregation case argued that the responsibility of the court was to achieve the greatest practicable actual desegregation and that this could be achieved best by requiring all community districts within Boston to have student populations similar to the citywide school population which was 36 percent black, 13 percent other minority, and 51 percent white. The attempt by the court to achieve this goal resulted in the elimination of a predominantly black school district which the masters had proposed. Thus, whites initially were the dominant group in terms of numbers in each of the new school districts ordered by the court, although in time some predominantly white districts became predominantly black.

In summary, the masters proposed a new approach to school desegregation that attempted to reunite method and purpose. Ultimately desegregation is to achieve quality education, and the courts have found that both are intertwined. In a pluralistic society, there is not quality education where there is not desegregation. But desegregation can go forth in a constitutional way without facilitating quality education. How to prevent separation between method and purpose in education is a problem in need of serious study. An editorial in the *New York Times* summed up the issue quite nicely: "Integration must be made synonymous with better education."[10] I am inclined to agree.

### Notes

1. Curtis Wilkie, "Phase 2 Order Raises Many Questions, Fears," *Boston Globe*, May 12, 1975, p. 1.

2. Thomas Pettigrew, "Racism and the Mental Health of White Americans: A Social Psychological View," in Charles V. Willie et al., *Racism and Mental Health* (Pittsburgh: University of Pittsburgh Press, 1973), p. 272.

3. Gregory Anrig, "Our Goal: Elimination of Racial Isolation," *Harvard Graduate School of Education Association Bulletin*, Vol. XIX, No. 2 (Winter 1974-75), p. 11.

4. William J. Leary, "Boston: The Way It Is and the Way It Might Be," *Harvard Graduate School of Education Association Bulletin*, Vol. XIX, No. 2 (Winter 1974-75), p. 13.

5. James S. Coleman, et al., *Equality of Educational Opportunity* (Washington, D.C.: U.S. Government Printing Office, 1966), pp. 22, 29.

6. Ibid., p. 23.

7. James S. Coleman, "Equality of Educational Opportunity," *Integrated Education*, Vol. 6, No. 5 (Sept.-Oct. 1968), p. 25.

8. Gloria Johnson Powell, "Self-Concept in White and Black Children," in Charles V. Willie et al., eds., *Racism and Mental Health* (Pittsburgh: University of Pittsburgh Press, 1973, pp. 299-318.

9. Morris Rosenberg, and Roberta Simmons, *Black and White Self-Esteem: The Urban School Child* (Washington, D.C.: The American Sociological Association, 1972).

10. *New York Times*, May 20, 1975, p. 36.

# 3

## White Flight, Community Control, and the City-Suburban Connection

An issue that has insinuated itself into most discussions of school desegregation is that of "white flight." This phrase refers to the movement of white families from the central city to suburban communities in the metropolitan area. White flight is not a legal consideration in school desegregation cases and cannot be permitted to excuse the failure to correct deprivation of constitutional rights, particularly those denied because of the operation of a dual school system that discriminates against blacks and other racial minorities. Where people live is a matter of personal choice. Whether balcks or whites move into or out of the central city, therefore, is an action that legally is unrelated to a finding of officially sanctioned discrimination. Public action that is governed by the Constitution for the common good cannot be subordinated to private action that is a function of personal preference. Yet, the white-flight controversy, which has to do with private living arrangements, continues; and the threat of it is seen by some educational planners as the basis for modifying city school desegregation plans.

It is true that the court has required more and more dual school systems to desegregate and that more and more white families have migrated to the suburbs. But there may not be a cause-and-effect relationship between these two experiences. Rapid suburban development began in the United States years before court-ordered school desegregation affected many cities. A report entitled *Guiding Metropolitan Growth*, published by the Committee on Economic Development shortly after the landmark school desegregation decision of the Supreme Court when there was little litigation regarding enforcement, stated that "middle income families with children have been departing for the suburbs since the end of World War II." The beginning of the trek to the suburbs in significant numbers occurred, therefore, nearly a decade before the *Brown* v. *Board of Education* court decision.[1]

The Committee on Economic Development attributed the increasing suburban growth rate to "the strong desire for lower-density living on the part of families with children . . . Federal policies in the field of mortgage insurance, which have generally favored single-family construction as against apartment developments . . . public policies in the fields of highway construction and education." The report stated that "these and related factors portend a more widely dispersed pattern of metropolitan development in years ahead," and predicted that before the end of the twentieth century three-fifths of the people living in metropolitan areas would be living outside the central cities.[2]

27

All of this is to say that the pattern of suburban growth in the United States is a phenomenon that came before court orders for school desegregation in most cities. The two issues should not be confused as linked together in a cause-and-effect relationship.

School desegregation and integration are difficult enough to understand and plan for without confusing the issue with the white-flight theory, as sociologist James Coleman has done. To repeat, the fact is that the movement of whites from the cities to the suburbs has been going on at an accelerated rate since the midpoint of the twentieth century.

In addition, evidence is mounting that suburban growth is not limited exclusively to whites or to the United States. Harold Rose reported that "by 1970, the nation's metropolitan rings were the place of residence of 3.5 million blacks, an increase of almost one million blacks, an increase of almost one million during the decade."[3]

Within a two-year period, Tokyo, Japan, experienced a net population loss of almost 340,000. The *New York Times* reported that "37 percent of Tokyo's workers spend more than one hour commuting each way." The reasons given for living outside the city by suburban dwellers in Japan, where there is no court-ordered school desegregation, are similar to the reasons given by suburban dwellers in the United States: "the hills and the sea and [the] peach tree."[4]

Thus, it is inappropriate to attribute the prevalence of suburban growth in the United States or elsewhere to court-ordered school desegregation. Yet that is precisely what Coleman did in a deposition that was submitted to the Dallas Division of the United States District Court for the school desegregation case involving that city. He said, "Based on my research, it is my opinion that extensive desegregation of schools within the larger central cities has two effects: first, by reassignment of children within the district, it has a direct and immediate effect in eliminating predominantly black schools. Second, *it increases the loss of white children from the district*, and as a consequence, it has the long-term effect of re-establishing predominantly black schools in the central city" (emphasis added). On the basis of such information as this, the Home and School Association in Boston concluded that the United States District Court's sweeping order would "exacerbate the very racial isolation and segregation it is attempting to remedy." This is the message that was sent to the Supreme Court in an appeal that was rejected.

Reynolds Farley examined 125 school districts, each with 100,000 people or more, in northern and southern regions of the United States, and discovered "that changes in white enrollment were not strongly linked to changes in school segregation." He found that some school districts, from which whites had moved, experienced much desegregation, while others experienced little, if any, change in the segregation pattern of their schools. These findings led to the general conclusion that "there is not a significant relationship between school integration and white flight."[5]

Even if the rate of increase in suburban growth is greater immediately after court-ordered school desegregation than before for whites, it does not continue at the accelerated pace for a long period of time. Thus a distinction must be made between the *prevalence* rate and the *incidence* rate of white suburban growth in relation to school desegregation. In view of the facts that (1) the suburban growth pattern has been going on for several decades and that (2) the Committee on Economic Development predicted a suburban plurality for most metropolitan areas before the end of this century on the basis of trends observed near the middle of the century, one must conclude that any asserted correlation between the prevalence rate of suburban growth and school desegregation is spurious. The incidence rate which may have a modest association with school desegregation occurs during a short period of time, a year or two after the court order. Moreover, the fact that suburban growth is occurring in Japan and else-where indicates that events other than court-ordered school desegregation are contributing to this worldwide phenomenon during the second half of the twentieth century.

We know that students learn from each other as well as from their teachers. If this statement is true, then it can be concluded that the suburban schools whose student bodies consist of people of markedly similar backgrounds are deficient as educational environments; that is, they are deficient if one has a broad view of education and sees it as more than a percentile rank in an array of verbal and mathematics test scores.

If segregated education is inherently unequal education, as determined by the Supreme Court, one should be appropriately suspicious of those who advo-cate a slowdown in school desegregation to prevent white flight from the city for the benefit of blacks and other racial minorities, and who do not at the same time call for a speed-up in black and brown flight to the suburbs to facili-tate school integration there for the benefit of whites. Black segregated cities are no more or less harmful than white segregated suburbs in terms of cultural isolation and race relations in education. If integration is a significant compo-nent in education, it is good for whites as well as blacks; and it is good for the suburbs as well as the cities. There is no need to slow down school desegregation to prevent white flight from the city when a more manageable solution is avail-able for speeding up school integration by facilitating the movement of blacks and other racial minorities to the segregated suburbs. Already there is evidence that blacks are finding their way to the suburbs in greater numbers, since the beginning of the 1970s.

The issue of local control is related to the movement of families to suburban communities and also to the larger and generic issue of who shall be in charge. This is an issue that has troubled whites for years, especially middle-class, middle-age men, the customary community decision-makers. For example, metropolitan government involving the consolidation of city and suburban political jurisdictions cannot be analyzed on its own merit as an effective and

efficient or ineffective and inefficient form of government without considering
also the racial ratio of city and suburban populations. Whites campaigned for
metropolitan government in Dade County, Florida, under the banner of "good
government" and as a way of retaining political control as their numbers in the
central city of Miami began to dwindle, but they resisted metropolitan education in Detroit and its environs under the banner of maintaining "quality education" and as a way of resisting city influence in suburban schools, as the
numbers of blacks in Detroit, Michigan, increased.

Suburban growth since World War II has been a movement to fulfill a
number of goals, including the goal of gaining control over local resources. The
modern suburban movement has taught us that neither people nor communities
are self-sufficient. The unit cost of education and other common services is
exorbitant in communities with relatively small populations, and some services
cannot be effectively developed by one community or political jurisdiction
because of the small population base. Soon after suburban dwellers gained
control over their schools, they negotiated away their new prize because local
resources were inadequate for effective operation of local schools. Eventually
regional and central schools were developed. Through these necessary arrangements, the suburban dwellers gave up exclusive local control to obtain the
greater benefits that flow from a consolidated school district that can draw on
a larger population and tax base.

Despite the increasing evidence that educational services in many suburban
communities that are under the exclusive authority of a locality are insufficiently
financed, groups which have not experienced failure associated with a local base
that is too small now are calling for local control. Blacks and other minorities
are beginning to ask, "Who shall be in charge?" One reason they are calling for
local control is that central planning has failed. Blacks and members of the
Hispanic community, for example, had neither local control nor quality schools
in the past. So they now are opting for the antithesis of central control, since
it did not serve their interests in the past. In this instance, the call for local
control is not so much a judgment about the beneficial effects of local authority
as it is a negative assessment of the consequences of centralized authority. Moreover, it is a way of asserting the self-interest of blacks and other minorities in
public decisions, as whites have made public policy in terms of their self-interest
in years gone by.

Some blacks and other racial minorities look upon local control as an
enhancement of cultural identity. The suburban movement after World War II,
which was in effect a push for local control, never achieved that goal. The condition of alienation in some suburbs as well as the oppressive conformity of some
ethnic and other closed communities are well known. The suburban movement,
from the very beginning, was a political or power movement and not a cultural-
identity matter. It was an adaptation by white middle-class people to the increasing pluralism of the city and the encroachment of racial and ethnic groups

and other social classes upon their decision-making power. Thus, the suburban growth after World War II was, among other things, an attempt by middle-class whites to go where they could remain in charge.

In some respects, this power play on the part of the middle-class worked to their advantage. While the power play did not provide the necessary local resources for all common community services such as schools, the suburbanites who became a recognized population were able to pressure government into reordering expenditure priorities. For example, funds were shifted to the erection of highway systems rather than to expansion of city mass transportation.

The current movement for self-determination and local control over neighborhood services within cities will work only if leaders of such movements recognize that they are frankly political and do not get sidetracked on a cultural-identity binge. Such movements should enable cities to bargain effectively with the suburbs for the setting of federal and state as well as metropolitan community priorities. If such movements are not recognized as political, then they are nothing more than aimless motion. As a political move, some cities are on target in requiring residence within city limits for employees of the municipality. Support of such a requirement for local government workers should be a priority of the advocates of local control.

The city-residence requirement in many municipalities will enhance their capacity to make trade-offs with suburbs that surround them. For example, city dwellers might offer to support the funding of commuter transportation so that suburban dwellers can have access to the central city and its employment opportunities (or even permit  suburban residents to work for the city) only if suburban dwellers facilitate access, for example, to suburban schools and educational opportunities there for the children of city families. Such would be in the nature of a trade-off, which is an honorable political tradition in the United States. The benefits of local control come alive only to the extent that they enable the locality to negotiate and bargain effectively with the larger metropolitan community. Used as a political instrument, local control fosters genuine integration rather than cultural isolation and has little, if anything, to do with cultural identity.

Thus far, the suburbanites have not had to bargain with city dwellers about metropolitan community priorities. In the past, they took their case directly to the state government, which they and rural interests controlled. This period is rapidly coming to an end. The suburbanites have touted the propaganda that the city is dead, while guaranteeing daily access to it because they know it is the heart of their existence. The time is coming soon when city dwellers will recognize the metropolitan value of the locality which they control, their political power in the federal government, and consequently will extract a price from suburban dwellers for access to the city they left behind. That price could be access to the suburbs, which have been sealed off to racial minorities and the poor. The city and suburbs are interdependent. The suburbs cannot go it alone.

White flight, therefore, is no cause for real alarm when one realizes that the city and its suburbs are interconnected. Eventually they will embrace each other, although they may appear to be drifting apart.


## Notes

1. Committee on Economic Development, *Guiding Metropolitan Growth* (New York: Committee on Economic Development, 1960), p. 18.

2. Ibid., p. 4.

3. Harold M. Rose, *Black Suburbanization* (Cambridge: Ballinger, 1976), p. 2.

4. Andrew Malcolm, "In Japan, Too, They Dream of a Little House with a Graden," *New York Times*, March 3, 1976, p. 31.

5. Reynolds Farley, "School Integration and White Flight," *Symposium on School Desegregation and White Flight* (Notre Dame: Center for Civil Rights of Notre Dame University, 1975), p. 7.

# 4

## Involving the Disadvantaged in Education and Community Decision-Making

At the base of much of the controversy pertaining to urban education and intergroup relations is the failure of the United States to eliminate the oppression of women, racial and ethnic minorities, and poor people and to effectively involve them in the mainstream of society. The old way of handling this failure was to deny that a problem existed. Thus the people of this nation proclaimed that they were a melting pot in which racial and cultural differences were dissolved and that they had only a moderately stratified society in which all had equal rights.

Reality confronted the rhetoric in a series of freedom movements for workers, women, and minorities during the twentieth century. The problem of integrating the pluralistic populations of this nation would not go away. The practice of ignoring or denying the problem brought much more pain than pleasure and resulted in several serious challenges to the unity of this nation.

School desegregation has focused the attention of this society upon the continuing revolution for freedom, justice, and equality. The oppressed no longer are invisible. Their presence has been acknowledged in courts of law by litigation. The issue now is how to involve women, minorities, and the poor in the mainstream of society for the mutual benefit of all.

Back in 1968, I attended a conference on People and Cities in Coventry, England. More than 150 delegates from thirty-five countries were present. There were differences among the delegates which, in part, were associated with the various societies, systems of belief, and cultures from which participants came. Yet, group members arrived at a consensus about some principles for community living. Consensus emerging from such a group is something of value. My small group in the conference wrestled with the issue of participation in the community and came up with the following conclusions:

1. Participation has intrinsic value as a self-corrective in human associations.
2. The best way to learn about participation is by participating. There is no real education for participation.
3. Participation varies directly in proportion to the degree of communication within an organization.
4. Effective participation in the community involves an interaction between individuals at the grassroots level and groups of individuals at the intermediate level that have the power to influence the larger social system.

Another discussion group at the conference spoke directly about violence in the city and came to the conclusion that "violence will generally occur where no dialogue exists between social groups and authorities." This conclusion suggested the further idea that the possibility for disorder in the community increases as communication and participation among the people decrease.

The conference expressed great concern for participation of the disadvantaged. This is a universal problem. All nations have some citizens who are considered by others or by themselves to be disadvantaged. Their condition of disadvantage may be age, sex, race, ethnicity, family status, or wealth. Any of these may be utilized by a society as the basis for extending differential privileges and opportunities that result in more or less power and that affect the well-being of individuals. Those with less power—the subordinates—are disadvantaged in comparison with those of more power—the dominants. Dominants have direct access to the resources required to implement community programs, while subdominants can implement community programs only by gaining the cooperation of a sufficient number of other subdominants who are willing to pool their resources, or by winning the support of dominants who have or control sufficient resources.

School-board members recruited from a variety of localities and subpopulations, including the disadvantaged, are likely to be better decision-makers and more representative of the people. Educational policymakers should be affiliated with dominant and subdominant groups. Those recruited at large who are affluent and experienced may have outstanding skills and talents in problem-solving and in ways of maintaining an organization. But they often lack constituencies or do not acknowledge that they represent special interests and are therefore not accountable. So it is beneficial for a policymaking board such as a school board to have a mixture of members with local loyalities and members who represent special-interest groups, as well as unaffiliated members-at-large. Such diversity increases the sense of participation directly and indirectly by all. Such diversity can serve as a means for group self-correction.

The appropriate ratio has not been determined, but one can certainly say that representatives of disadvantaged populations ought to be present in numbers large enough to have an impact upon deliberations, beyond that of mere token participation. The number of board members representing the disadvantaged should be determined as a function of the size of the policymaking board, rather than as a function of the proportion of disadvantaged people in the total population. In general, I believe that a homogeneous majority should be not more than two-thirds of the total membership of a governing board. When this principle is followed in allocating positions on policymaking boards, it is true that disadvantaged people may be disproportionately represented. But this is probably as it should be sociologically.

The hazards of life are greater for people in disadvantaged circumstances. Crises in daily living are experienced more frequently. Thus attendance at meetings may be less regular than for other board members. A sufficient number of representatives of the disadvantaged is therefore needed to guarantee a self-correcting struggle at all meetings.

Black and brown people, other ethnic minorities, and women have unquestionably experienced a disproportionate share of inequality. In allocating positions for representatives of disadvantaged interest groups, several with common experiences may be considered as a collectivity. At the same time, while policymaking boards are advised—even admonished—to diversify their membership, the practice of selecting two of each, as Noah did in stocking the Ark, is not required. True enough, this practice could result in a well-balanced board— so well balanced that it could only quiver, making decisive action out of the question. Yet organizations should be counseled against selecting only one member of a disadvantaged group or only token representation.

A diversified policymaking structure in educational and other public policy groups is recommended, on the one hand, because democratic decision-making in a pluralistic community requires input from many different sources, and on the other hand because representatives of special-interest groups who are present to compete with the majority or dominant power interests serve as a mirror for an organization, reflecting its capacity to be compassionate. In a political democracy, the people—all of the people—have a right to participate in the governance of the community and its educational and other institutions, either directly or indirectly through representatives.

Yet the Establishment-oriented writers of contemporary social science act as if public policymaking is not affected by the thrust from below, by the subdominant people of power in the community.

In his book *Maximum Feasible Misunderstanding*,[1] for example, Daniel Patrick Moynihan discussed the Johnson Administration's war on poverty as if it had been concocted out of the minds of university professors and as if the main issue were a contest between the Columbia and the Harvard professors about the appropriate way to fight the war. According to Moynihan, the Columbia professors won and thus the war on poverty was lost. Although it had a subtitle, "Community Action in the War on Poverty", Moynihan's book contains not a single reference to Martin Luther King, Jr. It is as if his demonstrations during the 1950s and 1960s had been of no effect, which, of course, is patently untrue.

It is interesting to note that the courageous community-organizing activities of King to change the established systems of oppression in America were recognized internationally but ignored in books about community development and community action written by American social scientists. Such, one must conclude, is the writing of Establishment-oriented In-group social analysts who attempt to ignore the Out-group in a racist society.

Marshall Clinard is another of these analysts, whose book entitled *Slums and Community Development*[2] also managed to ignore Martin Luther King, Jr., in both text and bibliography. In this volume, he stated that "reports on urban developments [throughout] the world have suggested that effective relations between politicians and citizens' self-help projects are generally difficult."[3] Maybe this is why the politicians and professors, when they write about each other, attempt to ignore the unpleasant community organization experiences of subdominant or disadvantaged people that intrude into the social system and demand a redefinition of the existing social structure. The members of citizens' self-help movements are ignored in many social-science publications as if they were invisible people.

Clinard, for example, accepts the idea set forth by Carl Feiss that the basic weakness of slum programs is that slum people have not been storming City Hall. Yet he does not see the storm once the storming has started. As late as the mid-1960s when Martin Luther King, Jr., students, and others were demonstrating in the city streets, Clinard discounted protests by the average American black slum-dweller as an effective way of doing anything for himself or herself. For example, Clinard described self-help for black slum-dwellers as "self-initiated changes in [their] norms and values . . . relating to delinquency and crime, violence, illegitimacy, drug addiction, lack of family responsibility, and apathy toward educational opportunities."[4] It is clear that he supports self-help that focuses on disadvantaged individuals, their families, and values but not on the social system, its institutions and norms that generate and perpetuate slum conditions. In fact, his orientation to the existing order of things is clearly revealed when he sets forth a conceptual framework for changing the slums: "any effective solution requires changes within a balanced framework in which all ingredients are recognized."[5] Protest activity often creates disequilibrium and imbalance. Yet it has been an effective way of changing society for the benefit of dominants as well as subdominants. Clinard, however, prefers a balanced framework which does not upset the existing social order.

James Allen, Jr., former Commissioner of Education of the State of New York (and later of the United States), assigned credit for the new initiatives taken by school boards nationwide to achieve quality education for all, to the pressure from below, from community subdominants. He said that blacks, in their peaceful demonstrations, have done more than any other segment of our society to push us to the point where we have now gone.[6] He urged blacks to continue to push. Subdominants are a fruitful source of social change in schools and in all institutions in society. They make their contributions to change through the community-development approach. If a balanced framework, a dynamic equilibrium, or a smoothly functioning program is the goal of community action, then protest activity is ignored as it has been by several social scientists studying community development and community action. The continuation of these omissions in books and other publications is questionable social science, contributes to bad public policymaking, and should no longer be tolerated.

Following the race riots in Los Angeles, New York, Detroit, and other large cities in the United States, George Gallup sent his pollsters into black and white communities to discover what could be done to prevent civil disorders in central city ghettos. The white dominant people of power listed better law enforcement as the number-one priority, while disadvantaged blacks said the provision of more and better jobs was the best way to prevent race riots. Most riots occurred in black ghettos, but the nation acted upon the white priority and began teaching the national guard and the army better techniques of riot control. Not only did the nation act upon the priority of whites, who are dominant in the power structure, but it also summarily rejected the number-one priority of jobs that was listed by blacks, who are subdominant in the power structure.

Six months after Gallup published his findings, the President of the United States asked the Office of Economic Opportunity to reserve only $35 million to pay for emergency operations for the approaching summer. Congress had appropriated $75 million to finance summer programs the preceding year. The *New York Times* called this reduction in funds for antipoverty programs a "squeeze on the poor." And a squeeze it was. Summer jobs for slum youngsters in New York City were cut from 43,000 the year of the riots to 25,000 the year following the riots for lack of funds to finance them.

Consider this sequence of actions and how the dominant people of power continue to ignore the priorities of subdominants. One year after the riots, and a year after the people who disrupted the orderly way of life of many urban areas said that more and better jobs would prevent future riots, the dominant people of power ignored or rejected their analysis. Jobs were decreased and police power was increased. What, then, was there for poor, disadvantaged, oppressed people to do? They protested and demonstrated. And, as subsequent events proved, the protest was an effective self-help effort.

A crowd of 1,500 youths demonstrated at City Hall in New York. They were demanding more summer jobs. The mayor was annoyed by the behavior of the demonstrators. He called it disgraceful. The day following the demonstrations, however, the mayor dug into what he described as the city's "empty purse" and came up with enough money to finance at least 10,000 more jobs for youngsters from poor and disadvantaged families.

Why did the city and federal governments not act earlier upon the request of poor and disadvantaged people for more and better jobs? The request had been made known in the Gallup Poll that was published following the riots. But the city and federal governments ignored or rejected it. By failing to act on the priority of people who are subdominant in the community power structure, the city and the federal governments were inviting the demonstrations and protests which erupted like a summer storm at City Hall. Apparently there was no other way for these subdominants to make their needs known. Their opinions, expressed in an orderly fashion to the interviewers of the public-opinion poll, were ignored. Opportunity for participation in local and national decision-making was nill. Disadvantaged people were not members of most of the public policy-making authorities. So they had to force their priorities upon the community, by way of a demonstration.

The demonstration at city hall for jobs revealed that all people have power, subdominants as well as dominants. Only dominants may have the power to implement educational and community programs that require substantial resources. Both dominants and subdominants, however, have the capacity to veto. It is important to recognize the veto power that exists among subdominants. They too are people of power and can disrupt the social order and community equilibrium.

In place of poor people, black and brown people, or racial and ethnic minorities, substitute young people in the United States and elsewhere in the world. They also have experienced alienation and have had to utilize protest and the community-development approach to change oppressive institutional systems.

John Hess of the *New York Times* wrote that the French government announced that it is "committed to the most profound change in French education since [the day] of Napoleon."[7] This commitment came about largely because of the student demonstrations and confrontations.

At first it appeared that the French government had defeated the students. The student revolution had been soundly put down, and the ranks of student demonstrators were in disarray. Yet an address by the Minister of Education only a month or two after the confrontation "adopted in large measure the program of the student rebels."[8] Even the Minister of Education described the earlier French educational system as centralized, authoritarian, and outmoded. Yet nothing had been done to change it significantly until the students rebelled. The French government's first reply to the student riots was to wave a big stick. There was the threat of harsh police measures to maintain order. But in the end fundamental reforms were drafted.

Proposals for students to participate in the governing of social life in the dormitories and procedures to replace the authoritarian one-way professor-to-pupil teaching method are under consideration. Because of the confrontation, it appears that genuine change in the educational system of France is coming to pass. Could such change have been brought about without the trauma of confrontation through demonstrations from subdominants?

Community development is a process: a process of getting the people in the community to take action in their own behalf, based on goals of their own choosing. Political action is one important end-result of community development. Each person benefits as a result of collective effort. He or she benefits in personal and concrete ways, such as obtaining more food, higher wages, better housing, or improved education. The purpose of community development is to take collective action that will change the circumstance of individuals. Community development consists of organizing people into powerful groups in order to get the bureaucracy to do that which it would not do unless pressured into acting. Community development is helping people to organize and make decisions about their own destiny. Community development is concerned with institutional change. In community development, the people choose their own representatives to negotiate major issues with the society at large. They are not selected by the Establishment.

A free society remains free only if there is continuous participation of the governed in the instruments and associations of government. Community development as a method is applicable not only to the housing and employment problems of the poor and racial minorities, but also to the educational problems of students and other subdominant populations.

Orderly participation in urban communities that have larger, pluralistic, and dispersed populations usually is through representation. Representatives play a direct part in governance while the people who send them participate indirectly. Because representative decision-making is necessary for the efficient operation of institutions in urban communities, representatives must have sufficient knowledge of, loyalty to, and links with a particular constituency to make known adequately their needs, interests, and way of life. This means that subdominants must serve along with dominants in the community decision-making structures, for they are connected with different populations that ought to participate in the formulation and implementation of policy for education and other public affairs.

The dominant people of power have difficulty in dealing with the demands of subdominants. Dominants want to act on their own list of priorities, which may not be the priorities of the people of poverty, oppression, or alienation. And as long as dominant people of power continue to deal on their own terms with the subdominants—young people, poor people, black and brown people, ethnic minorities, or women—they will continue to add fuel to the protest movement. Community conflict is bound to escalate and shake the foundations of our educational institutions and other agencies.

What sort of individual, then, is the "ideal" participant in a policymaking body? What kind of person should be appointed or elected, for example, to a school board? Ability to generalize, to see the whole, to recognize how the individual parts fit together, and ability to promote the general welfare are desirable characteristics of one who participates directly as a representative in the policymaking activity of a community institution, or agency, including a board of education. If the participant is a good representative he or she should also be able to particularize, to assess the needs of his or her constituents, to articulate their self-interest and determine what is in their best interest. The good representative is ever alert, determining what policies and plans for the larger community may harm or help those to whom he or she is accountable. A good representative protects the particular welfare of his or her people while promoting the general welfare of the total community. In a decision-making body that is truly representative, tension always exists. Harmonizing particular interests with the general interest is a never-ending process of fine-tuning.

Conflict is inevitable in community development pertaining to education. Ward H. Goodenough describes one goal of community development as a "search for self-respect." He goes on to say that the efforts which acknowledge the legitimacy of this goal are more likely to be distressing to many influential persons in the dominant sector.[9] Jay Schulman says that "issues must be drawn that are specific [and that have] direct and immediate payoff . . . ." He further states that "there must be a commitment to the use of conflict tactics and an eagerness to engage in direct confrontation with authority-holders."[10] The community-development approach recognized the existence of incompatible desires among the people in a pluralistic society. Conflict, then, is a legitimate process by which a community attempts to harmonize the many different desires for education of its various members.

Indeed, when the deliberations of governing bodies become too peaceful, the possibility arises that they have become too homogeneous and unrepresentative of the various interests in urban communities. While the ability both to generalize and to particularize is required of representatives, these two characteristics are not always present at the same time in all persons who are eligible to serve as representatives. If priority must be given to one of these characteristics as opposed to the other, it should always be given to the ability to particularize. In the process of protecting local or parochial interest or self-interest, a good representative will learn that he or she must promote the general interest, too, because the whole and its parts are interdependent. One is more likely to move from exclusive concern with self-interest to concern with the general welfare, because this is necessary in gaining allies to fulfill self-interest, than to move in the opposite direction.

In summary, a free society depends on continuous participation of the governed in government. A special-interest group should select its own representatives. A policymaking board needs a mixture of members. Tension among representatives of different special-interest groups may have creative results. Disadvantaged populations ought to be adequately represented to have an impact on deliberations. Policies and plans which promote the public interest are likely to be those which are forged on the anvil of controversy by competing interest groups. It is more appropriate to encounter controversy around the conference table, where it can be dealt with in a controlled way and where bargaining, trade-offs, and compromises can be worked out. For these reasons, decision-making groups ought to be diversified. Otherwise, beautiful plans may be formulated, technically perfect, but rejected out of fear, suspicion, or misunderstanding on the part of those who were left out of the process of formulation.

The public interest for education and other efforts does not reside in any single sector of the community, poor or affluent, blacks or whites, males or females, the young or older people. It resides in all of the people and is a function of their political compromises. This is precisely why all people ought to be represented in all aspects of educational planning and policymaking in the community.

Disadvantaged people who are members of a board must be looked upon as partners with an equal say about what is and what ought to be, just like any other board member. The governing boards and bodies of all our community organizations and agencies, including those concerned with tax-supported schools, should become heterogeneous, consisting of representatives of the various economic, age, sex, ethnic, and racial populations in the community. But we will not set out to bring about this kind of participation deliberately, we will not create truly democratic and diversified educational decision-making structures until men, older people, affluent people, and white people can acknowledge that they do not always know what is best for women, the young, the poor, and racial and ethnic minorities.

It has been suggested by the nineteenth century Italian social analyst Vilfredo Paredo, and others, that an organization could contribute to orderly change by deliberately introducing within it dissident interests to which the total system must respond. Paredo believed that "leaders maintain themselves in power by . . . bringing into the governing class . . . individuals who might prove dangerous to the governing group. If such recruiting does not take place, in the absence of a free use of force, sooner or later there will be an uprising."[11] This is to suggest that if racial and ethnic minorities, poor people, young people, and women were invited to help make the rules, to have genuine power in policymaking, perhaps they would be more inclined to abide by these rules and would be less oriented to disruptive revolutionary change.

When disadvantaged people are introduced into the community policymaking structure for educational planning and development, the possibility for new alliances and coalitions with existing interest groups is present. It is important that representatives of established interest groups recognize that a new political arrangement has been introduced, that new power potentials are available. Thus the special interests of the disadvantaged must be taken seriously. Only in this way can the community encourage flexibility and provide a fluid environment for continuous change in the formations of alliances and coalitions and at the same time avoid polarization. In other words, representatives of the disadvantaged must be recognized, accepted, and negotiated with as power people, and not as pets, nice to have around but considered to be outside the real decision-making apparatus. Representatives of the disadvantaged must therefore be invovled not only on boards of education or other educational authorities, but also in executive committees of these bodies when there are such, and as officers of the organizations.

Their very participation will tend to change some of the established rules of the game and the ways in which the rules are enforced. New participants will tend to evolve new games. This is as it should be in a democracy. As it is, the rules that currently govern our communities and their educational institutions are created largely by decision-making structures whose members are predominantly white, affluent, older adults, and male. These are unquestionably today's dominant people of power. They must learn to share their power with subdominants if necessary social change is to evolve rather than be forced through revolutionary action.

The tendency is for affluent members of the board of education and other community agencies to listen to poor people as reporters on "the way it is" in those distant slums. Then the dominant people of power make their own decisions in a paternalistic way about what ought to be done. Under these conditions, the representatives of the disadvantaged are permitted to describe their situation but not prescribe appropriate solutions. This is not to suggest that disadvantaged people inevitably know best what ought to be done to alleviate their unpleasant experiences. Such a suggestion would be nothing more than a romantic extension of the equally farfetched notion that the affluent know what is good, better, and best for everybody. Certainly the example cited earlier of action taken to beef up law enforcement as a means of quelling race riots, while turning a deaf ear to the cry for more jobs emanating from the ghettos themselves, provides a persuasive illustration of the lack of wisdom on the part of the dominant people of power. People who experience adversity are most capable of describing it; but they, too, can be humanly fallible in giving the answers. The proposed solutions should be the product of a commingling of the ideas of all.

If full partnership comes hard in a diversified decision-making structure, this may be in part attributed to the lack of leadership preparation on the part of representatives of the disadvantaged. This is an area in which our colleges and universities could have a strong and positive impact on the community at large. In the past, these institutions of higher learning have looked upon themselves as developers of leaders, as mentioned in Chapters 1 and 2. Leadership development is still a useful goal, but today it must apply to more than just the Establishment. We must develop leaders for people of high and low status, leaders for the rich and leaders for the poor, leaders for black people and other racial or ethnic minority populations and for white people, leaders who are male and female. In the past, our colleges and universities tried to sensitize the sons of affluent white men to the problems of women, blacks, and other disadvantaged populations. Now colleges are called upon to educate women and people connected with a variety of races, religions, and social-class categories. Schools are not being asked to change their bias functions. Rather, they are being asked to be inclusive of all populations in offering leadership training.

Controversy is the creative kernel of history when negotiating sessions are engaged in by men and women, young people and older people, affluent and poor, black, brown, and white people, who trust and respect each other. Conflict, conciliation, and cooperation: this is the creative action process in public education and other community efforts.

## Notes

1. Daniel P. Moynihan, *Maximum Feasible Misunderstanding: Community Action in the War on Poverty* (New York: The Free Press, 1969).

2. Marshall B. Clinard, *Slums and Community Development* (New York: The Free Press, 1966).

3. Ibid., pp. 275-76.

4. Ibid., p. 311.

5. Ibid., 313.

6. Testimony of Dr. James E. Allen, Jr., Commissioner of Education, State of New York, at a hearing before the United States Commission on Civil Rights in Rochester, N.Y., September 16-17, 1966 (Washington, D.C.: U.S. Government Printing Office, 1967), p. 207.

7. John L. Hess, "In France, Victory from the Ashes of Defeat," *New York Times*, August 4, 1968, p. E-11.

8. Ibid.

9. Ward E. Goodenough, letter to the author (August 21, 1967).

10. Jay Schulman, letter to the author (August 17, 1967).

11. W. Rex Crawford, "Representative Italian Contributions to Sociology," in *Introduction to the History of Sociology*, ed. by Harry Elmer Barnes (Chicago: University of Chicago Press, 1948), p. 567.

# 5 Biological and Cultural Differences and Race-Related Behavior

During the height of the school desegregation crisis in the United States, some blacks insisted, "It's not the bus, it's us." That little ditty did two things: it implied that busing is a fake and phony issue, as mentioned in Chapter 2, and it identified racism as one of the fundamental factors in the controversy. One out of every two children in public elementary and secondary schools in this country is transported at public expense to and from school daily. Thus busing is the norm; it is not unusual or extraordinary.

The *Report of the National Advisory Commission on Civil Disorders* stated that "race prejudice has shaped our history decisively."[1] Court orders to use transportation if necessary to achieve desegregated education also have been decisive events in our history that have revealed the residue of racism in this society. The resistance to desegregation in the public schools has been intense and widespread,[2] and it has been shaped by a history of racism.

Racism in urban education has been difficult to deal with because of the persisting misconceptions of race that abound. Race refers to biological characteristics of individuals that are inherited. Anthropologists and biologists classify people into races in terms of the presence or absence of several different physical characteristics. Thus race is a statistical concept, an abstraction, or a model that includes several different traits. Race is not a single trait that can be inherited. Rather, it describes a complex or set of traits that are inherited.

According to John Bennett and Melvin Tumin, "The concept of 'race' is employed by biologists to designate a group of animals who share a statistical majority of inherited, relatively unmodifiable, physical and biological characteristics which set them off as a relatively distinct group from other animals."[3] Among the inheritable physical characteristics most frequently used in classifying human populations by race are skin color, eye color, head shape, nose shape, hair color, hair texture, the presence or absence of body hair, and stature. Persons with long heads, wide noses, dark skin, tightly curled dark hair on the head, dark eyes, little body hair, and tall stature are classified as members of the Negroid race. The Mongoloid race consists of people of medium stature, with almost no body hair, straight black hair on the head, medium-sized noses, and light brown skin. Caucasoids tend to be people of beige skin color, light brown or blond wavy hair on the head, light-colored eyes, medium to tall stature, much body hair, and relatively long noses.[4] These are useful characteristics that are customarily referred to collectively as indicators of one or another

45

race; but each of these traits is not more or less important in human terms than other inherited traits (such as blood type) that are not commonly used as racial indicators.

Most people in the United States exhibit some physical characteristics that are found in races other than the one with which they identify. They simply are classified as members of one or another race because they have a preponderance of traits that more closely resemble the ideal type of a particular racial category. Races, therefore, are not mutually exclusive of each other. One is more or less Negroid, Mongoloid, or Caucasoid.

Since race is a statistical and abstract concept, it cannot be inherited. People inherit specific biological traits. As stated above, it is the combination of specific traits that are classified as a race. Failure to distinguish between what can and cannot be inherited has contributed to some of the confusion surrounding the issue of race. The confusion is increased because of the fact that specific traits that are inherited can be modified in appearance by the environment. An inherited trait that can vary in appearance or manifestation is called phenotype and refers to the physical manifestation that is a result of interaction with the environment. The basic and inherited trait is called genotype. While the genotype such as skin color may have varying phenotypical manifestations depending on environmental circumstances such as exposure to sun rays, the phenotype cannot be inherited. Only the genotype or basic skin color is inherited.

Most of our measures of intelligence, for example, assess the phenotype— the cultivated mind—rather than the genotype, the basic ability or capacity to think, reflect, and reason. Misunderstanding of the difference between genotypic and phenotypic characteristics of individuals further has contributed to confusion about learning, inheritance, and race-related behavior. Much that is attributed to inheritance, the good and the bad, is phenotypic and can be explained only in relation to the cultural as well as physical environmental context within which it occurs. Populations are said to be polymorphic when a genotype or basic inherited trait can be manifested in several different forms. A single genotypic characteristic may take on several different forms in a human population of biologically related individuals. One should be careful not to assume ´ that the phenotype is the genotype. This is an error frequently made by people who do not know the difference between these two biological features.

Theodosius Dobzhansky has tried as much as anyone to clarify the concept of race, the process of inheritance, and their genotypic and phenotypic aspects. Born in Russia in 1900, Dobzhansky was naturalized as a United States citizen and became a famous American geneticist. For many years he taught zoology at Columbia University. His early research focused on the fruit fly. In later years he discussed the implications of his findings for cultural as well as biological evolution. Eleven principles are extracted from his writings that contribute to a theory of cultural and biological differences.[5]

1. "A Mendelian population is . . . a reproduction of individuals who share in a common gene pool" (p. 15).
2. "Gene frequencies and variances, rather than averages characterize Mendelian populations. All Mendelian populations are polymorphic" (pp. 108-109).
3. "A species [is] polymorphic if it contains a variety of genotypes, each of which is superior in adaptive value to the others in some habitats which occur regularly in the territory occupied by the species . . . " (pp. 132-33).
4. "Polymorphic populations [are], in general, more efficient in the exploitation of ecological opportunities of an environment than genetically uniform ones . . . " (pp. 132-33).
5. "Racial differences are more commonly due to variations in the relative frequencies of genes in different parts of the species population than to an absolute lack of genes in certain groups . . ." (p. 176).
6. "Race and species are populations . . . which remain distinct only so long as some cause limits their interbreeding" (p. 18).
7. "The sum of genes of an individual or a population constitutes the genotype . . . the resulting bodily forms . . . are different phenotypes . . . A genotype is potentially able to engender a multitude of phenotypes . . ." (pp. 20-21).
8. "Any phenotype that may be formed is necessarily a response of the environment to the activity of the genotype. The genotype reproduces itself regardless of what phenotype it happens to evoke in a given instance" (pp. 20-22).
9. "Some genotypes permit a greater amplitude of modifications . . . than others, and some traits are plastic while others are more rigidly fixed" (p. 23).
10. "Human intellectuality [or] emotional development is an example of a great plasticity and susceptibility to environmental influences. Environment, upbringing, schooling, association with other people and the manifold variations of individual biographies are powerful moulders of human personality. The genotypic determinants of human personality are easily obscured by the environmental ones" (p. 23).
11. "The populations of most species vary, often within an enormous range, from generation to generation (p. 163).

It is appropriate to close this review of findings pertaining to population genetics by returning to Dobzhansky's discussion of the Mendelian laws. According to Mendel, *the fundamental units of racial variability are populations and genes, not complexes of characters.* Dobzhansky goes on to say:

Many studies of hybridization were made before Mendel, but they did not lead to the discovery of Mendel's laws. In retrospect we see clearly where the mistake lay: they treated as units the complexes of characteristics of individuals, races, and species and attempted to find rules governing inheritance of such

complexes . . . . Mendel was the first to understand that . . . the inheritance of
separate traits [and] not [the inheritance] of complexes of traits . . . had to be
studied . . . . Some of the students of racial variability consistently repeat the
mistakes of Mendel's predecessors (p. 177). [That is, they try to trace inheritance through complexes of characteristics.]

Dobzhansky concludes that "race is not a static entity but a process . . . .
Racial variability must be described in terms of the frequencies of individual
genes . . . in groups of individuals occupying definite habitats. Such a description is more adequate than the usual method of finding the abstract average
phenotypes of 'races' . . ." (pp. 177-78).

Note that this review has focused on population genetics and not on the
genetics of individuals. As stated by Dobzhansky, the rules governing the genetic
structure of individuals are different from those governing the genetic structure of
a population. Moreover, he states that "every human individual is unique, different from all others who live or lived" (pp. 15, 4).

J. McV. Hunt states that "heredity is clearly primary" with reference to
intelligence.[6] Lloyd Humphreys warns us that "the functions measured by
intelligence and aptitude tests are not stable in the individual over time."[7]
Eleanor Maccoby and Carol Jacklin conclude, "It is still a reliable generalization
that there are not sex differences [on measures of total or composite abilities
such as IQ tests] ."[8] From these statements we may determine that populations
with obviously different hereditary characteristics such as those associated with
sex respond similarly to intelligence tests, and that a person whose hereditary
characteristics are obviously the same at birth as in later years responds differently to intelligence tests at different periods in time.

If heredity is primary, as Hunt has asserted, it is primary for the continuation of the species. Only a genotype may reproduce a genotype. As Hunt has
said, only an elephant can reproduce an elephant.[9] After that, much is left to
the habitat and environment. He further states that life under different circumstances can produce differences in a given genotype or a given population of genotypes. He makes specific reference to children from poor families who have
lived under conditions of poverty.[10] Humphreys states that children who are
much below average in achievement may suffer the deficit from a number of
possible sources, starting with genetic differences and including the totality of
the environment.[11] Maccoby and Jacklin state that data on the incidence of
specific deficits in learning abilities indicate that these occur considerably more
frequently among boys than girls. However, they explain that the greater vulnerability of the male child to anomalies of prenatal development, birth injury,
and childhood disease is well known and that this vulnerability probably does
affect the incidence of very low scores on tests of intellectual abilities.[12]

These statements are similar to those of Dobzhansky, that a phenotype is a
response of the environment to the activity of the genotype and that the genotypic determinants of human personality are easily obscured by the

environmental ones.  A genotype is potentially able to engender a multitude of phenotypes.  Apparently most of our tests have been measuring genotypic *responses* to the environment, or phenotypes, which account for the instability of such measurements on the same individual at different periods in time. Dobzhansky's finding that "human intellectuality . . . is an example of a great plasticity and susceptibility to environmental influences" is confirmed by other scholars.  For example, Hunt has shared with us the results of studies conducted by him and associates in the Parent and Child Center in Mr. Carmel, Illinois. He and his colleagues found that child-rearing of parents from a lower class had been improved by a parent education program so that the behavior of their children in the development of object permanence surpassed that of the middle class, at least during the first two years of infancy.[13]  These findings are illustrative of the great plasticity of intellectuality.

Humphreys states that there is some evidence that the size of the correlation between phenotype and genotype differs as a function of social class.[14]  This evidence may or may not indicate genotypic plasticity; but it certainly does point toward phenotypic variability, possibly related to differential environmental circumstances of life, especially with reference to intelligence.

Most black students enrolled in four upstate New York colleges which we studied did not perform as well academically as most white students.  About 23 percent of the blacks compared to 49 percent of the whites had self-reported cumulative grades of A or B; 64 percent of the blacks compared to 49 percent of the whites had cumulative grade averages at the C level; and 13 percent of the blacks compared to 2 percent of the whites had self-reported cumulative grades of D or less.  Averages like these tend to mask so much and contribute to our misunderstanding about variability in adaptation.  When analyzed by year in school, we discovered that black college seniors had better grades than black college freshmen.  But not only that; black college seniors had better grades than white college seniors:  52 percent of the black college seniors compared to 42 percent of the white college seniors had cumulative grades at the A and B levels.[15]

Do these findings mean that black college seniors came from intellectually more gifted parents than black college freshmen?  I doubt it.  Do these findings mean that black college seniors came from genetic pools that are intellectually superior to the genetic pools from which white college seniors were drawn?  I doubt this possibility too.  Our conclusion is that the superior achievement of these black seniors compared with other students is a function of the way in which they adapted to the difficult situation in which they found themselves. It is probably fair to say that both the low achievement of black students during the first three years and the high achievement of blacks during the fourth and last year were due to environmental circumstances and adaptations thereto.  (An unanswered question is whether the grade average for black seniors is as high as it was because low-achieving blacks dropped out during the first three years.)

On the basis of our study (which unfortunately is inconclusive because it is limited to cross-sectional data), we assert that black students in predominantly white colleges are neither superior nor inferior to their white college mates, that each group has an overlapping range of intellectual capacity which is capable of making a variety of responses to different environmental situations, and that black seniors tend to respond by superior academic performance while black freshman, sophomores, and juniors respond by inferior academic performance compared to whites.

We can understand this only if we can remember four principles earlier set forth by Dobzhansky: (1) that "a genotype is potentially able to engender a multitude of phenotypes," including those which function in superior and inferior ways; (2) that "genotypic determinants of human personality are easily obscured by the environmental ones"; (3) that "racial differences are more commonly due to variations in the relative frequencies of genes in different parts of the species population than to an absolute lack of genes in certain groups"; and (4) that "environment, upbringing, schooling, association with other people, and the manifold variations of individual biographies are powerful moulders of human personality."

A common limitation of much research is our common tendency to rely upon statistical measures of aggregated characteristics to get at the problem of biological difference between the races, particularly as it relates to intelligence. Even though, as a total racial group, their cumulative average attainment was lower, black senior college students in our study performed better than whites academically. They could not have performed better than whites academically the last year of college if they had not had the capacity to do so, a capacity which was probably present during the earlier three years but was dormant, had not been cultivated and made manifest.

In populations of poor performers the capacity to perform well probably is present and could become manifest, given the appropriate set of circumstances or motivational components. One reason for not recognizing this fact is our tendency to rely either on composite measures of intelligence or on composite descriptions of a population. And thus we commit the same error committed by Mendel's predecessors, that of treating as a unit the complexes of characteristics of race or intelligence rather than recognizing as did Mendel that what must be understood is the inheritance of separate traits and not the inheritance of complexes of traits. Moreover, it should be stated again and again that geno-typic traits may be present even though they are not observable in the pheno-type. This simple fact is frequently forgotten. In a gentle way, we are trying to say that although our statistical methods and techniques for studying varia-tions in the association between intelligence and race appear to be sophisticated, conceptually—especially with reference to the nature and form of heritability—some are pre-Mendelian and, therefore, dated.

Mention of the need to disaggregate traits for the purpose of studying heritability leads directly into a discussion of race. It is time we ceased the silly

business of discussing variations in behavior by racial categories as if the races
which we commonly recognize were pure. Indeed, racial purity would be a
liability. Such a population would be less adaptable and less able to exploit
the environment.

Dobzhansky tells us that the genetic structures of populations can be molded
into new shapes through the influences of selection, migration, and geographic
isolation, and especially the breeding of species.[16] To be sure, there have been
laws against the intermingling of the races in this country. But historian John
Hope Franklin tells us that "the slave woman was frequently forced into
cohabitation and pregnancy by . . . her master." He describes the miscegenation
which went on during the slave period as "extensive."[17] Moreover, he indicates
that there are records of marriages of black-white couples and black-Indian couples
in New England during the colonial period.[18] We know that there was considerable interbreeding between whites and the Native Americans, also known as
American Indians, when the West was settled.[19] In summary, there has been a
lot of race mixing and interbreeding in the United States. The diversity of inherited characteristics exhibited by the people in any public gathering is ample
evidence of the extensive cohabitation between all sorts and conditions of
people over the years in this land. Lloyd Humphreys is right when he states that
any given individual belongs to a very large number of different demographic
groups.[20]

It is inappropriate to measure intelligence as a complex of characteristics,
if one wants to understand something about inheritance. Maccoby and Jacklin's
approach of looking at specific skills is more promising than the search for an
inheritable composite.[21] Also it is inappropriate to relate a faulty measure of
intellectual heritability which Humphreys calls a "hypothetical capacity" to race,
which Dobzhansky calls an "abstract statistical phenotype," if one wishes to
understand the association between innate characteristics. Neither intelligence
as presently measured nor race as presently defined are innate. Yet we persist
in correlating the two and thereby compound our error by making what
Humphreys would call "unfair inferences about native capacities."[22] The discussion about race and intelligence in the United States, then, is so much talk
about nothing. Measures of intelligence are unsatisfactory, and so are the
definitions of race. So what is all the fuss about?

I am inclined to believe that the controversy has little, if anything, to do
with science. It seems to me that the controversy is a continuation of the
social Darwinism in American thought. Hofstadter's discussion on "Racism and
Imperialism" details how Americans rationalized oppression of Outgroups in the
past as a natural development in which "backward races would disappear before
the advance of higher civilizations."[23]

Herbert Spencer, William Graham Summer, and nineteenth century white
Americans may have believed these thoughts. They used the findings of population genetics as a way of putting people down as inferiors and explaining

Outgroup failures. But twentieth-century Americans have been exposed to more enlightened thoughts. They know "that the physical well-being of [human kind] is a result of their social organization and not vice versa." They know that "social improvement is a product of advances in technology and social organization, not of breeding or selective elimination."[24]

If twentieth-century Americans know these things, why do they continue to use social Darwinism? Social Darwinism is used today not so much to put down the Outgroup as subhuman as to build up the Ingroup as superhuman.

The article by Arthur Jensen on IQ and scholastic achievement is a classic example of the use of social Darwinism to explain away the lack of success of the Ingroup. One does not have to read far into that article to pick up a twentieth-century tone of Manifest Destiny. Read this: "The remedy deemed logical for children who would do poorly in school is to boost their IQs up to where they can perform like the majority . . . ." This is a direct quotation from Arthur Jensen. He goes on to say, "This is in fact essentially what we are attempting in our special programs of preschool enrichment and compensatory education" (p. 3). He develops a series of questions. "Why has there been such uniform failure of compensatory programs whenever they have been tried? What has gone wrong? In other fields, when bridges do not stand, when aircraft do not fly, when machines do not work, when treatments do not cure, *despite all conscientious effort on the part of many persons to make them do so*, one begins to question the basic assumptions, principles, theories, and hypotheses that guide one's effort. Is it time to follow suit in education?" (p. 3; italics added). He asserts that preschool and compensatory programs are successful if they develop gains in IQ and in scholastic achievement. And then, in a bold attempt to stake out the public definition of the problem, he states that "our diagnosis should begin . . . with the concept of the IQ."[25]

By what line of reasoning did Jensen determine that the intellectual adaptation of the majority should be the determinant norm for the kinds of adaptations which the minority ought to make? Remember our upstate New York study of black college students. Minority black seniors functioned better than majority white seniors. It is an arrogant act to establish the Ingroup as a model for all others to follow. Jensen's position with reference to black youth was quite similar to one advocated by Daniel Patrick Moynihan for black adults. Moynihan advocated overhauling the black family because, he declared, "It is so out of line with the rest of the American society."[26]

Again the majority is used as a model for the minority, without recognizing that the minority has found survival value in the kinds of adaptations to which it has grown accustomed. Moreover, minority adaptations are sometimes beneficial for all.

The poor and disadvantaged have some ideas of their own about what they would like to get out of formal education. Manipulation of their children's IQ may not be their highest priority. Learning how to endure,[27] and how to develop a positive concept of self,[28] and how to gain a measure of control over one's environment,[29] probably are as important to the poor as gains in IQ.

And so the great experiment failed which was fashioned by the Ingroup for the Outgroup. The affluent, majority, Ingroup tried to make over the poor, minority, Outgroup in its own image. Rather than accept the failure as an inadequately planned program, improperly imposed upon a population, the Ingroup with Arthur Jensen as philosopher-king has turned once more to social Darwinism, this time to explain the lack of success of the Ingroup rather than to put down the Outgroup. The compensatory educational programs that failed were misguided efforts to remedy the irremediable and were not failures in educational planning and social organization, according to twentieth-century social Darwinists. Others view these failures as inappropriately organized programs based on inadequate consultation with the poor, involving little, if any, participation in the planning process by representatives of the groups they were intended to help.

The time has come to deal with cultural and biological differences as they ought to be dealt with, in the tradition of the social and behavioral sciences, and not in the tradition of social Darwinism, which tends to justify existing patterns of privilege and power in society as if they were inherited.

The Boston experience in school desegregation is an example of what happens when the perspective of the social sciences as an explanation of racial differences is abandoned in favor of a political doctrine like social Darwinism. Members of the Caucasoid race, according to social Darwinists, are superior. In years gone by, Boston had one of the nation's best school systems. In the last quarter of the twentieth century, after the court order to desegregate, it became a school system in which black and brown students were the majority. Of the 68,000 students enrolled in public schools in 1976, 29,000 were classified as blacks and 9,000 as other minorities. Subsequent to this change, a report about declining test scores that was prepared by the Boston School Department for the federal government "[sought] . . . to show how various aspects of desegregation . . . [had] affected student performance" in mathematics and reading skills.[30] According to the *Boston Globe*, "the decline, as measured by reading and math tests, has been an ongoing process for decades. . . ."[31] The decline, therefore, should not be attributed to the fact that minorities now are the predominant population in Boston and many other big-city schools. Yet this is the conclusion suggested by some of the authors of studies of skills development by students in schools undergoing desegregation. For example, a report on reading released by the National Assessment of Educational Programs in Denver, Colorado, concluded that "Society's attempts at providing equal educational opportunities apparently have not yet resulted in equal educational benefits."[32] The basis for this statement was a finding contained in the report that nearly half of the seventeen-year-old blacks tested in the nationwide survey had reading difficulties.

The social Darwinists too easily have concluded that the deficiencies exhibited by blacks are inherited and therefore are race-related and relatively unmodifiable. But Richard Lewontin, a geneticist, has asserted that intelligence levels are chiefly determined by environmental factors. Arthur Jensen disagrees. He has insisted that 60 to 80 percent of the variability in IQ is genetic.[33]

One of the most severe blows to the social Darwinists' linkage between race and intelligence resulted from the discrediting of the findings of British psychologist Cyril Burt. According to the *New York Times*, Burt's writings, based on his alleged studies of identical twins reared in separate homes, had been a major buttress of the view that blacks have inherited inferior brains. Further investigations into Burt's findings by psychologist Leon Kamin found "many instances of questionable scientific thought" including statements that reflect deep racial prejudice. Indeed Kamin said some of Burt's findings were "fraudulent."[34]

These developments support the earlier statement by Dobzhansky that intelligence is inherited but is susceptible to environmental influences. It is inappropriate, therefore, to attribute skills development and the performance of blacks, browns, or whites to a racial origin without also examining the environmental contexts to which the members of each racial group are exposed. A valid theory of biological and cultural differences must include information about the individual and information about the individual's environment. The two are interrelated and should not be separated in studies of race-related behavior.

## Notes

1. *Report of the National Advisory Commission on Civic Disorders* (New York: Bantam Books, 1968), p. 10.

2. Charles V. Willie and Jerome Beker, *Race Mixing in the Public Schools* (New York: Praeger, 1973).

3. John W. Bennett and Melvin M. Tumin, *Social Life* (New York: Alfred Knopf, 1948), pp. 7-8.

4. Ibid., pp. 9-10.

5. Taken from Theodosius Dobzhansky, *Genetics and the Origin of Species* (New York: Columbia U. Press, 1951), pp. 15-178. Published by permission of Columbia University Press.

6. J. McV. Hunt, "Heredity, Environment, and Class or Ethnic Differences," in *Assessment in a Pluralistic Society* (Princeton: Educational Testing Service, 1973), p. 7.

7. Lloyd G. Humphreys, "Implications of Group Differences for Test Interpretation," in *Assessment in a Pluralistic Society* (Princeton: Educational Testing Service, 1973), p. 3.

8. Eleanor Maccoby and Carol Jacklin, "Sex Differences in Intellectual Functioning," in *Assessment in a Pluralistic Society* (Princeton: Educational Testing Service, 1973), p. 37.

9. Hunt, p. 4.

10. Ibid.

11. Humphreys, p. 67.

12. Maccoby and Jacklin, p. 4.

13. Hunt, p. 17.

14. Humphreys, p. 62.

15. C.V. Willie and A. McCord, *Black Students at White Colleges* (New York: Praeger, 1972), p. 86.

16. Dobzhansky, p. 15.

17. J.H. Franklin, *From Slavery to Freedom* (New York: Alfred Knopf, 1967), p. 204.

18. Ibid., p. 109.

19. Dee Brown, *Bury My Heart at Wounded Knee* (New York: Bantam Books, 1970).

20. Humphreys, p. 58.

21. Maccoby and Jacklin, p. 44.

22. Humphreys, p. 58.

23. R. Hofstadter, *Social Darwinism in American Thought* (Boston: Beacon, 1955), p. 171.

24. Ibid., p. 204.

25. A.R. Jensen, "How Much Can We Boost IQ and Scholastic Achievement?" *Environment, Heredity, and Intelligence* (Cambridge: Harvard Education Review, 1969), Reprint Series No. 2, pp. 1-123.

26. U.S. Department of Labor, *The Negro Family* (Washington, D.C.: U.S. Government Printing Office, 1966).

27. F. Douglass, *Life and Times of Frederick Douglass* (New York: Macmillan, 1962), p. 39.

28. M. Rosenberg and R.G. Simmons, *Black and White Self-Esteem: The Urban School Child* (Washington, D.C.: The American Sociological Association, 1972), pp. 21-30.

29. J.E. Teele, "Sociocultural Factors Relating to Mild Mental Retardation," *Social Science and Medicine*, 3 (1970), 363-69.

30. Peter Mancusi, "Report Cites Negative Effects of Desegregation," *Boston Globe*, January 16, 1976, p. 1.

31. *Boston Globe,* "Misplacing Blame," January 22, 1977, p. 8.

32. *Boston Globe*, "Many Students Still Cannot Read," January 16, 1976.

33. Boyce Rensberger, "Briton's Classic I.Q. Data Now Viewed as Fradulent," *New York Times*, November 28, 1976, p. 26.

34. Ibid.

**Part II:**
**Education Planning and Policymaking**

# 6

## Basic Features of a Good School Desegregation Plan

The distinguished journalist and former editor of the *Atlanta Constitution*, Ralph McGill, said that the "careful and wise phrasing" of the Supreme Court's decision in *Brown* v. *Board of Education* "anticipated that the knowledge and skills of educators, of social psychologists and of the social sciences, would assume direction of the processes of desegregation." But such was not to be. "That this did not happen," said McGill, "is a rebuke chiefly to the political and legal leadership of the states involved."[1] But Harold Howe II, former Commissioner of Education of the United States, said there may be a reason why social scientists were bypassed, and that reason as he sees it is ". . . the difficulty of translating research findings into forms that the schools can use."[2]

This chapter is a modest attempt by one who is a research social scientist (in sociology) and a practicing educator (at the college level) to synthesize principle and practice in a way that results in operational guidelines for the development of a workable school desegregation plan.

A beneficial effect of school desegregation is that it has focused attention upon education as a process of social interaction rather than as a product. The person is not an inanimate object into which education, a good thing, is poured. Education, like economic and political activity, is a function of exchange.

School desegregation has emphasized these exchange relationships in terms of the racial characteristics of the participants involved and the context within which they take place. School desegregation for the purpose of achieving quality education demands modification of an institution when formerly we had focused largely on the individual. Individuals—students and teachers (whites, blacks, browns, and other minorities)—are dependent upon institutions for personal fulfillment, including the attainment of an education. Institutions are collectivities of people and materials, using agreed-upon means of interacting in group structures, within prescribed situations and settings, for the purpose of achieving a goal or goals which are held in common. Education is an institution which exists for the enhancement of individuals who must receive such enhancement in communion with each other. The benefits of education cannot be obtained in isolation.

It is the nature of education as a societal goal and a community institution that I wish to examine for the purpose of determining the basic components of a school desegregation plan. In a good school desegregation plan: (a) there is a systemwide approach; (b) the school and not the student is the basic educational unit; (c) such units or schools that complement each other may be grouped

59

into common attendance zones, districts, or regions for more effective and
efficient operation and administration; (d) a uniform grade structure facilitates interchange between and easy access to all units or schools within the
system; (e) opportunities are provided to pursue specialized interests as well as
common concerns; (f) the existence of a monitoring structure insures good-faith
implementation of the systemwide plan; (g) faculty is diversified.


## Systemwide Approach

The systemwide approach has been troubling and troublesome to many. Some
contend that only those schools should be desegregated which are segregated
because of official action by school authorities. The suburbs have attempted
to exclude themselves from responsibility for city-school system segregation.
They successfully resisted participating in metropolitan desegregation in areas
surrounding Detroit and Richmond by claiming that their official actions did
not contribute to segregated schools in the city. Yet, a practice for years—
though now discontinued—in the South was to send the children of black private
household workers who lived on the suburban premises of their employer into
the nearby city to attend segregated schools as a way of preventing desegregated
education in the suburban community. Moreover, several studies have docu-
mented racial discrimination in the sale and rental of housing in the suburbs—in
the North, South, East, and West. Such practices have not been challenged by
local governmental authorities in the communities surrounding central cities;
which is to say, the governments in the suburbs have not insisted that equal
protection of the laws be granted to all who seek the services of real-estate
agents who are licensed by public authorities. There is culpability in condoning
housing and consequently school segregation by omission if not by commission.
    In biblical literature, Paul said, "We who are many are one body," and
"If one member suffers, all suffer together" (I Corinthians 10:17; 12:26). In
English literature, John Donne concluded that no one is an island entire of
itself, that each person's death diminished him. In American political rhetoric,
Abraham Lincoln said a house divided against itself cannot stand; and John
Kennedy declared, "The rights of [all] are diminished when the rights of one . . .
are threatened." This principle of the interdependence of humanity has
stretched across the centuries and around the world. It has stood the test of
time and space. The particular affects the general and the whole affects its
parts.
    So far as school desegregation is concerned, however, the Boston Home
and School Association asserted that the court should not have required desegregated schools for the entire Boston public school system. The association, as
we said earlier, believed that the remedy of desegregation should be applied only
to those schools which were segregated because of illegal "state action" and that

schools segregated because of residential population patterns should not be covered by the court order.

Operating on a similar premise, the Dallas Independent School District, in a proposed desegregation plan not accepted by the court, exempted fifty-five of its 173 schools because, according to the district, these schools were "naturally integrated." By exempting these schools which incidentally contained two-fifths of all white students, the district, therefore, was unable to desegregate forty-eight other schools which contained more than three-fifths of the black students in that city. The desegregation proposal for Dallas would have left about two out of every three black students isolated in segregated schools because more than one out of every three whites was not available to participate in a systemwide desegregation plan. Such are the difficulties of desegregating an illegally segregated public school system when part of the system is exempted from participating.

Beyond the logistical problems of effecting equitable desegregation when part of the system is uninvolved or exempted from the plan, such an approach could become the basis for community strife. Sociologists Robin Williams and Margaret Ryan came to this conclusion several years ago and published their findings in a book entitled *Schools in Transition*.[3] After studying desegregation efforts in several communities they said, "Partial desegregation that affects only . . . a few schools in a community opens the door to charges [of favoritism]." Those who are required to participate in the desegregation process feel put-upon while those exempted boast of special treatment for one reason or another. Such was the experience of South Boston, Roxbury, and other inner-city Boston neighborhoods included in the first-year partial desegregation plan that was limited to about eighty of 200 schools, largely in working-class areas.

The rationale for special treatment sometimes is a function of fantasy that nevertheless has a debilitating effect upon the total community. For example, East Boston (largely a working-class, ethnically homogeneous community), separated from the rest of Boston by a tunnel, was not included in the second-year citywide desegregation plan, for one reason, because of logistical problems in transporting students to and from the community during the hours of congested automobile traffic on the city streets. Some East Bostonians claimed that they were exempted from the second-year citywide desegregation plan because of a rumored threat that the tunnel would be blown up. Because of their belief that the threat was efficacious, although it actually was not the basis for the exemption, some East Bostonians engaged in demonstrations as further proof of their capacity to disrupt when the court proposed to desegregated East Boston High School the third year of court surveillance. Thus a fantasy about the reasons for the earlier exemption stimulate violence when the third-year plan was announced; also other homogeneous working-class communities heavily populated by ethnic groups followed suit (even those included in the second-year citywide plan) and participated in disruptive demonstrations

for the purpose of inducing the court to change its citywide desegregation
order.

To avoid fantasies and charges of favoritism, all parts of a system should
be included in any citywide desegregation plan. A systemwide approach
facilitates the development of an equitable plan, contributes to unity and total
community involvement, and is in keeping with the principle of human interdependence wherein the many are one body who suffer and rejoice together.


## Basic Educational Unit

Because of our belief in self-determination, we tend to look upon the individual
as the basic unit of analysis in all human associations. Commemorating the
two hundredth anniversary of the Declaration of Independence, the President
of the United States said, "In this country individuals can be the masters . . . of
their destiny. We can make our own opportunities and make the most of them."
Such a statement exalts individuals as primary in our national life, but also
contributes to a distorted perception of the function of groups and institutions
that support and encumber individual effort. Human behavior should be analyzed
as the activity of individuals, groups, and institutions. Either may be the basic
unit of analysis, depending upon the problem under consideration, the preferred
outcome, and the level of social organization responsible for effecting the indicated solution. Thus the classificatory scheme for human associations is groups,
institutions, and communities or societies. Human groups are separable into
those that are primary and secondary, and individuals are dominant or subdominant in terms of their power within groups.

Groups are the basic units of analysis in institutional systems; and individuals
or their various status and role relationships are the basic units of analysis in
groups. When we speak of human associations we are including all institutions
and all groups.

Individuals may experience opportunity and indeed their humanity only by
participating in groups and institutions. Unassisted, individuals cannot make
their own opportunities and make the most of them, as asserted by the President
in his Bicentennial message. They need the help and support of a community.
The ultimate goal of all human associations is enhancement of the individual.
The individual who is dependent on associations is not entirely in charge.

Failure to understand the function of different levels of social organization,
and particularly the basic units responsible for the solution of different problems,
has contributed to faulty diagnoses, misguided planning, and defective proposals
of remedial action. For example, poverty in a capitalistic society is a problem of
equity. The solution requires modification in earning opportunities or consump-
tion privileges—in short, some form of income redistribution or transfer. Such
modification involves coordination and integration of the various units of a

society, including individuals and groups, concerned with the production and distribution of goods and services and, therefore, is an economic institutional problem. Yet Daniel Patrick Moynihan identified the kinship system as the principal institution within which remedial action was necessary to reduce poverty among blacks. He directed attention to the wrong institution, and to the family which is the wrong group if his goal was elimination of the differential prevalence of poverty among blacks compared with whites. His mis-diagnosis caused him to overlook the economic institution which is the basic unit of analysis for the production and distribution of goods and services and the distribution of income at the community or societal level. This mis-diagnosis led him to a faulty proposal that black family groups should be strengthened.[4] The action he recommended missed the mark on two counts: first, it focused on a group as the basic unit of analysis when the problem required an institutional response; and second, he directed attention toward the wrong institution, the kinship system rather than the economy.

A similar problem of mis-diagnosis was exhibited by Arthur Jensen.[5] He tried to define the differential performance of blacks and whites in school as an individual rather than an institutional problem. Socializing the young into effective adults by sharing with them the accumulated knowledge of the past and cultivating their capacities to create and exchange information, to compare, synthesize and reflect upon it, to reason and to anticipate the future in relation to the present and the past is the business of education. These activities are so important for the welfare of the community that they cannot be left to chance or personal caprice. Thus, most societies have institutionalized them into a formal education system.

When the average performance in calculation and communication of a population of students such as blacks is consistently different from that of another population such as whites, and both populations participate in a common society, it is probable that the educational system is relating to the student of each population differently. Robert Merton has said that ". . . patterns of human behavior are largely a product of the modifiable structure of society."[6] Education, an institution with its multiple units or groups, is one such structure; and teachers and administrators, the dominant people of power in this institutional system, have a good deal to do with the quality of the learning experiences provided for black and white students. Merton described the operation of the education system with reference to black students as an example of the self-fulfilling prophecy in which the dominant people of power defined blacks as incompetent, saw to it that funds for their education were disproportionately limited, and then justified providing fewer resources and opportunities for racial minorities because of their lower level of educational attainment.[7]

This is precisely what happened in Boston. A very high proportion of the graduates of the elite examination schools—Boston Latin School, Boston Latin

Academy, and Boston Technical High School—go on to college. Racial minorities have been underrepresented in the student body of these schools. The federal court required that at least 40 percent of their entering class the second year of court-ordered desegregation consist of black and Hispanic students. This approach was necessary to desegregate these schools, since low-income and minority students tended not to perform well on standard examinations such as the Secondary School Admission Test that had been used as a major basis for admissions decisions.

Despite the fact that an education in one of Boston's Latin schools or in the Technical High School would enhance the possibility that racial minorities would be accepted in college and thereby have their future employment opportunities increased, the Boston School Committee, the mayor, and the Boston Home and School Association challenged the court's mandate that a minimum percentage of black and brown children be admitted to these elite schools. It was a case of some of the dominant people of power damning the racial minorities for not graduating from the elite high schools of Boston which would have enhanced their opportunity for acceptance by a good college, and then damning the court for insisting that these elite schools make their extraordinary educational experiences available to black and brown students.

Placing the blame directly on the system, Reginal Jones stated unequivocally that ". . . the school as an institution and its agents have failed many black children." Further, he said that "teachers, administrators, and the school curriculum are all implicated."[8] Yet Jensen, as we saw, tried to define the differential academic performance by black and white children in school as a problem of the individual having to do with intelligence or heritability. His prescription that we should start with IQ and attempt to boost it for each minority child so that he or she "can perform like the majority" is a defective prescription,[9] largely because he has misdefined a problem of the educational system as an individual problem. If differential learning by black and white children is largely a function of their inherited capacities, then the individual is the appropriate focus for intervention. But if the problem is one generated by malfunctions in the educational institution, then the school is the appropriate point of intervention for correction.

In addition to Jones and Merton, others such as James Conant and John Kenneth Galbraith believe that the school is the basic unit for intervention to increase the skills performance of low-income or poor children. For example, Galbraith said we ought to invest "more than proportionately in the children of the poor community . . . [so that] . . . high quality schools . . . [may] . . . compensate for the very low investment which [poor] families are able to make in their offspring . . . ."[10] Conant's statement is simple and direct: "More money is needed in slum schools."[11] Elsewhere I have pointed out that the call for more resources for inner-city schools is not likely to be heeded as long as they are part of the overall community pattern of racial segregation, *de facto* or *de jure*, because "the only reason for separating persons in the first place is to accord them differential treatment."[12]   It is indeed difficult to solve a problem of resource allocation compounded by racial segregation in the public schools (and the consequence of this for differential learning by black, brown, and white children), when the prescription recommended directs our attention away from the appropriate unit for intervention.

A good school desegregation plan determines where corrective action is required and recommends intervention strategies that are appropriate for the defects and deficiencies.  We tend to place the onus for failure on the individual rather than the institution and do not make the necessary changes in schools, the basic units of the educational institution, so that they may meet the learning needs of all of the children.

A recent example of mis-diagnosis and faulty prescription was associated with the assessment and educational outcomes presented in Christopher Jencks's book *Inequality*, published in 1972.[13]   Harold Howe II described the public response to the defective assessment this way: "Jencks' view that luck and personality factors were more important than education in producing differentials in income was rapidly parlayed in popular articles and editorials across the United States into arguments that schools didn't matter and that money spent on schools was wasted . . . .  The initial result of Jencks' work was to hurt children.  The counter-fire from knowledgeable critics . . . did not appear in time to get the public notice to undo the harm."[14]

Segregated schools or the tracking of students by ability within schools, as well as excessive suspensions and expulsions of racial minority and poor children, are devices used to disguise the real problem of inflexibility in an institutional system.  The students too often find their needs bypassed in favor of the need of the more powerful teachers and administrators who sometimes use the schools exclusively to promote their professional goals and personal interests.

The school should be the basic and target unit in educational reform; the principal, for the purpose of implementing reform, holds the most significant status position within the school.[15]   The way he or she performs the various role requirements of that office determines whether a school will meet the needs of all of its participants in an honorable way.  School desegregation plans that do not desegregate individual schools but simply provide desegregation experiences part of the day in resources centers visited by students of segregated schools are of some value; but they violate the basic principle that a school is the basic unit in the educational system.

Each school building should have an administrator who has the power and authority to create a sense of community within that building and to help its occupants learn how to turn toward, rather than against or away from, each other.  Each school building should have a program that has an integrity of its own, consisting of students, faculty, and staff who identify with the setting. Effective school desegregation cannot be achieved by moving selected individuals in and out of different school buildings for portions of a day, as if the education were a product and schools were manufacturing assembly lines.

Too many schools have been fashioned in the image of the machine. Some schemes for desegregation are under the influence of this image. Desegregated education should be understood as a way of life and not merely as a technique. The Supreme Court has stated that a desegregated education is the constitutional requirement. The law mandates a desegregated education and not just a desegregated experience. A desegregated education in our society takes place within a school where there is sufficient continuity in interaction by the participants to build up relationships. Because desegregation is a systemwide phenomenon of the educational institution, each school building should be the basic unit within the system for implementation.

## Common Districts or Attendance Zones

Having identified each school as the basic unit of a systemwide program, a good school desegregation plan should indicate clusters of complementary units so that schools dependent on each other are linked together in a rational way. The creation of a common district or attendance zone for schools that share a common geography creates a sense of place and belonging, and also contributes to continuity if schools with responsibility for varying levels of education in the system are combined into an academic cluster. A desegregated education is a societal value sanctioned by law. A sense of belonging and continuity are methods that may contribute to the process of achieving this value. And so it is fitting and proper that the basic educational unit, the school, should be combined and united with other units of the system for the purpose of achieving a more effective academic program and a more efficient system.

The overall purpose should be kept in mind when delineating common districts or attendance zones. The contiguous geographic areas combined should include a sufficiently diversified population so that, ideally, any identifiable racial group is not more than two-thirds or less than one-fifth of the student body of any school.

If the population of minorities is too small to achieve one-third, then a critical mass of not less than one-fifth should be assigned to target schools. Target schools should be those that offer extraordinary educational opportunities. Beyond assignment to target schools, the privilege should be available for students who are a majority to transfer to a school in which they would be part of the minority. When the minority population is small, not all majority schools may be desegregated. This will be discussed in more detail later.

The common attendance zone should consist of one or more senior high schools, and junior high or middle schools that feed students into the senior high school, and then elementary schools that feed students into the middle

or junior high buildings. Such an arrangement with a common feeder pattern
not only creates a sense of belonging and continuity, but facilitates planning
for class size, facility usage, transportation, and staffing beyond the elementary
grades.

If transportation is necessary to achieve integrated education in a particular
building with a population mix within the range mentioned earlier, this can be
accomplished while limiting the distance which students must travel to and from
school. A desegregation plan using these guidelines would transport students
to and from school only within a common district or attendance zone. Such a
limitation should result in a bus trip of not more than thirty minutes for any
student.

Despite the residential segregation which characterizes most American
cities, neighborhoods of dissimilar races are sufficiently near each other to be
combined into a common district to create a population pool from which an
appropriate racial and social class mix can be drawn for the student body of
each school. A common district consisting of schools in contiguous geographic
areas is one way of overcoming segregation and cultural isolation. Neighborhood schools that admit only those children who live within walking distance
of them often are more homogeneous in the ethnic and racial composition of
their student bodies than district schools that admit students from a larger
area that combines several neighborhoods. When a district rather than a
neighborhood is the attendance zone, students within a district are available
for assignment to any of the district schools to achieve a desegregated student
body. Though the distance traveled is held to a minimum by restricting
transportation to within the boundaries of a district, some busing is necessary
to overcome the isolation imposed by segregated neighborhoods. As pointed
out by John Finger, who has worked on several desegregation plans, "There
is no way to achieve desegregation except by busing."[16]

The delineation of districts or attendance zones consisting of contiguous
neighborhoods for a series of schools at elementary, middle or junior high,
and senior high school levels is not difficult, if the proportions of majority and
minority students mentioned earlier are an acceptable operational definition
of desegregation.

The rationale for these proportions is given. An identifiable racial population with a majority of not more than two-thirds of a student body must be
compassionate not only of the minority but also of members of the majority
so as not to risk their defection. When the majority is greater than two out of
every three, it tends to be overwhelming to the minority and less sensitive to
dissidents among the majority who represent little if any real threat to the continuing dominance or control of the current people of power. Oppressive tactics
are ever-present dangers and constant temptations for the many who dominate
because their numbers are overwhelming. Thus a student body of not more than
two-thirds of any one racial population is a way of building in restraint and

consideration on the part of the majority. These would appear to be valuable learnings for life in a democracy, and a desegregated school of the racial ratio recommended presents an excellent opportunity for such learnings to take place.

Any population not of the identifiable racial group in the majority is part of the minority. Ideally, all minority populations combined should not be less than one-third of a public-school student body. The minority may consist of several different identifiable racial or ethnic populations. So far as practicable, the members of any particular minority group should be clustered if necessary so that they are not less than one-fifth of the students in a school. When the members of an identifiable group are less than one out of every five students in a school, their critical mass in terms of numbers is too small to have a significant educative effect upon that learning environment. This means that the proportion of a specific minority population needed to enhance the educational quality of a desegregated school—which is set at one-fifth—may be greater or less than the proportion of that group in the total community population. When the critical mass is less than one-fifth, the minority students tend to experience a greater sense of isolation within the school environment and even estrangement among themselves.

The concept of a critical mass sufficient for a significant impact on a particular setting is important to keep in mind in designing a school desegregation plan. Any combination of minority groups is sufficient to reach the one-third minimum level. For a community that has many different minority groups, some may not be present in all schools if clustering is necessary. The particular racial or ethnic minority group with which the majority must deal is not so important as long as the majority receives a desegregated education in the presence of a significant number of students dissimilar in some ways from the racial or cultural group that is in control. One obvious purpose of school desegregation is to enhance the education of students by facilitating the exchange of ideas between those who can teach each other problem-solving methods based on their unique cultural experiences. This is why any combination of majority and minority students is appropriate, so long as no individual is excluded in an arbitrary and capricious way from any school.

Finally, with reference to the multi-racial composition of the attendance zones of school districts, it really does not matter which race is the majority. A majority of the students may be black, brown, or white in any district. There are assets and liabilities attached to majority and minority statuses. An important learning by minorities is trust, since ultimately they are dependent on others for the fulfillment of their needs that require community resources greater than those in the population of the subdominant people of power. Also, to continue to participate in a situation that one does not control means that minorities must learn how to endure. Trust and endurance are learnings which are valuable for whites, blacks, and all people. Thus, whites ought to have the privilege of obtaining these learnings that are unique to the minority status and should be enrolled in schools in which they are a minority as well as in schools in which they are a majority. Likewise, the majority learns some things that are unique to that status position—for example, the need to exercise restraint and compassion when one is in charge and to be generous. These learnings are beneficial for black and brown people as well as for white people. Thus, black or brown populations ought to be enrolled in some schools in which they are a majority When functioning as a majority, blacks too need to experience a desegregated education in the presence of a minority of whites and others so that they may learn to exercise the responsibilities of the dominant status.

Some state-supported, predominantly black colleges in the South and in the North are beginning to provide whites with a desegregated education in which they are the minority. Blacks in these schools are experiencing the responsibility of being a majority. In the mid-1970s, the proportion of whites in such colleges was 9 to 10 percent; this proportion should increase to a point where whites are not less than one out of every five students in these predominantly black institutions. The same could and should happen in secondary and elementary public schools. The learnings of the members of any people who have always been a majority, who have always been in charge, are inadequate and possibly defective, just as the learnings of the members of any group who have always been a minority, who have always been dependent on others, are constricted and inadequate. A good school desegregation plan delineates several common districts or attendance zones, some of which are majority white and others of which are majority black or majority brown so that some students in all groups may have both kinds of experiences.

It was the failure to abide by this principle that got the Boston School Committee in trouble (*Morgan* v. *Hennigan*, June 21, 1974). Judge W. Arthur Garrity, Jr., of the Federal District Court in Boston, found that overcrowded schools are "educationally damaging," that the Boston School Committee "often acknowledged that fact," but that it "responded on at least one occasion to the problem of overcrowding with actions contrary to sound educational practice. In alleviating overcrowding at [a] junior high, 91 percent white students were assigned to [an] already overcrowded and relatively distant white . . . high school. There were closer schools with available seats but these schools were identifiably black." According to Judge Garrity, "[The] Deputy Superintendent [of Schools in Boston] did not consider assigning students from overcrowded white schools to black schools with available space because he 'thought it would create a problem' of white parents protesting." Apparently, the School Committee cooperated with prejudiced white parents in every way, even to the point of deliberately engaging in segregative acts that were unconstitutional, to keep whites from the privilege of experiencing the learnings that flow from a minority status in a predominantly black school.

If it is educationally sound for whites or blacks to be the minority population in a school, then a good school desegregation plan should provide the full range of opportunities to the children of all races to be in the majority or minority, and parental protest cannot be the basis for denying white children their constitutional right to a desegregated education even if they are required to be a minority. The test is whether it is educationally sound for whites to assume the minority status. This analysis and the findings of the court point toward an affirmative answer.

## Uniform Grade Configuration

A basic characteristic of a unitary, well-functioning system is the ease with which one part has access to another which it needs. Most educational systems are organized in a hierarchical fashion, with students progressing from kindergarten to a new grade each year through a final grade twelve in senior high school. There are competing theories about the best organizational pattern by grade level for a school system. Some school boards have adopted a three-tiered pattern which groups kindergarten through grade five as the elementary-school component of the system, grades six through eight as the middle-school component, and grades nine through twelve as the high-school component of the education system. An alternative pattern used by many begins with kindergarten but ends with grade six for elementary school; junior high school includes grades seven, eight, and nine; and senior high extends from the tenth through the twelfth grade. The essential difference between the patterns has to do with the intermediate grades. Some systems prefer a middle school which educates in the same building children who are eleven, twelve, and thirteen years of age while other systems believe it to be a more felicitous educational experience to group children who are twelve, thirteen, and fourteen years of age in a junior high school. Each organizational pattern has its advocates and each has merit. For the system as a whole, however, it is important to choose one or the other pattern or any standardized way of grouping all of the schools by grade level so that there is easy access to all schools for all students. The accessibility of schools by grade level is a basic way of demonstrating the presence of a unitary school system.

Indeed, the court found that Boston had used multiple patterns of grouping students by grade level to create a dual system of secondary education: "Black students generally entered high school upon completion of the eighth grade, and white students upon completion of the ninth. High school education for black students was conducted by and large in city-wide schools, and for white students in district schools." The race of students as well as the grade configuration in citywide and district high schools tended to be different. Essentially, the middle schools were for blacks and the junior high schools were for whites. Middle schools had to feed into high schools that had a different grade configuration than senior high schools that received students from the junior high buildings.

While the court found that the Boston arrangement was deliberate, other school systems throughout the United States have evolved multiple grade structures in schools that serve similar age grades for various reasons that may have been forgotten, although the arrangement persists. The Dallas Independent School System, for example, at one period in its history had junior high schools which included grades seven, eight, and nine. At the same time, it had two sets of middle schools—some with grades six, seven, and eight and one with grades seven and eight only. The educational rationale for these unique arrangements is hard to come by. They must be classified as aberrations and defects in the organizational structure of the educational system because they limit residential mobility, interfere with the transfer process, and are off-limits to the graduates of schools that do not link up with their unique grade configuration. Students who move from one residential area to another in the same school system are disadvantaged when the grade configurations are different for schools in different sections of the city. Also students with special needs who discover, for example, after enrolling in a district high school that they can obtain greater benefits from education in a citywide school, and vice versa, have difficulty transferring when the grade configurations are not the same in all schools.

The achievement of a uniform grade structure is a basic component of a good school desegregation plan and should receive high priority in any program of educational reform. Justification for such a structure is found in the principle that public education as an institution in our society was created to fulfill in a systematic way our common as well as our unique needs.

Freedom of movement, of course, is a common need for all in an open society. The school system should support and not block the attainment of freedom. A uniform grade structure facilitates mobility and guarantees the accessibility of the educational system to all.

## Specialized or Magnet Citywide Schools

Specialized citywide schools, sometimes called magnet schools, as mentioned earlier, are appropriate in any educational system and as part of a good school desegregation plan. The schools in each district or attendance zone should be staffed and equipped to meet the common needs of all students, while a few citywide schools may provide extraordinary educational experiences to meet the special needs of students. It should go without saying that the number of specialized schools should be few in number. The function of an educational system is to provide a common learning experience that is adapted to the individual needs of students. It is inappropriate, therefore, to attempt to build an entire school desegregation plan around magnet or specialized citywide schools. Such schools, when they are structured into a school desegregation plan, should be for the purpose of serving the unique needs of students in the entire system. Schools such as the Bronx School of Science and Boston Latin School are important units that should relate to other schools in the system in a complementary way by demonstrating how an effective learning environment should operate and by sharing information with other units of the system on effective methods and techniques of instruction.

The panel of court-appointed masters in the Boston school desegregation case recommended that the Latin schools add on a thirteenth year in which any college-bound graduate of a Boston high school could enroll. The post-high-school year would be a college-preparatory year for those who felt that their high-school education was inadequate to gain them admission to a selective college. Such a program would give a second chance to local high-school gradu-ates who (because of immaturity or lack of motivation or lack of guidance) did not diligently or appropriately prepare for higher education. By including a post-high-school college preparatory year in its offerings, the Latin schools in Boston, which emphasize high academic achievement, would serve the entire community in addition to their regular enrollment of gifted students. This way, the special school would serve a general purpose and the total community. Presently some students who do poorly in high school but wish to go on to college take an extra year in one of the prestigious private preparatory schools. Families with limited financial resources cannot afford this arrangement and, therefore, cannot purchase the second chance for their offspring as can the wealthy. The Latin schools could make the second chance available to all at a subsidized lower cost.

Another function of specialized or magnet citywide schools is to diversify the curriculum and make available special courses of study for the total system. Such specialties may fulfill the common needs of some students; but the num-bers of those students may be too few to warrant specialized offerings in each of the several districts schools. Special courses of study in music, art, health care, technology, business, science, and mathematics could be offered for all students in the system in magnet schools. These and other special programs of study are appropriately taught in magnet schools. Thus the attendance zone for the few specialized or magnet schools should be citywide.

Magnet schools, like other schools, should provide a desegregated education. The ratio of majority to minority students in each citywide school could vary within the limits mentioned above and the race of the student body could be predominantly black, brown, or white with a significant minority unlike the prevailing group. When magnet schools assume a disproportionate responsibility for desegregating a system, strict racial ratios are necessary; they should be similar to the citywide racial ratio of students.

Magnet schools introduce a measure of choice into a system that is more or less coercive. Freedom and choice are essential in a democracy. But the freedom *and* choice which a few desegregated magnet schools offer are quite different from the freedom *of* choice to attend any school in the system. In the past, freedom-of-choice enrollment programs, not connected with any special course of study, were used to frustrate and hinder rather than to facilitate and help achieve desegregation. Magnet schools as described in this chapter commit one to a special program of study unlike the common comprehensive curriculum of a district school and to a guaranteed desegregated education. Thus, specialized or magnet citywide schools can enhance and become an adjunct to but not the sole component of a school desegregation plan.

## Monitoring Structure

The implementation of a good school desegregation plan must be monitored. In most instances, school boards are defendants in court cases. Even when there is no litigation, the school authorities who must oversee a new desegregated approach to public school education are responsible to the dominant people of power in the community who had sanctioned and become accustomed to a dual system of education. Thus, one should not expect a school board or school department, in good faith, to implement a school desegregation plan without being monitored by some group other than itself. All ought to be anxious about being honest, including a school board and professional educators. An effective monitoring system contributes to honesty and accountability.

Speaking of the South, Ralph McGill said that "in almost all the cases, school desegregation plans have been created not by educators, but political office-holders and lawyers . . . ." He further observed that "the planners involved themselves needlessly with all the varied demands of local politics" and that "not one of them planned simply to meet the undenied need of children. . . ." It could be said that many of the plans "had the objective of preventing desegregation" and "hardly met the test of equal protection of the law."[17]

The Boston School Committee was ordered by Judge Garrity "to formulate and implement plans to secure for the plaintiffs [black parents and children] their constitutional rights." One could hardly expect such to be accomplished in good faith by school authorities who had resisted for nearly a decade other legal mandates to desegregate the city public schools. Before the court order, the Boston School Committee unsuccessfully attacked the Massachusetts Racial Imbalance Act, which prohibited any school from being more than 50 percent black or other racial minority. A group that did not wish to abide by that law could hardly be expected to formulate a good desegregation plan for the total system and implement it in good faith, unassisted and unmonitored. In the North as well as the South, most school desegregation plans initially proposed by school boards had the objective of preventing or minimizing systemwide desegregation.

School desegregation plans that are mandated by the court should have monitoring structures that are recognized by the court. The monitors should have access to the court for the purpose of reporting from time to time on the extent to which its order is being followed and whether the plaintiffs are receiving relief from the segregative acts which violated their constitutional rights.

A monitoring structure should not consist of individuals unsympathetic to the court order. It is not a forum for harmonizing conflicting views on the wisdom of racial desegregation and the operation of a unitary school system. The decisions on these issues are for the court to render, if there has been litigation. Issues that come before the court because the plaintiff and defendant have irreconcilable differences concerning their lawful rights and responsibilities are resolved by a judgment in which one party wins and the other loses. The monitoring structure therefore cannot be impartial. It exists for the expressed purpose of overseeing the implementation of injunctive relief mandated for those who won the court case. The monitors may be sympathetic to the agony that new adaptations evoke from those who lost. But beyond such feelings and sentiments, the monitors must firmly believe in law and order, including the belief, as stated by Judge Garrity, that "the constitutional principles which mandate duty to desegregate cannot be allowed to yield simply because of disagreement with them."

Monitors are sometimes chosen as if they were a jury. An impartial group is appropriate for sifting through claims and counterclaims and from these determining what is factual. A monitoring group should not function in this way. For it, the facts and the law already are determined, including who was right and who was wrong. It oversees the implementation of the court order, which is for the purpose of redressing the grievances of the offended party. Yet, the tendency is to appoint monitors representative of all points of view in the community, including those who favor and are against school desegregation. A monitoring system so composed cannot carry out its mission effectively. The monitoring group should not reargue the court case in each and every meeting. The eyes and ears of the court should look and listen and report what they see and hear.

### Affirmative Action Plan

Finally, an affirmative action plan should be developed for the recruitment and appointment of teachers and administrators of diversified racial and ethnic backgrounds. The teaching and administrative staff should reflect the racial and ethnic composition of the local community, the metropolitan area, or the state. It is essential that students trust the teachers, the dominant people of power in schools, if they are to learn from them. All students may feel that the school system is trustworthy and is acting in their best interest if people like them or who have had experiences that are similar to their own are people of power in the system. The affirmative action plan should require a diversity in the

teaching and administrative staff of a school system that reflects the diversity
of the school-age population of the state, even if specific populations are not
present in the local communities that are part of a statewide school system.
When the racial and ethnic populations in the local area are greater than their
statewide population, then the proportion of minorities at the local level
should be the guideline for the affirmative action plan.

An affirmative action plan implemented is its own reward. But communities
must experience negative sanctions for disregarding the plan, if their school
systems are to effectively desegregate their administrative and teaching staffs.
After an appropriate guideline has been established, local systems should be
required by the state education authority, and by the court if there has been
litigation, to hire one minority for every majority teacher or administrator
hired, until the minimum guideline has been reached. Such a sanction essentially
denies a system the privilege of filling positions and therefore of having the
required personnel unless the affirmative action guideline is adhered to. Insuf-
ficient personnel, of course, is harmful to the entire system. Such a sanction
as mentioned, then, would encourage the entire system to work together to
diversify its teaching and administrative staffs.

A diversified staff is of educational value. Majority and minority teachers
tend to analyze problems from different perspectives. The presence of minority
and majority teachers in a school system helps prevent the knowledge-dispensing
institution from issuing biased information.

There are many other features of a good school desegregation plan that
could be discussed. A few are mentioned merely by title, such as: (a) *curriculum
reform that eliminates racist and sexist language, images, and stereotypes* from
books and other learning materials and that includes examples and illustrations
of a range of life experiences of minority as well as majority people in the community; (b) *a discipline code of reasonable and acceptable sanctions*, one that
provides opportunities for students and others accused of wrongdoing to
challenge such allegation if they should so choose, and that is administered in a
just and equitable way; (c) *an equal opportunity plan to facilitate participation
by all students in extracurricular activities that are school-sponsored or school-
connected*, directly or indirectly.

These and other features should be included in a good school desegregation
plan, are not elaborated upon at this point because they are not as central as a
systemwide approach, a correct determination of the basic educational unit of
the system, the establishment of common districts of attendance zones, the
development of a uniform grade structure for all schools, and the implementation of an affirmative action plan for diversifying the teaching and administrative staffs. On these features hang the success or failure of a school desegregation plan.

**Notes**

1. Ralph McGill, *The South and the Southerner* (Boston: Little, Brown and Company, 1964), p. 249.

2. Harold Howe II, "Educational Research—The Promise and the Problem." Invited Address presented at the Annual Meeting of the American Educational Research Association, San Francisco, April 21, 1976.

3. Robin Williams, and Margaret Ryan, *Schools in Transition* (Chapel Hill: University of North Carolina Press, 1954).

4. U.S. Department of Labor, *The Negro Family* (Washington D.C.: U.S. Government Printing Office, 1965).

5. Arthur R. Jensen, "How Much Can We Boost IQ and Scholastic Achievement?" *Environment, Heredity, and Intelligence* (Cambridge: Harvard Educational Review, 1969), Reprint Series No. 2, p. 3.

6. Robert K. Merton, *Social Theory and Social Structure* (New York: The Free Press, 1949), p. 185.

7. Ibid., p. 193.

8. Reginal L. Jones, "Racism, Mental Health and the Schools," in Charles V. Willie, Bernard M. Kramer and Bertram S. Brown, eds., *Racism and Mental Health* (Pittsburgh: University of Pittsburgh Press, 1973), pp. 319-52.

9. Jensen, p. 3.

10. John Kenneth Galbraith, *The Affluent Society* (New York: Mentor Book, 1958), pp. 256-58.

11. James B. Conant, *Slums and Suburbs*, pp. 145-46.

12. Charles V. Willie, "Education, Deprivation and Alienation," *Journal of Negro Education* (Summer), 1965.

13. C. Jencks, et al., *Inequality*, New York, Basic Books, 1972.

14. Howe, "Educational Research."

15. Charles V. Willie, and Jerome Beker, *Race Mixing in the Public Schools* (New York: Praeger, 1973).

16. John A. Finger, "Why Busing Plans Work," *School Review* 84 (May), 1976, pp. 37, 364-72.

17. McGill, p. 249.

# 7

## School Desegregation and Public Policy: The Boston Experience

Many of the features of a good school desegregation plan, discussed in Chapter 6, were derived from my experience in Boston. Because the court order for Boston and public reaction to it have been discussed often in the mass media, a more detailed analysis of some of the public policy issues is presented in this chapter. Particular attention is given to an analysis of the role of social scientists in the making of public policy and of public officials in maintaining public order pertaining to school desegregation. I begin by linking the present with the past.

Queen Elizabeth II of Great Britain, a descendant of King George III, came to Boston to celebrate the bicentennial anniversary of the United States. With 200 years of hindsight, she tried to explain what went wrong. The queen's version of the American Revolution is that England lacked the statesmanship to know the right time and the manner of yielding what is impossible to keep. The vicar of Old North Church in Boston, where the candles to alert the colonists were placed, liked what he heard and echoed the queen's ideas in his Sunday sermon. The Reverend Robert Golledge said, "Stubborn pride shouted out in every situation is nonsense and evil, not bravery and steadfastness." Then he said, "Knowing when and how to relinquish something you have but cannot hope to keep in the face of another's fair claim is a strength found in brave [people], not a weakness." This was his commentary on the school desegregation revolution in Boston during the bicentennial year. Unfortunately, many of the residents of Boston heard neither the vicar nor the queen; and if they heard them, they—like the queen's ancestors—would not listen. And so the school desegregation revolution flamed in Boston and elsewhere in the nation, fueled by stubborn pride, nonsense, and people fearful of losing their ethnic purity.

There is common ground and similarity among the queen's analysis of Britain during the last trimester of the eighteenth century, the vicar's analysis of Boston during the last trimester of the twentieth century, and the sociological analysis of social conflict. My purpose here is to focus on the latter and to examine selected aspects of the school desegregation issue in Boston in the light of some sociological principles.

There is and indeed must be a place for sociology in public policy pertaining to school desegregation plans and their implementation. The determination of guilt and innocence or what is legal and illegal is a matter of law and not sociology in disputes that are settled in the court. The responsibility of the court, however, is not limited to making such a determination. If the court arrives at a decision based on law that is in favor of the plaintiff and against the defendant, then the court has the added responsibility of fashioning a remedy or a means of granting relief to the person or persons who were treated unfairly. Blacks and other racial minorities, according to the court, were treated unfairly and not granted equal protection of the laws in public education. Public officials intentionally created a racially segregated or dual public school system that was educationally harmful. Blacks and other racial minorities could not be treated fairly until the harmful social arrangement was changed. How to change a segregated system is a sociological as well as a legal and political problem, as mentioned in Chapters 1, 4, and 6.

The court knows something about justice and interpretations of the law. Sociologists know something about social organization and social change that may be required to fulfill the law. The remedy in school desegregation cases must provide for new social arrangements in the public school system to replace those that were found to be illegal. Sociologists are experts in understanding social arrangements and should participate in the formulation of school desegregation plans. Often they do not because the court cannot determine which sociologist to believe.

Whose advice should the court act upon? This is a major problem. The answer thus far has been elusive. It is a problem, however, not limited to sociology or to sociologists. Indeed, the law is similarly confronted. Five justices of the Supreme Court may believe one thing, and four others may believe another thing. Yet the common opinion of the majority is the law, despite the differing opinions of the minority. Thus, justices of the Supreme Court differ even as sociologists differ. But our society has developed a procedure for handling the varying opinions of a panel of judges. The opinion of a Supreme Court justice is followed only when it is concurrent with that of a majority. This procedure enables the Court to cope with diversity in the opinions of its members. I am not suggesting that this is the only procedure for dealing with diversity of expert opinion. Indeed it may not be the best way and probably would be the wrong procedure for dealing with the diversity of expert sociological opinion, which seldom is unanimous. In our society, then, we have no agreed-upon procedure outside the court for determining when to accept or reject expert opinion in the making of public policy. In the absence of agreed-upon procedures, we rely upon unreliable indicators such as the race, religion, or reputation of the expert and his or her Ingroup or Outgroup status. Members of the Ingroup, for example, tend to doubt the expert opinion of members of the Outgroup.

The issue is not whether sociology can make a valid contribution to court-authorized plans for remedy and relief in school desegregation cases. The main problem is the development of a procedure for determining which expert opinion to use. Herein lies our difficulty. Social-science advice is necessary and needed. But our society knows neither which social-science advice to use in the development of school desegregation public policy nor how or when to use it. Even if our society developed an acceptable procedure for determining which social-science advice to use, that procedure could rule in advice that is wrong, and rule out advice that is right. We should not forget that a decision of a majority of the justices of the Supreme Court is lawful and legal, but could also be inhumane, such as the Dred Scott decision of 1857 that decreed that a black person whose ancestors were sold as slaves had no rights of citizenship or standing in the court.

Sociologists should not wait until their knowledge is perfect before offering it to the court and other institutions in society. Neither they, the justices, nor other professionals ever will be perfect. There are no ultimate guarantees in human society. In the absence of an agreed-upon procedure, our best protection against error is a self-correcting approach—one which seeks the advice of many different people rather than that of a single individual. This approach may escalate confusion because of the competing versions of truth that must be considered, but is better than not seeking any social science advice.

There are competing versions of social-science truth. School desegregation plans and practices, like other social events, are subject to various interpretations that may be valid or erroneous. Errors may be a function of analytic technique, perspective, or the time-frame considered. What is called for, then, is not the dismissal of sociology from the public policy process, but a rational way for the public to determine when an opinion is informed and the conditions under which an informed opinion should be used. The consequence for Boston of rejecting sociological principles in the implementation of school desegregation is the focus of this analysis.[1]

The Boston experience in school desegregation revealed a phenomenon that is increasingly characteristic of the entire nation—the tendency to view achievement in education in terms of performance on standardized tests of communicating and calculating skills.[2] These are skills of efficiency. Michael Katz has said that order and efficiency, values that have permeated public education since the nineteenth century, have strong social class overtones.[3] Thomas Pettigrew has complained about this focus in formal education, too: "Achievement-test scores are surely not the sole goal of education," he said. On the basis of his own research, he concluded that "desegregated schooling does in fact prepare its products—both black and white—for interracial living as adults."[4] The achievement of harmonious interracial living also is a skill that can be learned in school, although standardized tests for its measurement are not available. Maybe the development of this skill is what the Supreme Court had in mind when, in *Brown* v. *Board of Education*, it described an equitable education, in part, as one in which a student of one racial group is able "to engage in discussion and exchange views with other students." Obviously racial segregation prohibits this kind of learning and, therefore, is a harmful educational arrangement.

Living effectively in an interracial society consisting of majority and minority populations of unequal power because of their numbers, organization, or resources requires the development of systems of justice and equity. It was Reinhold Niebuhr who said that "a simple . . . moralism counsels [people] to be unselfish; [but] a profounder . . . faith must encourage people to create systems of justice which will save society . . . ."[5]  Thus justice and equity are major goals of the educational system in a free society. And if they are not, they ought to be.

We have witnessed in Boston and elsewhere in this nation what Aaron Wildavsky has called the *principle of goal displacement,* in which "the process subtly becomes the purpose."[6]  By focusing upon the effects of schooling for individuals (in terms of their communicating and calculating skills development) and ignoring the social consequences of segregated or integrated education (for the quality of racial interaction in community life), justice and equity, which have to do with purpose in society, have been deemphasized or displaced in favor of order and efficiency, which have to do with method of social organization. Reading, writing, and arithmetic, once upon a time identified as the methods of education, now have become goals or ends in themselves—so much so that they sometimes are classified as "the basics" in education. These are clear and present examples of goal displacement.

When the Boston news media were taking stock of the second year of court-ordered school desegregation, Muriel Cohen, a staff member of the *Boston Globe,* wrote the following as the lead sentences of her article: "The Boston schools are on their way up. Slowly. Reading scores are holding the rise of last year." Clearly, such improvement was considered a favorable outcome. The article continued, "Preliminary reading test results for the year . . . show improvement in a number of district high schools, gains for minority children but no loss for whites."[7]  In other words, school desegregation had benefited blacks and had not harmed whites, if test scores are taken as an indicator of educational benefit or success. There was no discussion of whether Boston school children had gained a better understanding of the functions of the court in a democratic society or developed a better understanding of justice and equity by going through the school desegregation experience.

Even under conditions of our present situation, where efficiency and skills-development are exalted, something beneficial has come out of desegregation in Boston. The benefit has been in favor of some whites as well as blacks and is directly attributable to their interracial experience. For example, South Boston whites profited from court-ordered school desegregation. Initially, they opposed school desegregation. South Boston is an ethnically homogeneous, largely working-class community. James Dougherty, a school official, told a newspaper reporter that the second year of desegregation at South Boston High School had its positive side. Said he, "The 'in' thing with blacks is going to college, and that was a boon to Southie, where almost no one goes [to college]." Dougherty further said, "The very feeling [blacks] had about going on to college had a good effect on the white kids." According to him, "The white kids have downgraded themselves, felt college was too tough or that they didn't have the ability." And, "Now there is a feeling [among whites]," reported Dougherty, "that if blacks are going [to college]; why can't we?" The school official said, "It's rubbed off on the white kids [of South Boston]," meaning, of course, the desire to go on to college.[8] Nowhere in any of the analytical discussions of desegregation success or failure is there acknowledgment of this fact as a benefit for whites.

Judge Garrity found that the Boston public school system was characterized by racial segregation and that the defendant, the Boston School Committee, did not dispute this central fact. Indeed, the School Committee had encountered administrative sanctions by the federal government for alleged violations of the Civil Rights Act of 1964 and had been hauled into court several times for rulings on whether or not it had complied with the State Racial Imbalance Act of 1965. Thus, the children of Boston were presented with a model of massive resistance to school desegregation public law for at least ten years prior to Judge Garrity's comprehensive plans for citywide desegregation.

After years of defeat in its attempt to enforce the Racial Imbalance Act, the Massachusetts Board of Education moved against the Boston School Committee and its dilatory tactics and began to withhold state funds. The State Board also demanded that Boston develop a plan to eliminate racially imbalanced schools. Winning on some fine procedural points, the Boston School Committee managed to get state action impounding city school funds overturned, although it never developed a comprehensive school desegregation plan. Frustrated by the flagrant violations of state law, both the State Board of Education and the National Association for the Advancement of Colored People (NAACP) charged the Boston School Committee with violation of the United States Constitution. Formal proceedings were brought by black parents and their children against the Boston School Committee in federal court in 1972. Meanwhile, the State Board of Education decided to draft its own plan for eliminating racial imbalance in the Boston public schools.

The State Board of Education's plan for Boston included some but not all sections of the city. It was not a systemwide approach, as recommended in Chapter 6. It reduced the number of predominantly black schools in Boston from seventy to forty-four. The initial response of the Suffolk Superior Court was that the plan was too limited. The State Board of Education made some modifications and it eventually was accepted by the State Supreme Judicial Court, which concluded that "the time for prompt action to implement . . . is at hand." Judge Garrity's finding that the Boston School Committee had deliberately maintained a dual school system for whites and blacks and other racial minorities was issued the last day of the school's spring term in 1974. With only the summer months available to prepare for desegregation, the judge ordered the Boston School Committee to implement the partial desegregation plan that was prepared by the State Board of Education.

Because so many neighborhoods of Boston were excluded from the partial desegregation plan implemented in Phase I of Judge Garrity's order, some behavioral scientists and long-term desegregation watchers such as Robert Coles called it an imposition "on working class people exclusively."[9] Further, Coles said that social change cannot just occur in one area while everyone else is let off the hook. The partial plan was implemented because the Boston School Committee had refused to prepare a comprehensive plan and also because the state and the court had not consulted social scientists to determine the consequence of implementing a partial versus a comprehensive plan. The outcome was great bitterness on the part of both blacks and whites in the affected communities. A comprehensive desegregation plan that was a modification of the one prepared by the masters and discussed in Chapter 2 was not implemented until the second year, or Phase II, of court-ordered school desegregation.

It was as late as June 1976, the end of the second year of court-ordered school desegregation, and after the Supreme Court had rejected a petition to review the appellate court's affirmation of Judge Garrity's order, that the mayor of Boston finally told the people of that city the facts of life: "That the process of desegregation will continue, . . . that schools that are now integrated will remain integrated," and that "where segregation remains, it will be eliminated." He further said that "busing will continue," and that "any who tell you otherwise . . . that the courts will change their minds . . . or that violent resistance will succeed . . . mislead you." One may wonder why it took the mayor of Boston so long to tell the people what he knew to be true.

Of the South, Ralph McGill said, "History already is drawing a harsh indictment of those political leaders who . . . took a decision delineating the rights of children . . . and dishonestly distorted it . . . ."[10] Shortly after the Court's decision in 1954, McGill believed that had public officials spoken out "when ears arched [sic] to hear from the . . . leaders," there would have been a different story.[11] This did not happen decades ago in the South and it did not happen in the North and in Boston.

McGill explained the violence in the South this way: "Before the winter of 1954-55 was done . . . the hoodlums were fired up by the hot definance from . . . city halls. . . . If the power structure could damn the courts and describe their actions as illegal, then the [people] who wished to dynamite or burn . . . felt . . . approved."[12]

The mayor of Boston, in his brief filed with the Supreme Court requesting a review of the district court's school desegregation decision and plan, indicated that the pairing of some communities would be acceptable in the redrawing of school districts, but that the pairing of others such as Roxbury and South Boston would not. Such an argument was at variance with the reasoning by Judge Garrity based on previous court decisions that "a preference . . . for neighborhood schools . . . can be validly maintained by school authorities only if it will not interfere with the authorities' constitutional duty to desegregate" and that "no amount of public . . . opposition will excuse avoidance by school officials of constitutional obligations to desegregate and [that] constitutional principles which mandate duty to desegregate cannot be allowed to yield simply because of disagreement with them." The mayor did not tell the people of Boston this until it was too late to avoid the violence caused by those who thought that they could resist a court order if they disagreed with it. The violence undoubtedly was stimulated by the actions of public officials that cast doubt on the legality of the court order.

The Supreme Court rejected the mayor's petition for review and the mayor eventually spoke out. He spoke in a forthright manner and taught the children of Boston a good lesson about constitutional democracy and the separate powers of the executive, the legislative, and the judiciary branches of government. It was a lesson in civics far better than those of yesteryear—a lesson that came late but still one worthy of remembering.

When public officials of northern or southern communities do not tell their constituents the facts and do not urge them to obey the law to desegregate the public schools, the result is the same: mob rule and violence. Hostility and hatred, prejudice and discrimination are the same whether found in the North or the South. This is another way of saying that the North could have learned from the South, that Boston could have avoided the experience of Little Rock. The South had experienced the futility of massive resistance to the constitutional requirement to desegregate public schools; but the mayor of Boston did not tell his people that massive resistance to a court order was futile until the end of the second year of court-ordered school desegregation.

The mayor of a community is responsible for and to all the people, whites, blacks, and other minorities, those in favor and those opposed to desegregation. It is not the privilege of one who occupies the position of the chief executive officer of a community or country to be selective in the rules and regulations enforced. The Boston community, like other communities in the United States, is based on law. These laws are for the purpose of maintaining social order in a pluralistic population. They are enacted by legislative bodies, interpreted by the courts, and enforced by an executive branch of government. Obedience of the laws of the community, then, is the ultimate basis of social order in the city. Antinomies are eternal. Always there will be people who disagree with some practices in community life such as school desegregation. But such people can be persuaded to abide by that which they dislike if they believe that the activity is lawful. The law, then, is the basis for achieving accommodation among people of the same community who have disparate interests. This principle is true for southern and northern communities, for Boston as well as for Little Rock and other urban areas.

When the mayor of Boston appealed the school desegregation order of the United States District Court, he let it be known to the citizens of Boston that he believed the decision was unlawful. By his actions, the mayor lost any legal basis for asking those who disliked the school desegregation court order to obey the law because he already had indicated his doubt of its legality. By officially expressing doubt, the mayor placed in jeopardy his law-enforcement authority regarding this matter. As proof that this indeed was what happened, one need only look at the violence which came like thunder and lightning. Ralph McGill said it is an old lesson that "the white Southerner will not join in mob violence unless he believes that laxity in law enforcement will make it possible."[13] The same may be said of the North. Sociologically, what we have learned from the Boston experience is that the appeal of a school desegregation court order is a proscribed policy for the mayor or any chief executive officer of the total community. Plaintiffs and defendants may appeal; citizens who are affected and are parties to the case may appeal; but mayors may initiate appeals at their peril.

A further example that race relations, northern and southern style, are similar came from Dallas, Texas, which behaved years ago in ways quite similar to the way Boston behaved recently. Before 1940, all blacks in Dallas attended one high school, Booker T. Washington. From East Dallas, West Dallas, and South Dallas, they used public transportation to go to North Dallas to Booker T. Washington High School, and the costs for this transportation to maintain segregation were assumed by the minority students and their parents.

There is a limit to the capacity of any school to accommodate one more student, even a black high school. Already Booker T. Washington was in double session. Finally, the Dallas Independent School District erected a new high-school building in South Dallas for blacks. What was unique about this move in the 1930s is that a *new* structure was erected for blacks. In the past, when practicable, new structures had been erected for whites and the abandoned white schools had been reassigned to blacks. The new Lincoln High School for blacks in South Dallas near white neighborhoods was a new development in school construction policy in that city. What do you think happened? Whites in Dallas were so outraged over the fact that a new building near their neighborhoods was to be occupied first by blacks that they went into court and obtained an injunction which prevented Lincoln High School from opening at the beginning of the academic year. In the end, the blacks obtained a just decision. The injunction was lifted and they marched into Lincoln High School for the spring semester, singing "God Bless America."

What happened to Dallas in the South decades ago is no different from what happened in Boston in the North in recent years. In September 1973 English High School, which is located in the Back Bay Fens section of Boston, was scheduled to move into a new $24 million facility, the first new high school opened in Boston in thirty-five years. When the new building was planned as a replacement for old English High six years earlier, the student body was 20 percent black. When the new structure was ready for occupancy, the English High School student body was 80 percent black. Although the structure was erected as a replacement for old English High, the Boston School Committee by majority vote reneged on the commitment to rehouse English High in the new structure and reassigned it to Girls Latin School. At that time, only 5 percent of the student body at Girls Latin was black; in fact, it was 89 percent white. If the new building had been assigned to Girls Latin, the only structure available for English High was the antiquated structure from which Girls Latin would have moved, since the old English High School building had been razed. The plaintiffs (blacks in Boston) obtained a court ruling that prevented the reassignment of the new building to Girls Latin.

The similarity between the North and the South in these cases is that whites believed that any new and modern building for educational purposes ought to be assigned first to whites. The difference between the North and the South in these cases is the use made of the court. The court was used by whites in Dallas in an attempt to maintain discrimination and the court was used by blacks in Boston in an attempt to eliminate discrimination.

And what of the future? Two social scientists, Robin Williams and Margaret Ryan, found that "few communities can sustain, over protracted periods of time, intense bitterness and tension involving only one of the functions of the community."[14] Little Rock and other cities emerged from a state of turmoil after desegregation was accepted as lawful, and so will Boston and other cities.

The mayor pointed toward the new Boston at the close of his speech in June 1976. He said, "If we choose to accept our realities, and to build on those realities toward a society in which tranquil equality is accompanied by real opportunity, then I know enough of this city's possibilities to believe that in a generation, Boston—and its way of life—will be the envy of the nation." The sociologists are inclined to agree with him and would make but one correction. The new Boston may come more quickly than he realizes, in less time than a decade, now that public officials are stating that the school desegregation law will be enforced.

Consider, for example, this 1976 report from Central High School, Little Rock, Arkansas, where federal troops were deployed around that building in the 1950s to maintain public order due to the uproar over court-ordered school desegregation. As late as 1959, black and white students were kicking each other in the corridors of Central High. But in 1976, a *New York Times* reporter found Central High School in Little Rock "one of the most effectively desegregated schools in the United States," with perhaps a slight majority of blacks. Reporter Roy Reed explained that "racial violence has practically disappeared. Athletic teams, cheerleader squads, and several . . . student organizations are integrated. . . . Both races participate vigorously in student government. Tension seemed to be nonexistent. . . . A few black and white students walked and talked together between classes, although a large majority still gathered with members of their own race. . . . Many of Central's white students are bused in . . . over the objection of some parents. . . . [The] School Superintendent, . . . who is white, said . . . that the district had done many things to try to make desegregation work. . . . A new principal, the second black principal since the school was desegregated, . . . enjoys exceptional rapport with black and white students and is spoken of with respect in and out of the school."[15] All of this has occurred in less than a generation where the officials did "many things to try to make desegregation work."

Florence Levinsohn summed up the desegregation situation for the nation this way: "Since 1954, there has been more peaceful integration of schools than violent."[16] John Egerton, an education writer who has studied the South in depth, concluded that "there has been no decrease in the quality of education as a consequence of desegregation."[17] These statements also apply to Boston, Louisville and other cities; but few realize that this is so because they have not seen or been told about it. Forence Levinsohn said, "These successful and peaceful efforts have not been brought dramatically to the attention of the American public . . . [because] television newspeople have not learned how, have not made the effort to dramatically convey these peaceful transactions."[18]

The court-appointed masters were partially successful in fashioning a desegregation plan for Boston that united the goal of education with the method. Moreover, in granting relief to the minorities, the masters were interested also in promoting interracial harmony. Their plan and the modified version that was implemented were defective in some ways. Yet the Boston school desegregation plan achieved a measure of success beyond that expected because the assumptions on which it was based were sociologically sound. To recapitulate these assumptions, the masters believed that:

1. Busing is a phony issue.
2. There is no correlation between how students go to school and what they learn in school.
3. Big-city schools cannot be desegregated without using some form of transportation.
4. Whites need not be the majority to receive a quality education.
5. Unique educational benefits accrue to people of the minority which whites should be permitted to experience.
6. Integrated education benefits whites as well as blacks.
7. A systemwide desegregation plan is essential.

**Notes**

1. Ralph McGill, *The South and the Southerner* (Boston: Little, Brown and Company, 1964), p. 246.

2. Report of the Masters, in *Tallulah Morgan, et al., vs. John Kerrigan, et al.,* March 31, 1975.

3. Michael B. Katz, *Class, Bureaucracy and Schools* (New York: Praeger, 1971), p. 108.

4. Thomas F. Pettigrew, *Racially Separate or Together* (New York: McGraw-Hill Book Company, 1964), pp. 246, 248, 249.

5. Charles V. Willie, "The American Dream: Illusion or Reality," *Harvard Magazine*, Vol. 78, No. 11 (July-August 1976), p. 37.

6. Aaron Wildavasky, "Can Health Be Planned" (Chicago: The Center for Health Administration Studies, Graduate School of Business, University of Chicago, 1976) p. 3.

7. Murial Cohen, "Report Card on Boston Schools: Slow Steady Gain for Students," *Boston Globe*, June 4, 1976, p. 56.

8. George Croft, "Graduate Joy Missing for Many South Boston Seniors," *Boston Globe*, June 4, 1976, p. 56.

9. Mike Barnicle, "Busing Puts Burden on Working Class, Black and White," *Boston Globe,* October 15, 1974, p. 23.

10. McGill, p. 246.

11. Ibid., p. 246.

12. Ibid., p. 248.

13. Ibid., p. 265.

14. Robin M. Williams and Margaret W. Ryan, eds., *Schools in Transition* (Chapel Hill: University of North Carolina Press, 1954) pp. 237, 238, 242, 243.

15. Roy Reed, "Little Rock School Now Integration Model," *New York Times,* September 8, 1976, pp. 1, 16.

16. Florence H. Levinsohn, "TV's Deadly Inadvertent Bias," in Levinsohn and Benjamin D. Wright, eds., *School Desegregation, Shadow and Substance* (Chicago: University of Chicago Press, 1976), p. 93.

17. John Egerton, *School Desegregation, A Report Card from the South* (Atlanta: Southern Regional Council, 1976), p. 47.

18. Levinsohn, p. 93.

# 8 Planning for School and Community Change

There is an association between the school and the community. Any discussion of school-community relations that is significant and meaningful is a discussion of community power relations. Schools, like other institutions in society, are instruments of social control and social change. One cannot plan for school desegregation or for any kind of social change without an understanding of the influences and forces at work in the community and their relationship to social planning.

The Utopian builders of old, in a sense, were social planners. Their major problem—which continues to be a problem for educational planners even today—was their inability to accommodate diversity. Bertrand de Jouvenel wrote of the Utopian designers that "they get rid of clashes by getting rid of the differences." He cited Plato's concept of the perfect republic as an example of this orientation: "Let [the citizens] all advance in step toward the same object, and let them have always and in everything but one common life." Elsewhere in *The Republic,* Plato aks, "Can there be any greater evil than discord and distraction and plurality where unity ought to reign?"[1]

Where there is social change, some discord and disunity are to be expected. Dealing with discord in a creative way is an important part of planning. This means that one must pay attention to planning as well as to the plan, for the process and the purpose are interrelated. As indicated in Chapter 7, the process should not displace the goal. Here, I emphasize that the process should not be ignored either and restate the principle that goal and method are complementary.

At a seminar on planning and evaluation in the Laboratory of Community Psychiatry of the Harvard Medical School, planners representing four disciplines presented their views. This chapter summarizes and analyzes those views and discusses their implications for educational planning and desegregation. One planner was a political scientist and professor, one a social welfare specialist and health-planning agency executive, the third a psychiatrist and staff member of a federal government agency, and the fourth an architect actively involved in planning the expansion of a medical center.

According to the *planner-political scientist,* one is unable to identify all the action alternatives, and it is impossible for anyone to know all of the consequences of a specific action. One should not conclude, however, that it is impossible to make a rational decision; some decisions are merely more rational than others. There is what one may call planning, and then there is opportunistic decision-making. The latter anticipates an immediate future; the former represents a long-term means-end change.

The American political system is radically incompatible with rational planning. This system consists of a number of veto groups designed to prevent the clustering of power or the centralizing of power in a common hand. These veto groups cause one to "roll with the punch" from moment to moment and try to "get in a hard knock" from time to time. Opportunistic decision-making is incompatible with a rational planning model. In such a decision-making system, planners are available, in general, to justify or legitimize decisions that have already been made.

In the view of the *planner-social welfare specialist,* the planner has to exploit and capitalize on unique features of the situation. Financing is always a problem. If possible, it is beneficial to get financing from multiple sources for a planning project so that the project is not beholden to one sponsor. When possible, one should marshal local, state, and federal contributions, as well as private funds.

There is some value in having a vague plan in the beginning. The planner should talk with some people—policymaking board people and policy-implementing agency executives—whose support is needed (or whose opposition should be neutralized) on a one-to-one basis. These people should be approached for the purpose of maintaining their support, neutralizing their opposition, and if possible winning them over to the position of the planning project. Time must be spent by the planner in building up relationships with people and their organizations and to assure them that the planning organization is trustworthy. Through interviewing and other means, data and information about a community may be obtained that, if presented at the appropriate time, will effectively confront the people of the existence of community problems that they managed to ignore or avoid.

Once the problems are understood, task forces may be established to determine what action to take. These task forces consisting of local people can accomplish much more than the outside expert who is the planner. The inclusion on task forces of professional staff people from local agencies will give them a greater stake in the planning project and its outcome. The task forces may develop proposals that are less than ideal. This must be accepted as a necessary risk in community planning. The major role of the planner is to anticipate problems that may result in territorial or domain conflict among community groups with vested interests. The major goal of the planner of human services is to develop a service pattern that will benefit his or her client.

The *planner-psychiatrist* said that looking at planning as a product rather than as a process has not been useful. Much of the planning in the United States has been done by persons not classified as planners. The planning process changes the way people think about things and helps to point out alternatives. Most planning models are static. The Constitution of the United States, however, is an example of a dynamic model. The Constitution can be reinterpreted in the light of the needs of the moment, while upholding some basic values.

The process of planning is the creation of a structure within which confrontations can take place continually. The opening up of the structure to dissident groups is one role of the planner. Once the confrontation is loud enough and the pain great enough, the planner can help devise a way to cope with the situation. This means that people must be pulled into the decision-making process who have responsibility in their various community associations for decision-making. The planner must bring into the discussion people both dominant and subdominant in the community power structure. Many planners focus only on the dominant people of power and forget that the sub-dominants have veto power.

The planner should anticipate problems that an organization will face and try to develop the alternatives so that, when problems arise, viable solutions are available. The quickest way to change an organization is to change its clients. The planner must be tuned in to all information centers throughout an organization and within the constituency.

In bringing about change in the local community, one has to identify the leverage points in which economic resources, preferably money from a source other than the resources of the planning agency, can be used. Then one must link up a program in one agency or institution with other systems. One cannot plan everything; sometimes one has to take advantage of circumstances. In a pluralistic community, some forces seldom mobilize until confronted. America is a crisis-oriented society and the public or the members-at-large in an organization seldom move into action until there is a crisis. Planners can try to anticipate the forthcoming crisis and pull the appropriate forces together to step in when the crisis occurs.

According to the *planner-architect,* the planner may consider how a particular project may interrelate with other planning operations in the community, but the planner must work from the point of view of a particular organization. By knowing the plans of other agencies, one may be able to develop packages that are attractive to them, and which at the same time fulfill the interests of one's own organization.

Planning is basically pragmatic. Judgment plays a very important role. Feedback from the organization in which one is working is helpful in planning and helpful in keeping a step ahead of the opposition. While some planning involves changing the physical setting, there are always social components involved that should be taken into consideration.

To be effective, a planning operation must be a strong organization. Planners have to have a concept of what is to be achieved and are sometimes required to take sides on an issue. This will probably make enemies. Thus, in terms of strategy, the planning office must be a step ahead of its potential enemies. Planners must use whatever resources are available, such as the professional authority and prestige of consultants, to achieve a goal.

To insure continuity in planning, it is sometimes necessary to "plant" personnel who are under the influence of the planning office in strategic positions throughout the system. Planners are innovators and are not likely to be around when the innovation is finally pushed through. Because so much disruption is caused in the system, planners may become casualties of the very change required by their bold new plans. Flexibility is important. Long-term plans should be wedded to short-term plans. Planners may have to help raise part of the funds to support a planning operation.

A comparative analysis of the four planners follows and indicates the themes on which their views diverge or come together. Three of the four emphasized the importance of money. Two saw the raising of money as one of the responsibilities of planning. One preferred to develop plans that use other people's money, and in this orientation he was joined by another who liked to plan packages that are attractive to other agencies as well as his own. Because of the near-unanimous agreement on the responsibility of the planner to help uncover funding resources, this function must be considered of high priority.

All four planners emphasized the value of flexibility. The political scientist spoke of being able to roll with the punches from moment to moment. The social welfare specialist believed in exploiting and capitalizing on unique features of the situation. The psychiatrist talked about taking advantage of circumstances. The architect simply asserted that planning is pragmatic and that flexibility is an important characteristic of the planning process if one is to utilize unanticipated opportunities.

The fundamental disagreements among these planners appear in their concept of goals in planning and in their orientation to full public disclosure of all possible effects of a plan. Here we find a continuum from the political scientist, who believed that too much honest talk about specific goals is destructive for an organization, to the architect, who believed that one must have a clear concept of the goals and an elaborate system of propositions supporting those goals. In between these two extremes were the psychiatrist, who believed in having goals but accepted as fact that they may not be achieved, to the social welfare specialist, who developed goals but would take what he could get. Thus the range extended from one planner who did not believe in setting goals, to another who set goals but did not care whether they were achieved, to a third who set goals but would effect a compromise if necessary, to the fourth who developed clear goals and adhered to them in a flexible way.

It should be noted that the one who professes to not having a goal may be a wolf in sheep's clothing. He or she may have a goal but may be unwilling to make it known to others, and thus may claim to have no goal. This is sometimes a stratagem for exercising leadership in an arbitrary way. As perceptively pointed

out by one of the seminar participants, someone is planning somewhere, although
one may not see the planning in the obvious places. The concealed planning is
concealed by the apparently innocent affirmation that one does not have a plan.
It should also be mentioned that the failure to establish goals as a matter of
policy means that evaluation of outcome is discouraged as a matter of policy.

Probably the greatest difference among the four planners was their operational concept of the planner's role. One saw the planner as a *figurehead* who is
available to justify or legitimize decisions that are already made. Another saw the
planner as a *broker and consultant* who brings together appropriate leaders in the
community to get the best deal possible for the client. Another identified the
role as that of *policy analyst and advocate*, who opens up the planning structure
and process to dissident groups so that they may confront the Establishment.
The fourth saw the planner as *decision-maker and change-agent*, who by hook or
by crook enables the plan to be put into operation.

The proper role of the planner is probably a function of the personal style
of each planner, on the one hand, and the kinds of situations with which one is
confronted, on the other. There is a delicate process, then, in matching up the
personal operating style of the planner with the unique requirements of the
planning situation. For example, to place a figurehead in a situation that requires a decision-maker and change-agent would be disastrous.

Whatever their style, however, the planners must be sufficiently flexible to
adapt their operating procedures to changing circumstances even as their plans
must be sufficiently flexible to accommodate unanticipated opportunities.
Planning always occurs within a context. It is inevitably linked to the circumstances and conditions at a particular point in time. Planning also is associated
with the redistribution of power within a system.

How, then, should the school relate to the community in planning for
desegregation and a program of quality education for all children? The *Report
of the National Advisory Commission on Civil Disorders* had this to say about
community-school relations and the disadvantaged:

Teachers of the poor rarely live in the community where they work and sometimes have little sympathy for the lifestyle of their students. Moreover, the
growth and complexity of the administration of large urban school systems has
compromised the accountability of the local schools to the communities which
they serve, and reduced the ability of parents to influence decisions affecting
the education of their children. Ghetto schools often appear to be unresponsive
to the community, communication has broken down, and parents are distrustful
of officials responsible for formulating educational policy.

The consequences for the education of students attending these schools are
serious. Parental hostility to the schools is reflected in the attitudes of their
children. Since the needs and concerns of the ghetto community are rarely
reflected in educational policy formulated on a citywide basis, the schools are
often seen by ghetto youth as being irrelevant . . . .

In the schools, as in the larger society, the isolation of ghetto residents from the policy-making institutions of local government is adding to the polarization of the community and depriving the system of its self-rectifying potential.[2]

One could say that the school has always related and been responsive to the community, but not to all segments of the community. The observations of this commission indicate that the curriculum and other aspects of schools are affected by who is in charge.

The position and role of the school superintendent are most important in educational planning for desegregation and other changes in the school and community. The plan of most school administrators tends to be that of following and adapting to the customs of the community at large; they seldom invoke a deliberate planning strategy for change. As pointed out by Robin Williams and Margaret Ryan, superintendents can become community leaders and contribute to community change rather than waiting to be directed to move in one way or another. Specifically, they discuss the need for ". . . firm policies advanced by the superintendent of schools and his staff . . ." as one way of contributing to school desegregation. "The evidence seems clear," they concluded, "that cooperative planning which recognizes established feelings can reduce actual discrimination long before it is possible to remove deep-rooted prejudice."[3]   Cooperative planning is possible only when all sectors of the community are involved.

Most superintendents are not likely to give innovative leadership as planners in education if they follow the advice provided in some textbooks of educational sociology. One textbook writer had this to say about schools and community decision-making:

Every community has a power system. . . . Power refers to the ability or authority to dominate or to compel action. There are people or groups in every community who make important decisions and have the ability to enforce them. This is an inevitable community social process, for without power, and therefore control, it would be impossible to have social order . . . . One cannot understand until he is able to locate the sources of power . . . . Decisions affecting the entire community may be made under informal circumstances at a poker game, luncheon, or party . . . . School people need to know the sources of power groups in the community if the school program is to function smoothly.[4]

It is because school administrators have been responsible only to dominants in the power structure that school-community relations are at a low ebb and that subdominants have shaken the foundations of the social order and the ground on which the schools once firmly stood.

Indeed, there are dominants in the power structure of all communities. But there are subdominants, too. They also have power. After analyzing the history of a hospital construction controversy in Syracuse, New York, the following observation was made:

Popular conceptions of the community power structure have resulted in our identifying industrialists, financiers, and merchants as people of power. However, our analysis reveals that they comprise only one category of the power system—the dominant category—which is inefficient without the subdominant category. So we must recognize the veto power of the subdominants. They, too, are the right people and must be recruited and brought along in effective community organization.[5]

Dominants, of course, have the power to implement and veto community programs. Veto power is not exclusive dominant power, however. This kind of power is found among subdominants. Because they use veto power less frequently, its presence is often forgotten. Thus, school superintendents and other public officials are surprised when their plans run aground due to veto actions of subdominants.

Because it is unanticipated and comes from an unexpected source, the veto power of subdominants is considered to be disruptive by some school administrators and board of education members. Yet there is a creative push in the activities of subdominants. School boards throughout the nation are agonizing over new and different approaches to quality education, mainly because of the fuss about desegregation which subdominants have raised. It is only because subdominants exercised their veto power that this nation is actively searching for solutions to inequality in public education and ways to improve the quality of education for all.

It is doubtful that school authorities would have taken new initiatives on their own, without pressure from below from community subdominants. This, in effect, is what an education administrator told the U.S. Civil Rights Commission at a public hearing in Rochester, New York.[6]

The creative impulse resulting from subdominant action in the decision-making process has been recognized by others, such as Dan W. Dodson. He pointed to the value of all sectors of the community participating in educational decision-making, not only for the wisdom that diversity brings to educational planning, but also for the sense of significance such participation may engender within disadvantaged persons. In an article about new forces in educational decision-making, Dodson said:

We had better realize that the smallest power among us can create disruption enough to block the whole . . . .
. . . New forces are emerging that are going to require our boards of education and superintendents of schools to move into new approaches to the issue of decision-making. If children are not going to get hurt in this process, we are going to have to develop new skills with which to approach this conflict of interest. People must honestly come to face each other and honestly say that we have differences and ask how we can reconcile and compromise and how do we work them out to some sort of viable solution.
From this process will come a new sense of education . . . . All the community will feel involved in the dynamics of the decision-making process and a new sense of worth will emerge. This may be threatening to some who feel that their status is jeopardized . . . .[7]

And so the successful school superintendent now must do more than play golf with the community business and governmental influentials. He or she must also come to know the subdominants. This may require eating chitterlings and corn pone with the poor as well as recreating with the rich, if one is to synthesize the disparate interest groups in the community into a phalanx of support for a creative public policy designed to achieve quality education for all.

## Notes

1. Bertrand de Jouvenel, *On Power* (Boston: Beacon Press, 1962), pp. 114, 133.

2. *Report of the National Advisory Commission on Civil Disorder* (New York: Bantam Books, 1968), pp. 436-37.

3. Robin M. Williams, and Margaret W. Ryan, eds., *Schools in Transition* (Chapel Hill: University of North Carolina Press, 1954), p. 48.

4. Wilbur B. Brookover, *A Sociology of Education* (New York: American Book Co., 1955), pp. 378-79.

5. Charles V. Willie, "A Success Story of Community Action," in *Nursing Outlook*, IX (January 1961), p. 20.

6. U.S. Civil Rights Commission, "Testimony of Dr. James E. Allen Jr., Commissioner of Education, State of New York, *Hearing Before the United States Commission on Civil Rights in Rochester, New York*, September 16-17, 1966 (Washington, D.C.: U.S. Government Printing Office, 1967), p. 207.

7. Dan W. Dodson, "New Forces Operating in Educational Decision Making," in Meyer Weinberg, ed., *Integrated Education: A Reader* (Beverly Hills: The Glencoe Press, 1968), p. 21.

# Part III:
# Desegregating Elementary and Secondary Schools

**Integration Comes to Two Elementary Schools**

In the earlier chapters, we defined the issues and discussed their implications for educational planning and policymaking. These chapters indicated what the school desegregation plan and policy ought to be. In Part III and Part IV, we analyze how desegregation is implemented in elementary schools, high schools, and in colleges. This way, the theoretical discussions of Parts I and II are linked with discussions of practical application. Most important, the consequences of school desegregation for minority students of varying age grades are indicated. Chapter 9 discusses desegregation in two elementary schools and Chapter 10 focuses on the junior high school level. Finally, the role of the principal and teachers in the desegregation process is discussed in Chapter 11. The contrasting social contexts of different schools should be noted and the varying administrative and teaching styles in these schools. They influence the desegregation and integration processes as much as the black, brown, and white children who have borne the brunt of social change in race relations in our society.

The community and schools discussed in the next three chapters were mentioned in the Introduction. The names are pseudonyms so that their anonymity may be protected as promised. What follows is the story of Centralia, a community different from and yet in many ways similar to most American cities. This analysis is based on our own research and was first reported in a book entitled *Race Mixing and the Public School*[1] that I authored with assistance from Jerome Beker.

The Centralia School Board's proposal to reassign black youngsters to the Simpson Elementary School and Highland School to deliberately improve racial balance presents a most interesting situation that is being repeated throughout the country. Our researchers, stationed in the two schools, were able to give us on-the-scene reports of the initial reaction of teachers, students, and principals.

We want the reader to have the feeling of being at home in the four schools. Thus we used the method of participant-observation to obtain the data for this chapter and the following two.

We were able to compare the pattern of desegregation in two schools that were relatively similar in the socioeconomic status level of neighborhoods surrounding them but that had different orientations to education. The Simpson School had a reputation for being a high-achieving school. While the Highland School had a good academic rating, it was better known in the community as the school for physically handicapped children, although nonhandicapped children also attend it and were enrolled in the same classes as handicapped children. Thus one school had been oriented toward the intellectually gifted while the other had been oriented toward the physically handicapped. Our analysis will help to determine if these two different orientations made a difference in the way black children who were new to these schools were received.

About 18 percent of the Highland students were black, and from 6 to 7 percent of the Simpson students were black. These two schools, then, present an opportunity to explore whether or not the number of blacks in attendance at a school makes a difference in the progress of integration. It has been asserted in the past that, the larger the proportion of blacks involved, the more difficult the integration process.

Highland Elementary School became a host or receiving school for black and white students who had formerly attended Bridges and Denison schools. The children who were transferred from these two schools were, by and large, from a lower socioeconomic stratum than most of the children already at Highland. This new enrollment brought the total number of black students to nearly 18 percent of the 530-member student population.

When the plan for desegregation was announced, the principal stated that "it is good and it is healthy. There has been too much parochialism in Centralia, with people living in certain districts and attending certain schools." He was pleased that the Board of Education had at last become committed to a policy of considering racial balance where it had previously ignored the question of integration. He believed that the official action taken by the board removed the feeling of confusion and of things being "left up in the air."

Highland had a higher academic rating than Bridges and Denison; the principal, therefore, was concerned about the reassigned students. Primarily, he was anxious *for* rather than *about* the incoming children; he said:

> I wanted to make sure that the teachers would accommodate the new youngsters at their pace in school, for I thought it might be difficult for them to be placed in a new school. But as far as the acceptance of them as being black, I was not concerned at all, since Highland has had black pupils before without any problems of discrimination. In other words, I was concerned for them as new students and not as black or white, rich or poor.

The principal hoped, too, that the teachers at Highland would be patient and understanding, for the students were, as he expressed it, "victimized by an uprooting complex of events." He further stated that the higher socioeconomic level of most children in the existing Highland student body was reflected in their home backgrounds and in their interest in school and their desire to achieve.

Although principals are often subjected to a variety of cross-pressures from parents and teachers, the principal at Highland seemed to have escaped much of the usual Ping-Pong. According to him, his problems lay with the parents of the incoming black children:

I did have quite a number of black parents call me. They asked me to help them not have their kids come to Highland because they lived nearer their old schools and seemed to be happy in them. These parents were upset about their children being transferred, they didn't want it, and they wanted me to know it. I pointed out to them that the problem was one of overcrowding at Denison and Bridges and, in view of the fact that Highland had more room, that obviously the children had to be moved and the boundary lines of the school area expanded. I did not receive any distressed calls from white parents. In fact, they didn't call me at all, either before or after the arrival of the new children.

The PTA was, in his opinion, inadequately informed of the board's plan. Initially, there was a feeling of confusion among its members, and they seemed to be wondering, "Where are we going, what exactly is the policy?" The Board of Education scheduled a meeting in which the Superintendent of City Schools spoke to the Highland PTA. The general tone of the questions put forth by the parents indicated a fear that their children might receive an inferior education as a result of a "slowing-down process in classwork to accommodate 'slow learners.'" The speaker said that he thought the quality of education would not be altered at Highland. If any individual qualms did in fact exist among the white parents after this meeting, the principal was not made aware of them. In his words, "These parents bought the plan one hundred percent."

Most members of the teaching staff were not apprehensive about the arrival of the former Bridges and Denison students. The placement of a research observer in Highland whose responsibility it was to report on the development of the integration process was a cause of annoyance for only a few faculty members. According to the observer, these were the teachers who believed that the presence of an outsider disrupted the classroom.

The principal held another meeting prior to the entrance of the students in September. At this session, the teachers heard a school consultant speak on the things to work for in the development of the integration process, reactions of old and new students, exclusion and inclusion in classroom and extracurricular activities, and self-concepts of the former Denison and Bridges students. This consultant was working at that time in one of the predominantly black inner-city junior high schools.

At the beginning of the school year, the teachers were not particularly upset, angry, anxious, or unhappy about the incoming youngsters. According to the principal, teachers felt that in spite of the potentiality for problems, integration in the classroom would be relatively problem-free because of the low teacher-pupil ratio. For the most part, Highland's teachers were experienced, and some of the former Bridges faculty members had been absorbed into the Highland School System. These factors may have accounted for the apparent lack of anxiety in confronting the new situation.

Some teachers tended to equate position of the new black students with that of the physically handicapped children in Highland. One staff member, for example, was heard to say the following:

Teachers are experienced here in teaching the handicapped children and this new situation is not anything different from our past work. The teachers have always stressed individual attention. We had been told in June that the children were coming, but it is within our stride and has not presented any problems.

In general, there was a common attitude among the teachers of "taking things as they come."

The average class at Highland was composed of about eighteen pupils, and the former Bridges and Denison students were distributed among the classrooms of all six grades. The distribution was uneven, however. In one class of third graders, for example, there were eight new black children; in another, the majority of new students were white and only two were black.

In the first few weeks of classes, it was evident that some teachers ignored or felt uneasy about the black children from Denison and Bridges. The observer noted the following incident:

In this second-grade class, reading books were being passed out. The teacher gave instructions to "take your dark crayon and underline the correct answer." Finally, after two questions from the children concerning the color of the dark crayon, Miss Z said, "the black crayon," hesitating before the word "black." While the class of twenty students was completing the work, the teacher had "a reading group," as she called it, which was composed of one blonde-haired white girl, Judy, who was a neighborhood student. She warned the class to be quiet, that this was "Judy's time." Antoinette's hand [Antoinette was a new black student from Denison] was ignored four times until finally the teacher recognized her with a very stern "What?" The teacher then changed to a softer tone to address Judy about the reading lesson. Judy appears to be a normal reader and was working on appropriate and average work for second grade.

In a first-grade class, the teacher chose to tell this story to her students:

The story was about Harry, a white dog, who got dirty from playing in the street. "Have you ever got dirty from playing in the street?" No one answered. "Well, Harry got black. In fact, he was so black and dirty that no one recognized him. The neighbors saw this dog doing tricks. These tricks were the same as Harry did—but Harry was white and this dog was black. Finally, Harry went into some loose dirt and started to dig. He dug up a brush, a scrub brush. When father, brother, and sister saw him, he was going into the house with the scrub brush in his mouth. Where do you suppose he was going?" Again, no answer. "He went right upstairs to the bathroom and got into the bathtub and here is where the father and the children found him. Father told the children to take the brush and scrub him. The children called their father to 'hurry, come and look!' Harry was the clean, beautiful white dog again."

The observer said that throughout the story Louis, a recently transferred black youngster from Bridges, kept turning around in his seat to sneak a smile at her. The observer is black. There were two other new black children formerly from Bridges in this class.

In still another classroom, the observer noticed that only the new black students were ignored. Some of these students reacted by seeking ways to demand attention:

It was recess time in the class and Bryan, a new black student, had not been chosen by the teacher during the "Dog and Bone" game. After a while, he took a spectroscope from the desk opposite his, proceeded to tear off the bottom, and let the glass prism lens fall to the floor and break. Mrs. Y said that it had been ruined and no one would be able to look into it anymore as the prisms were what made it work. She told him to put it in the wastebasket. His next move was to the bulletin board to look over the gold-starred papers exhibited there. He turned up his nose and returned to his seat, where he reached across to another desk, got a magic slate, and began to write upon it.

The nature of student-teacher interaction was satisfactory in most classes. Most of the teachers were quick to incorporate the former Denison and Bridges students into class work and make them feel comfortable at Highland.

In this sixth-grade class, the students are working on Social Studies. Erwin, who is a white neighborhood student who had attended Highland since the first grade, shoved his desk over to meet David's. David is a new student. He is black and he used to attend Denison. They sat together the whole period, at times laughing, at times working, and at times answering questions. The teacher showed no objection to this casual arrangement. He called on David often, prodding him when he gave a half-answer with, "I know you can tell me more, David," or "Yes, you have the right idea." After a while, the teacher announced that "all of you have been such good workers that I am going to let you see a few innings of the World Series game."

Early in the year the observer noted a similar atmosphere in a different class and a similar attitude on the part of the teacher toward the new students:

In this second-grade classroom the seating arrangement is interspersed with black and white children, old and new. There are three rows, with three blacks and two whites in the first row, three whites and two blacks in the second row, and two whites and three blacks in the third row. Bob, a new black student from Bridges, answered the teacher's questions more frequently than any other student. It was apparent that the new black students in general are the most active participants in the class and are encouraged by the teacher: "You did so well on the last question, Bob, do you want to try again?" The white neighborhood students who attended Highland last year do not respond as well. They seem to be more passive.

For the most part, the new students were not isolated from the other youngsters in the classroom. There was little differential treatment by the faculty, not only in terms of recitation but also, and especially, in terms of discipline. The former Denison and Bridges children were not singled out if disruptive behavior occurred. Instead, the observer remarked, "If any acting out took place in the classroom which either was initiated by or participated in by the new children, the usual response of the teacher was a verbal 'it's-time-to-settle-down' response." There seemed to be no assumption on the part of the faculty that new students would be disruptive.

There was, however, one particular fifth-grade class in which the new children were separated from the old students through seating arrangements and were in fact cut off from responding in class. The teacher's physical and social separation of the children seemed to reflect her attitude toward their "newness" to Highland and not toward their ability or race. The observer described the class:

There are many children in this class, especially the new students, both black and white, who do not receive attention. They are never called upon by the teacher and are never chosen to answer when their hands are raised. As a general rule, the teacher-pupil interaction in this room centers in the extreme front section of the room where the old, established students sit.

Among the classes, some transferees, both black and white, had to be placed in special reading classes which met several times a week. These children were not set apart from their classmates in their own rooms, but they had to leave classes to go to the reading sessions. When these youngsters returned from remedial reading classes to their own classrooms, they were sometimes helped individually, and sometimes at great length, in the regular classroom setting. This special attention could have caused the reassigned children to feel different, but apparently it did not.

Throughout the work in class, Jim, a new black student formerly from Bridges, showed discouragement. The teacher had to read each item for him. She had him try to read the sentences, but there were many words beyond his repertoire. Even though they occurred again and again in the lesson, he did not recognize the words from sentence to sentence. This student was severely handicapped in reading skills but Miss X was patient and devoted the majority of her supervisory time to him. She was not discouraged, but he was. Yet, he did not give up. He would raise his hand and try to answer the question put forth. At the end of the lesson, he began to recognize words more easily and the teacher felt that some progress had been made.

The observer recorded another example of a child, an out-of-state transfer student, who lacked adequate reading skills:

This third grade is composed of sixteen children: three new black girls, four new black boys, one new white girl. The rest are neighborhood students who have attended Highland for some period of time. One black student, new to the school, is a boy from Savannah, Georgia, and was pointed out to me in a whisper by the teacher as having been placed in fourth grade upon arrival but without having records or documentation. His fourth-grade teacher had sent him back to third grade, stating that he was not prepared in verbal or in reading skills and did not have the foundation necessary for fourth grade.  Miss X said, however, that he, like the rest of the students in her class, had an IQ above 110.

Some of the former Bridges and Denison students had difficulty in verbal expression, although it was clear that they had no problem in comprehending the material presented in class.  The following observation depicts the way in which one child began to manipulate conceptual work in her class:

This is a fourth-grade class.  The story was "The Secret Cave."  Mrs. W asked, "What do you think was the reason for Jeff's fear after the flashlight went out?"  Clara, a new black student from Denison, volunteered and answered, "He was afraid that he would slip on glass which was on the floor and bump into it around in the cave."  Bonnie, a white neighborhood student who had been at Highland for several years, expanded this comment by saying, "He could be injured on rock formations or could wander afar or into an underground lake or water system."  After this clarification of the composition of caves, Clara volunteered again to discuss the dark rocky interior in response to another item, this time using the words Bonnie had used.  I could not help thinking that her background had not included caves either in real or vicarious experience but Clara readily learned, altered her thoughts and descriptions, and relayed back to the group in a more meaningful way.

Throughout the year at Highland, the observer recalled only one class in which one of the new black students was considered a "behavior problem."  Furthermore, the friends with whom he disturbed the class were white neighborhood youngsters who, according to the teacher, "had always caused trouble."

In Mrs. W's class there are three definite behavior problems:  David, a white neighborhood student, and Ronnie, a white neighborhood student—both of them have been students at Highland for a few years—and Bruce, a new black student from Denison.  David and Bruce annoy their neighbors by talking to them and getting out of their seats to bother them.  When the other children ignore them, they sit and talk with each other.  Ronnie sits in the back of the room by himself and does what he wants to do—which includes talking aloud, banging on his desk, and drumming with his pencil.  All three boys are classed as above average in intelligence, but each requires more attention than any of the physically handicapped children in the room.

The observer noted that the relations between the bused black children and the neighborhood white students were friendly outside as well as inside the classroom.  The children played well together.  In the playground and lunchroom the children separated into groups on the basis of sex; only in the beginning of the year did they separate on the basis of race.

It was the first day of school in September. Two teachers were on playground duty and talked together intently, letting the children play at will. The children were first and second graders out for noon recess. In looking over the playground, I noticed sixty children broken up into four distinct groups: black boys, white boys, black girls, white girls. The black boys were playing tag, the white boys were standing around bicycles, white girls were playing a circle game, and black girls came over to talk with me. They told me how much they liked Highland. I could not tell which students were new and which were not.

A more common scene is described in the following observations:

As the children were getting into line for lunch, a black girl new to Highland this year left hand-in-hand for lunch with a white girl from Bridges who is also new. As I followed the children into the cafeteria, I saw two new black girls sitting with three white girls who are also neighborhood students. They were sitting at the first table and were all laughing. As I got closer, I could hear them asking each other riddles.

The majority of the former Denison and Bridges students found themselves involved both socially and academically in Highland School by the end of the first semester of the year. Because of the freedom in the school and the pervading attitude of acceptance exhibited by the principal and (with a few exceptions) the staff, the transfer students responded to their new setting enthusiastically. Most important was the fact that the uprooted youngsters of September became the solidly grounded youngsters of June. A typical example of the new students' perceptions of Highland may be seen in the remarks of a new black girl in the fourth grade:

I like school now. Here, everybody is nice to you. The teachers are nice and so are the kids. The stories in class are better. The teachers aren't mean here. In our school, they used to beat us if we did something wrong. They help us here and they're friendly.

Many reactions from the staff reflected the same enthusiasm:

Third-grade teacher:
I have a new black boy in class. I am proud of the way he works. He has made an excellent adjustment. In a few weeks, he'll be taking part in the Christmas play that the students put on.

Sixty-grade teacher:
She [a black student] is a new student and holding her own too, doing all right. She gets along well with the other children. They love her.

Second-grade teacher:
Last year, he [a new black student formerly from Bridges] hated school and would not work. F's and D's were the bulk of his grades. Now that he's at

Highland, as I was telling his mother, he is as different this year from last as night is to day. He's not an excellent student, but he is an average one and does like school. His mother wanted to know what I had done to change his effort and attitude. She said he likes me too and at home, even, he's a different boy. Well, last year he was in a large second grade and this year it's better for him. I can give him individual attention and his response has been good.

Fifth-grade teacher:
The new kids have certainly moved into the school well and have become a part of it. But I wish their parents would do the same. Not one of the parents of the new kids, black or white, came to Open House. [The Board of Education] should have bused every one of those students years ago.

Seven months after the arrival of the new students, the observer noted their achievement and integration:

These children have come a long way since last September. They now appear capable, poised, and involved in classroom situations. Perhaps the most important thing, however, is the fact that they are well accepted by their classmates. It is difficult now to think of them as "new students."

In conclusion, it can be said that integration at Highland displayed the markings of success. Recognizing the urgency of desegregation, Highland's principal not only accepted the change but acted as the primary agent in bringing about a cooperative spirit. Together, he and a majority of the faculty established a climate for the former Denison and Bridges youngsters that was responsive to their needs. They made an unfamiliar school familiar. Most of the new children felt comfortable at Highland after a relatively short period of time.

Some incidents during the year, however, served to create problems in the youngsters' adjustment to the school. A few teachers resented the change that had been thrust on Highland and seemed to be unwilling to take the extraordinary steps in their classrooms that would lead to satisfactory relationships between the former Denison and Bridges children and the "old timers." Thus in a few classes the new black children were ignored and isolated. But in most instances the adjustment of the school to the new students was favorable, and so was that of the students to their new school.

The second elementary school we examined was the Simpson School. The School Board's decision was made public in May, and Simpson had its first experience in planned integration the following fall. It was announced then that Simpson would be the receiving school for fifty to sixty students from Corliss Elementary School, located in the inner-city area of Centralia. The parents of the Corliss children had agreed to this transfer.

Corliss does not have a high academic rating in comparison to Simpson. The majority of its students are black and most of the students transferred were black. With this deliberate shift, the proportion of black students at Simpson changed from less than 2 percent to about 7 percent. The transferred students were distributed among fifteen classrooms of the first, second, and third grades with a maximum of seven in each class. The average class size was twenty-five.

Once the details of the board's plan were made public, many white parents ceased to be fearful. Others, however, were still not satisfied with this plan to achieve a better racial balance at Simpson.

The Board of Education scheduled one meeting at the school to answer the questions of parents. This meeting was so filled with bitterness and controversy that it merely served to solidify existing divisions within the PTA. After the meeting, the group opposing the plan grew larger and more articulate. Several members of the faction against the busing of inner-city black children to Simpson were white business and professional people who could present their views forcefully and convincingly. While some were against busing because it violated the "neighborhood school" concept, others opposed it on racial and class grounds. This opposition group has since become a very strong voice in the Parent-Teachers Association at Simpson.

Generally, there seemed to be two prevailing concerns. The Simpson School neighborhood parents feared that their children would receive an inferior education in a diversified student body. Teachers were concerned that the academic reputation of the school would be lowered. These concerns were seemingly based on similar assumptions that the Corliss children would present behavioral problems, have low IQ scores, and come from "bad families."

Simpson was proud of its few international students (some of whom were nonwhites) and of its highly respected academic reputation. Blacks who could meet the high academic expectations had been readily accepted in the past. With regard to the transferees from Corliss, however, many of the teachers were apprehensive about their ability to cope with the new students' reputed behavior and academic problems.

Since this was the first planned attempt to alleviate racial imbalance in Centralia, the central administrative staff was in constant contact with the principal and teachers, and a research observer was stationed in the school. This constant surveillance was annoying. For example, one teacher questioned the observer in the following manner:

I don't know what you're doing here. We don't need to be observed. These are just children. This school has always been a little United Nations with Japanese, Korean, Indian, Mexican, all sorts of children coming here. We had three Spanish-speaking children here last year, and they always segregated themselves on the playground; why aren't you studying them? We know how to handle all these different children. Why aren't you studying *them* [blacks] in schools where there are more of them? Who are they trying to kid? I know why you're here. We teachers all know. And none of us likes being observed. We are all experienced teachers in the primary grades, more so than you.

One teacher reported that she found the Corliss children "unnerving." Anticipating the problems of the coming school year, she said that "having all these extra children means that the lunchroom, which used to be a quiet place where children could relax and talk, will be bedlam." She said that with "all the running on the playground, teachers are going to have to do double duty and won't like it."

There seemed to be two prevailing attitudes among teachers concerning the transfer of students from Corliss. According to the observer, "The young teachers didn't care and the older and more experienced teachers were panicked."

A teacher typifying the latter category stated that she was further behind this year than she had ever been during any of her nine years in Simpson, and that it was because of the Corliss children. This teacher added, "Anyone who pretends that she has managed to maintain Simpson standards with these children around is not being honest."

Many of the teachers seemed ultrasensitive to any behavior on the part of the black children from Corliss that appeared to differ from the norm. Many teachers anticipated behavioral problems and therefore quelled any exuberant behavior by Corliss children before it produced the anticipated bedlam. As a result, Corliss children were watched closely. According to the observer, teachers often lectured to the former Corliss students about appropriate and inappropriate behavior. For example, the observer who frequently ate with the students noted the following episode with four blacks eating together in the lunchroom:

Mrs. V had the 11:20-11:45 duty; she began by lecturing our table, talking about how noisy and messy it had been the day before. (Actually this table was far quieter than her own class.)

In a discussion of some of the problems facing the teachers in the beginning of the school year, one teacher was asked whether she or the other teachers had talked with the principal about these problems. She responded:

No, because the principal has always been a very pleasant person who would do whatever was expected of her. However, this fall she is tense and stern, walking around the halls all the time, too busy for any person. Other years she would drop in any time with no fuss, and the children loved having her. This year she is stern.

Initially, the principal was quite disturbed that there would be a research observer in her school. She felt that this would be disruptive to the teachers and the students. After schedules for the observation of classrooms were established in advance, she became more accepting of the fact that Simpson was being closely observed by researchers as well as by representatives of the Board of Education.

In this early phase of the school year, the special attention given this school took its toll on the principal. However, about the middle of October the observer noted a change in the principal:

She has begun to relax. In the beginning of the year she did not know these children's older sisters and brothers; she had no contact with the parents. She did not know which were apt to be ring leaders, whom she could call on in a pinch. Now, she is getting to know these pupils as individuals. I noticed in the lunchroom she is no longer the principal with the big stick, but is doing her best to talk these children into good behavior, kidding them, smiling, a bit of cajoling.

The principal and many of the teachers expressed discomfort in their initial relations with the inner-city black children. Much of this uneasiness was due to the fact that they had had no contact with the children's parents or older brothers and sisters prior to the transfer.

The observer also noted a tendency to stereotype the black children:

For many of the teachers who are resisting this transfer, all blacks are automatically considered as being from underprivileged homes with inadequate backgrounds, and, therefore, intruders to the smooth sailing (S.S.) Simpson.

It should be recalled, however, that some of the black children lived in the Simpson District and came from middle-class families. But when the Corliss children came, the teachers tended to react to old black youngsters as they reacted to transferred children.

Some teachers were able to relate to the new students on an individual basis. Often, particularly in the second half of the school year, teachers would use some of the former Corliss students as "good" behavioral models for the class. For example, a teacher attempting to get the attention of her class said, "April [a black child from Corliss] is the only one in the whole room who is ready." This technique is used very widely by the teachers, who use both Corliss and non-Corliss children as models for the class.

Several techniques were used to aid the socialization process of the new students. These techniques were geared to the individual and the particular situational demands. For example, tardiness was widespread in the beginning of the school year, and the following episode is typical of how it was handled in a sensitive and creative manner.

Elizabeth arrives just after attendance is taken. She is chronically tardy. Elizabeth has a small doll with her. Mrs. T asked her to bring the doll to the front of the room. Mrs. T took the doll and as Elizabeth nervously answers various questions, she kept reaching for the doll. Mrs. T kept it out of the girl's reach. She scolded the doll for making Elizabeth late, even though the child stated that the family got up late. When she returned to her seat, with the doll, she started to comfort it, and Mrs. T asked her to put it into her own desk for a nap.

A teacher attempted to get total class involvement by asking members to demonstrate, for example, particular aspects of counting. In a second-grade class, a teacher asked one of the former Corliss students to draw six pairs of shoes on the board. This pupil drew six shoes rather than six pairs of shoes. To illustrate, the teacher asked all of the six children in this student's row to place their feet in the aisle for her to count. As a result of this illustration, the student learned the meaning of "pair." Most of these techniques were not used or developed especially for the Corliss students. The Simpson teachers have a reputation for being very creative.

Some of these techniques, such as permitting one student to call on another student for recitation, tended to isolate or exclude the former Corliss students from the main flow of class activity. This hampered new student participation, particularly at the beginning of the year. In the following observation, this method was used and the teacher apparently became aware that the new students were being excluded. To alleviate this, the teacher called on those excluded and "liberally praised" one new student for giving the correct answer.

Spelling was next . . . . Mrs. T called on a white girl first, and told her to "invite someone else to do the next one." This went on for five answers, involving three girls and then two boys, all white. Then Mrs. T called on John (white), Ruth (black), and Yvonne (black). Yvonne had a particularly difficult question, but she had raised her hand, and she had all parts of it right, even though more than half the class had missed one part. She was somewhat self-satisfied, but in a quiet way; Mrs. T praised her liberally.

Some teachers divided the students into reading-ability groups. The majority of the Corliss children were placed in the poorest reading group, which meant that they had to leave the regular class periodically to attend special reading classes. This method of teaching homogeneous ability groups tended to keep the Corliss students together and also tended to separate them from other students at Simpson. For example, in one class the observer noted that the best reading group contained twelve white children and no black students. The observer described the composition of one of the poorest reading groups, consisting of the three black children and two white students.

Starting from the first grade, there is a strong emphasis on reading and the use of words. Since Simpson had received predominantly middle-class students in the past, the majority of the teachers were accustomed to having children with highly literate parents and well-stocked personal libraries. The teachers therefore assumed that the children would be highly verbal and able to read even in the early grades. The observer noted that in the first grade "there is a tremendous emphasis on words in this room. Many items are labeled, and the teacher operated on the assumption that many children read."

For example, in the beginning of the year, one first-grade teacher said: "A number of our children can read. Would those who can read already please raise their hands?" About eight children out of about twenty raised their hands, and none of these children were inner-city and from Corliss. It should be recalled that no class had more than seven former Corliss children.

During the second half of the school year, the teachers seemed to have made a greater effort to incorporate the black students into the class routine. In April, the observer noted the following about a teacher at Simpson:

Today in particular I noticed how many times Mrs. S calls on those students who are new, and particularly those who are apt to be behind. Ali has spent most of his life in Africa, and then the past six months in Finland. Marcus spoke no English when he came three months ago, and the inner-city black children are academically wanting by her standards. The glaring thing is the number of times they could give the correct answers.

Again it should be noted that some of the neighborhood white children have similar deficiency problems that require special attention by the teachers.

The new students became more at ease in their new environment, and by the second half of the year they knew the majority of their classmates. One typical indication of this can be seen in the observer's comment about a game the children were playing.

She [the teacher] began to explain a game whereby she would appoint one child to sit in the front of the room, with his eyes covered, and back to the students, and try to guess who is knocking on his chair. The people who come are to disguise their voices. The children were very excited, and this game might have been new to them. Cynthia (a black from Corliss) was the first child in the chair. For the first four children, she was able to guess each time.

The observer indicated on many occasions that the students, both old and new, had no difficulty in playing together. The observer did not report any terms, such as "bused kids" or "those black kids," used by the neighborhood residents to distinguish themselves from the Corliss children. There was frequent opportunity for free interaction between the old and new students. The playground offered what was probably the best opportunity. Several teachers very candidly stated that they were amazed at the extent of the interaction between these two groups. One teacher related the following incident as a sample of the extent to which old students chose to play with new ones.

Last Friday, the children were to bring in kites, but only five did .... So she divided the class in five teams, and they were to take turns. Yvonne (a black from Corliss) was in a group with four neighborhood white girls, including Karen. When it was Yvonne's turn, the kite really took off, and soared far above the other four. Yvonne got a look of pure ecstasy on her face as she "entered another world," and the two girls in her group who were still to have turns gave them up so she could continue to fly it. In the afternoon, this teacher supplied them with twelve kites, so each had to be shared by only two pupils. The first person . . . to choose a partner was Karen, and she chose Yvonne. Since that time, they have been very close. Karen is just about the top student in the room.

It should be noted that this free interaction did not always occur. In the early part of the year, the observer noted a great deal of separation by race.

My impression was that the playground was the most segregated spot I had seen. There were clusters of girls, all black, in many spots, and most of the groups of boys playing were with predominantly black or predominantly white groups. There was not a sharp cleavage at all times, and groups would form, dissolve, and reform with a changing racial composition, but the impression was still that of some form of subtle differentiation. At times this would become almost overt. Once a group of four black girls, holding hands, started to approach the spot where I was sitting with four or five white girls and one white boy [the observer is white]. As they approached, one of the girls swooped up a second and called toward the four approaching blacks, "You cannot touch me" as the two ran off. This seemed to put the black quartet off, in spite of my friendly smile.

In the latter half of the year, the observer reported in every playground observation that there were no groupings or interactions based solely on race. The observer stated: "From what I could tell, pursuit was the only game. It took many forms, often mixing grades and definitely mixing races." On another occasion, the following was reported: "The entire playground was mixed by grades and races. There are no evidences of cliques." Increasingly, the observer began to describe the following as typical behavior:

Susan [a white neighborhood resident], the redhead from Missouri, had her arm around Dora [a black transfer from Corliss], and she introduced her as her friend. On my other side, Michelle [a white neighborhood resident] and Mary [a black from Corliss] were holding hands, and vying for my attention. We walked two thirds across the playground like this, talking. Once I stood still, they used me as a sort of base for a tag game. Then one of them got the idea of Ring around the Rosie because of the way we were standing.

This pattern of free interaction became increasingly common for both new and old students. However, the observer did report a few cases in which this interaction was hampered by the white neighborhood residents. In one case, "A girl in a group of about three white girls started to hold the hand of another girl next to her. Realizing she was black, this girl said something I could not catch as she veered away and joined the circle at another point." In another, incident, a group of white neighborhood residents were playing a game and they seemingly pressured another white girl to play with them instead of with a black girl from Corliss. The observer explains:

One little first grader [who is a white neighborhood resident] kept protesting she did not want to play, though three girls from Mrs. R's class were trying to make her. She told them she was playing with someone else, and the someone she was referring to was Annette, a black girl from Corliss. They had been playing together when they first came up to me.

In the classroom, a few teachers were faced with what they considered to be very delicate situations in regard to the new students. Some of these children were chronically absent. The reason for this and the ramifications it had for the children can be seen in the following example. The observer reports:

This child [Flossie] is out of touch with the progress of the class. She has missed so many times, she is lost. Two siblings are in basic classes. Two nurses have made three home visits and told me the mother claims there is no money to buy bread so she cannot let Flossie go to school without lunch.

The effect of chronic absence on the student's classroom performance, and the extra time required of the teacher is apparent in the following observation:

Paper was being passed out. "First and last name on your Paper" was the only verbal direction until Mrs. T showed everyone how to fold the papers in four sections. Flossie, who is left handed, had written FL, and then erased it. From this early point in the lesson on she never again did catch up. She stood, borrowed an eraser from Gail, used it, and returned it to Gail. She wrote her name, but in mixed lowercase and uppercase letters. Mrs. T was walking around checking.
"Oh, Flossie, that's not the way you write your name. Stay in the lines." The teacher erased what Flossie had done up until this point, and the child began again. She wrote Flossie ____ in the lines. The next time the teacher checked on work, Flossie was behind. "Flossie, let me see your paper. Did you fold it right?" She had.
The lesson was spelling, *am, all, so, said, then, mother, father.* Spelling is brought into the first grade curriculum the last third of the year, and Flossie might not have had much spelling before. The proper way to do it is to write the word in a column all the way down the paper. Flossie, instead of writing *am* six times, wrote six *a*'s, then six *m*'s. Twice the teacher came and helped Flossie, but she didn't realize the way Flossie was writing. She had publicly reprimanded Nancy for doing her words that way, and though Flossie watched the reprimand, she didn't change her methods. She continued to erase as much as she wrote.

This behavior typified Flossie's classroom performance throughout much of the school year. For many of the Simpson teachers this type of performance tended to confirm their initial assumptions and stereotypes about the abilities of the Corliss children. With this impetus, there was a tendency in the early part of the year for the teachers to assume that most of the black students who were bused would perform on the same level as the student in the above example.

As the year progressed, it was found that the majority of the Corliss students did not conform to these assumptions made by some of the teachers. In fact, there were former Corliss students giving superior performances. Some teachers did not know how to respond to this unanticipated behavior. The following observation is a typical case in which a teacher was obviously confused, as indicated in her final statement, "I give up." Michael's performance had been discussed prior to this observation, and the teacher stated that he had very low IQ and achievement scores. As will become apparent, Michael's performance did not conform to the achievement expectations indicated by his low scores.

"Open to page 248," was the only direction. Michael began to turn to it, without looking at any other student's book. Then he sat with his head in his left hand, and seemed to be staring at the page. The first group of practice sentences were eight sentences or groups of words, and the children had to read the words, telling whether or not it was a sentence. All but three or four hands went up on every one, and near the end Miss P waited longer and longer before calling on a child each time, hoping for those new to also volunteer. No response out of Michael. Then she said, "Now, we shall do these again. Remember, read it out loud, and then tell me the answer." Michael's hand shot up, and she called on him. He read the sentence, and gave the correct response. His reading was slow of pace, but accurate. She praised him liberally but not overly. The second section, on the next page, involved correcting sentences. The class was on the third one before Michael realized they had turned the pages. He turned it, and in one more sentence caught up. Then he volunteered for the next one, and was called on. This time he read "that" for "what" in the middle of the sentence, but no one else noticed it; and he was not corrected but again praised. During the rest of the lesson, which lasted twenty-five minutes, Mike stayed with the class. He was called on two more times, and each time was correct. Then the assignment was to write an article which had just been read orally. I [the observer] left the room as the paper was being passed out. Miss P handed me a note: "I give up." According to a standardized reading test, Michael scored on the first-grade level. This teacher explained later that she was surprised he could keep up with the class at the third-grade level.

Thus, many of the Simpson teachers were presented with a conflict. On the one hand, they were led to believe for various reasons that all or most of the new black children could not perform on the level of achievement of the white students already at Simpson. They feared that these children would cause the achievement rating of the school to drop. On the other hand, many of these students performed well in the class and did not present "behavior problems." As a result, many of these teachers were forced to take a second look at their prior assumptions. Some of these teachers, at the end of the year, stated that the year had been a learning experience for them as well as for the new students. They said that these children did not fit one "type" in terms of performance or behavior.

Based on the data presented here and the qualitative analysis, it would appear that the integration process was smoother and less turbulent at the Highland Elementary School than at the Simpson Elementary School. While the Highland School received more black youngsters and had a much higher proportion of them in its student population, the integration experience was less stressful for the teachers and apparently for the parents of that school. Much of the ease with which Highland approached this new situation of an enlarged non-white population was probably due to the kind of leadership which the principal gave. But part of the absence of anxiety was probably due also to the school's experience with physically handicapped children. As a matter of custom, Highland had accepted all sorts and conditions of children in the past. The orientation the school had developed in dealing with the physically handicapped provided guidelines for assimilating the economically disadvantaged. Also the larger number of minorities may have been a critical mass sufficient to facilitate a good adaptation by blacks.

These findings mean that the orientation of teachers and administrators, the educational environment, or the school climate and the critical mass of minorities are probably more important variables in racial integration than is the socioeconomic status level of the children. The findings further suggest that an educational environment or school climate that fosters the integration and assimilation of all sorts and conditions of people, including all races and social classes, must include an orientation among teachers and administrators of accepting persons as they are, as well as an orientation toward achievement. It would appear that the development of both knowledge and compassion are worthy goals for formal education. Teachers with compassion were able to impart knowledge effectively.

**Note**

1. Charles V. Willie with Jerome Beker, *Race Mixing in the Public Schools* (New York: Praeger, 1973).

# 10 Integration Comes to Two Junior High Schools

As we follow the word-by-word accounts of the teachers and students, we get some idea of the unexpected problems that arise as racial integration comes to the schools. The schoolrooms described in this study are no doubt typical—almost anyone could find similar schoolrooms in his or her own area. It is interesting to see what happened at two junior high schools as they cautiously moved toward integration.

Lincoln Junior High School was located in a middle-class neighborhood. There were about four white students to every black student. About thirty new black students, most of them from the inner-city area of Centralia, were reassigned to Lincoln in order to achieve a better racial balance. Monroe Junior High School was located in the inner city. There were about three black children to every white child at Monroe. About thirty new white students were transferred to Monroe to bring about a better racial balance; most of them lived in another inner-city lower socioeconomic status area similar to the one surrounding the Monroe School.

In a qualitative manner, we can indicate the similarities and differences in the way new black children were received at a predominantly white school and in the way new white children were received at a predominantly black school. This also provides us with an opportunity to compare the integration process of students with a social-class background different from and similar to that of the existing student body. It should be borne in mind that the new students were strangers and, to anticipate the findings briefly, that strangers of any race often have similar experiences.

Although the thirty-two students who were transferred from the inner city to Lincoln Junior High School constituted a small portion of the 237 new children who entered that school in the fall, they were nevertheless significant in terms of the school's reaction to their presence.

Lincoln's principal expressed the following attitude about the new situation in his school:

De facto segregation is when you take a district such as Lincoln which has a black population of 7 percent and create a new district including more disadvantaged, culturally handicapped students and raise the black population to 18 percent.

Commenting upon what should be done, he also stated that

117

. . . the new black students have to be socialized before they can be educated. It is not right to take kids from one junior high school and drop them into another. We have to be careful not to give the white kids the impression that we let black kids get away with things. The children coming in under the board's plan cannot cope with the kids already here.

The principal's attitude about the former Monroe students was similar to his reaction toward the research observer's presence at Lincoln. He often expressed suspicion and uneasiness. This is apparent in the observer's account of his first meeting with the principal:

On September 23rd, at 8:00 in the morning, I met the principal in the secretary's office at the school. I was trying to obtain a locker. After he had directed me to see someone about it, he began a tirade against the City School Board and accused me of spying for the Superintendent of Schools, whom he referred to as "Boss." The vice-principal and three teachers were in the office at the time.

I told the principal that I wasn't a spy for anyone and that all of my observations were strictly confidential. As I started for the door he called me saying that no one scared him because he had the security of the big "R." He then asked me if I knew what the big "R" was and I said I didn't. He explained it stood for retirement. He said he had worked in this "racket" for forty years and neither I nor "Boss" worried him in the least. I left the room.

A few weeks later, the observer again encountered the principal in the faculty room. In this conversation, the principal's original idea of the observer as a spy remained intact:

As I entered the room the principal informed those present that "Boss's spy" was here and everyone should be careful of what he said. I apologized to the principal, saying that I was sorry I hadn't convinced him that I wasn't a spy. He didn't bring the topic up again until Mr. N, a school social worker, came in the room. He greeted Mr. N by saying "Be careful what you say—or he'll report you to the 'Boss.'"

Another incident occurred in which the observer noticed the principal's stereotyped opinions of blacks. The principal revealed his feelings in a conversation with the observer, the school nurse, the coach, and another teacher in the faculty room:

As I sat down to have a cup of coffee with the people assembled in the room, the principal began to speak. I realized that he was addressing me. He told me that they had just admitted a "Wonder Boy" to the school. He was a black boy who had been ordained a minister when he was three years old. The principal said he thought the boy would earn a lot of money because "they" make good preachers and "a lot of people will pay good money to have one of them."

The reactions of the Lincoln parents, according to the principal were not hostile when they were informed about the board's plan. In his words, "They

showed much less resistance than did parents in other districts, such as the
Simpson School District. Lincoln received only two phone calls from the
parents concerning this matter of racial balance. I attribute this low resistance
to the PTA, which, at Lincoln, is very fair-minded."

When the plan to transfer students from an inner-city school was announced, the teachers at Lincoln were apprehensive. They seemed to be afraid
that the achievement of the existing students would be hindered by the presence
of the former Monroe youngsters. One teacher asked the observer, "What do
you do to get these transfer kids to take on responsibility like the other students?"
Early in the year, the former Monroe students were branded by many of the
teachers as "irresponsible," "troublemakers," "slow learners," "potential failures." These feelings were apparent to the observer both in and out of the
classroom:

I observed in Mrs. W's homeroom today. Before the class started she told me
that I didn't have to observe in her homeroom if I didn't want to because there
were no problems in the class. She did, however, feel that I should come to
her second-period class because there were "You know, the transfers," in that
particular class. I explained to Mrs. W that I was at Lincoln to look at all of
the students in general and at the new students, black and white, in particular.

Another instance was recorded in which a member of Lincoln staff, the
librarian, displayed a negative opinion of the youngsters who had transferred
from Monroe to Lincoln:

I arrived at Lincoln School at 12:50. The classes had begun for the fifth period.
I went to the library on the second floor. As I was going into the room, Mrs. O,
the librarian, came up behind me and I opened the door for her to go in. We
were the only people in the library. Mrs. O explained that this year she very
seldom left the library. "Last year if I had to leave to do something I knew that
the students would put their passes in the box and there would be no trouble.
With the students we have this year I don't dare leave this room." I said, "Why,
has there been any kind of trouble?" Mrs. O said, "No, but that's because I
don't go anyplace where I can't see the door. Whenever anyone comes in, I get
back before any trouble can start."

One seventh-grade teacher was engaged in a "case study" approach that
was limited to only the new black transfer students. This teacher, in giving
special attention to the youngsters from Monroe, distinguished the black
transferees from old students at Lincoln by labeling the former "potential
failures." The observer remarked that this seventh-grade teacher, who looked
upon the new black students as "potential failures," singled out these youngsters
in the classroom by administering special tests to them while the rest of the class
worked on classroom material. Thus, in some classrooms, the transferees were
made to feel "different" at Lincoln.

Particularly at the start of the year, the observer noticed racial groupings and other signs that seemed to show that the former Monroe youngsters were isolated from the ongoing processes of life at Lincoln:

This is the first week of school for the fall session. The bell rang for the end of the first period and the students came out of the classrooms and filled the hall with noise and confusion. Teachers took up their posts as traffic directors in the center of the halls.

I decided to go upstairs to the boy's gym class. The boys were standing in a line against the western wall of the gym. There were twenty-three boys in this class. Six of the boys were black and the rest were white. Although the boys were supposed to be lined up according to height, they had divided themselves into racial groups. Five black boys who did not have their uniforms with them stood together and three white boys who were without theirs were standing on another side of the room . . . .

I arrived at Lincoln School at 12:35. The first lunch period was nearly finished. I got in line with the rest of the students who were waiting for the second lunch period to begin. By the time I was ready to sit down I noticed that the cafeteria had filled up already. I also noticed that there seemed to be many tables at which all white or all black children sat . . . .

This is a ninth-grade home economics class. There are thirteen girls in the class, and nine of them are black. Four of the white girls are new, and four of the black girls are new at Lincoln. The home economics room is the best furnished, best lighted, and most attractive room in Lincoln.

There was a definite racial difference in grouping. The nine black girls sat along the table on the northern and eastern sides. The four white girls sat at the southern end of the table. Each group interacted only with its seated members. One of the white girls, Tone, tried to show off for her group and Mrs. H, the teacher, made her move her chair to the front of the white group and away from them somewhat. Tone went through a few antics after she was moved, pushing her chair back and forth and making comments to the other white girls. This behavior drew no comments or attention from the black girls . . . .

I went to a ninth-grade history class. There are twenty-five students in the room, including one new white boy and one new black girl, formerly from Monroe. The rest of the class is composed of three black students who live in the area and twenty white students who live in the area.

Michael, the new white child, didn't know any answers and left blanks on his paper. He looked around the room while the other students wrote on their papers. The new black student, Leslie, kept her eyes on her own desk and apparently knew the answers. There was a racial grouping to this class. All four black students sat in the first two rows. All the white students were sitting in the remaining four rows.

Adjustment to Lincoln was difficult for both the new white students and the black youngsters who had previously attended Monroe School. Throughout the year, various teachers complained to the principal that the new children were "defiant" and engaged in "agitating behavior" in their classes. The observer noted that the principal responded to the complaints by stating that he would "get the School Board representative after them" (that is, the new school social worker). Many of the teachers consistently separated the "troublemakers" from the other students:

There are twenty students in this art class, ten boys and ten girls. It is composed of seventh-grade students listed as a "slow" group. Joe, a new white student, got up from his seat and faced the class. He had heard Miss P call for the girls only but he stood up anyhow. She reminded him that he wasn't a girl and Joe sat down with a pleased look on his face. He was sitting at a table which is pulled away from the rest of the class. Miss P usually puts "troublemakers" by themselves at this desk. During the period Joe was constantly badgering the teacher for attention. Miss P has a policy of calling students to her desk to look at their work. Normally she goes by alphabetical order and only speaks to the other students if they are causing trouble or need special help. Joe was the first one called. He went to her desk and an argument ensued about his work. Miss P said he had done a good job, but it was the same thing someone else had done. Joe said, "I did what you told me to do," and Miss P denied that she had said that. He informed her that he would not do another project. He finally left her desk, loudly protesting and claiming he had been wronged. As other students went to confer with the teacher, Joe would interrupt and ask questions. He was seeking attention which he did not receive.

Although both black and white new students were treated differently from the established students in many of the classrooms, the former Monroe children suffered by far the greater injustice. When disciplinary situations arose, the new black students often received unusually "harsh punishment." The observer recorded an incident that reveals the type of action taken by the administration against a new transfer student from Monroe:

The bell rang for the start of the third lunch period at 12:11. While I was standing in line outside of the cafeteria I noticed James, a white area student who has regularly attended Lincoln. He is a ninth-grade boy whom I have seen in gym class several times. He was fooling around with several other boys and the horseplay was quite rough. The boys were hitting each other and pushing each other out of line. Mrs. A, a ninth-grade teacher, walked past but said nothing to the boys. (All were white.) Mr. P. who was serving as the hall monitor, did not come up to do anything to the boys, Miss J, a ninth-grade teacher, also walked by but did nothing.

I mention this incident because it was at this same spot in the lunch line where Larry, a former Monroe student and a black boy, was caught for doing the same thing as James was doing and it led to his suspension. Yet, nothing was done to the white area students and in particular to James. James has a reputation for being a troublemaker and I have seen him exhibit nothing but disruptive and malicious behavior in the school.

Some of the new black pupils were so acutely aware of the manner in which they were treated by various faculty members that they reported their perceptions to the vice-principal. The observer reports that at one point during the spring semester two of the former Monroe students, both eighth-graders, went to the vice-principal concerning their feelings:

The school board representative at Lincoln told me a seventh-grade teacher was reported to the administration by two new black boys, Ray and Jerry, for what they considered to be prejudicial treatment in class.

The boys told the vice-principal, in his presence, that their teacher made them say "please" for everything they requested but did not make this demand of the white students, in the same class. The boys have Miss L for a study hall and she will not let them go to the library during this period. The vice-principal listened to the boys and then suggested that since they only have this teacher for one period, they should try to overlook her behavior. One of the boys, Ray, said he didn't feel they had to overlook her treatment of them since they had her study hall several times a week. He was insistent that something be done about the situation. Ray then stated that he would call up his mother for support, if this was needed to back his position. According to the school board representative, the boy's mother did arrive at Lincoln the next day to find out whether her son could be supported in his claims.

Several times during the school year the Lincoln School Board representative (the social worker) spoke with the observer about the problems of the school. The school social worker made this statement:

I have had a feeling that some of the teachers and others here at Lincoln are quite prejudiced. Some people from CORE were here to investigate the violation of one of the student's rights. I know that several of the kids' civil rights have been violated. A new black student in the seventh grade, Tom, had refused to say words, "with Liberty and Justice for all" when his class pledged allegiance to the flag. He, instead, said, "with Liberty and Justice *for Some.*" This caused some concern with the teacher. Tom explained to the teacher that he felt the "for all" portion of the pledge is false. He was reported to the principal and the CORE officials became involved in the incident in support of the boy.

The school board representative's charge of prejudice at Lincoln was directed toward the principal. One issue that came up at Lincoln involved complaints from some businessmen in the school area who threatened to close their stores during the time that the students were coming to and returning from school. It was their opinion that Lincoln students were stealing items from their places of business. When the principal heard of the complaints, he said, "They don't even know if it was someone from Lincoln. It could have been kids from another school. I don't think it was a Lincoln student, not even the colored ones." The sentiment invoked in this remark seemed to fit with the general pattern of response displayed by some teachers in their attitude toward Lincoln's black students.

Some of the new pupils, both black and white, were unable to conform to the structure of learning at Lincoln. The reactions of these youngsters were identical. As the observer reports, they simply withdrew from the class setting:

Mrs. Y began this eighth-grade science class by giving a practice session of questions which would be similar to those asked on the test the children were about to take. It lasted ten minutes and then Mrs. Y read twenty-five multiple-choice questions to the class. Carl, a black neighborhood student who has been at Lincoln, seemed to have no trouble and answered all the questions. John, a white neighborhood student who has also attended Lincoln for several years, puzzled over some questions and left two of them blank. As the last question was being asked by Mrs. Y, a black boy walked into the room, took a seat away from someone, and stared straight ahead with no expression on his face. Mrs. Y went over to him and said, "Take out a piece of paper, Alan, and I'll give you the questions while the rest of the class is finishing up." Alan said, "I'm not taking a test." "Come on Alan, get some paper." "I told you I'm not taking a test." Mrs. Y finally said, "Alan, if you don't take the test you'll get a zero. Now get some paper out." The rest of the class was watching them. She said, again, "Alan, get a piece of paper." "What did I tell you? I'm not taking the test and that's it." Mrs. Y walked toward her desk, obviously shaken, and said, "Well, I guess it's up to you but don't blame anyone else." Alan sat until the class ended and then left the room ahead of the others. He is a new transfer from Monroe . . . .
I took a seat in the middle of the northern section of this ninth-grade classroom. Joel, a new white student, came into the room with Ron, a black student who has been at Lincoln for two years. Mr. D began to take the attendance. A voice came over the loudspeaker and Joel responded to it with a resounding "Hello." The class laughed and Mr. D told Joel to be quiet. Mr. D was quite provoked, and Joel continued talking. He was again reprimanded with the threat that if he persisted in this behavior he would have to stay after school. Joel said he didn't care because he had to be there anyhow. Mr. D, voice rising and face flushing, informed Joel that if he kept it up he would stay after school for the entire week. Joel said, "That's up to you. I don't care." The teacher got very excited and asked Joel to leave the room, and said he would be in detention for two weeks. Joel complied and left the room.

It was a common experience for the new students to help one another in class if they were having difficulty in answering the questions posed by the teacher. In such cases, there was a good deal of interaction between the former Monroe students and the new white youngsters. The observer noticed that this kind of mutual-assistance behavior was exhibited particularly during the latter half of the year as a defensive measure against the older, established students:

This eighth-grade math class has three new black students and three new white students, all girls.
The class began at 8:40. The first part was devoted to homework. After the papers were handed in, the class started working on new problems and Mrs. H picked different youngsters to go to the board and put the answer up for the class. During this time, none of the new students volunteered to go to the front of the room. They were holding conversations with each other while the

students who were not new were giving the answers. Cindy, a new white student, was chosen to go to the board and work. She didn't appear to be too sure of what she was putting down. She turned around and gave a "help me!" look to Deborah, a former Monroe student. Deborah shook her head as if to tell Cindy that her answer was not right. She then held up some fingers and Cindy, nodding, turned around and did the problem again. This time it was completed correctly and Mrs. H chose someone else to take Cindy's place at the blackboard.

In certain classes, the new transfer students acted as informal class leaders and, at times, were able to control the work at hand and manipulate the teacher's direction of it:

In this ninth-grade business class, the work consists chiefly of Mrs. P reading the correct way of organizing the balance sheet. All of the students, except three, appeared to be involved in the material initially. The three students who were not participating were Elliot, a new white student, Eugene, a black student who has been attending Lincoln for several years, and Janice, a white student who also is part of the existing student body. Elliot sat staring off in space or turning around to look out the window. Mrs. P asked him what he was doing and he replied, "Nothing." She said, "As long as you are in the room you'll go through the motions." He didn't respond to her or do any work. Mrs. P then asked Eugene if he was "with the class." He said he got lost the day before and hadn't caught up. Janice was talking and laughing continually. The teacher told her to be quiet and stop distracting her neighbors.

Debra and Susan, both black students formerly from Monroe, would ask questions and answer them by calling out "Mrs. P!" before they spoke. They changed the whole tempo of the class. Debra frequently made noises such as clearing her throat to emphasize her responses. She threw her arms up in the air at times. Her answers were always correct. Once, she caught a mistake Mrs. P had made in labeling one account. Debra belabored the point after the teacher admitted her mistake, doing it in such a way that she was congratulated for sensing the error. Debra was in complete control of her gestures and explanations. Mrs. P was moved to remark that Debra would be a good bookkeeper because of her attention to detail. Both Debra and Susan, who had answered many questions correctly, were held up as "models" for the class which, in effect, centered around them.

Activities outside the classroom, as in gym period, provided other opportunities for informal leadership. The observer noted an eighth-grade gym class in which a former Monroe student acted as a leader:

Eleven boys were present in this gym class. The only new, and black, boy was Ted. He seemed to be relaxed with the other boys. They, in turn, seemed to be attracted to him and he was involved in quite a bit of "chatter" while the activity was taking place. Ted was chosen to head one group of five boys for drills. He lined his boys up and told them how to do the particular drill they were working on. One of the drills called for someone to stand in the center of the circle. A short white boy who lives in the area and has been at Lincoln two years took his turn in the center of Ted's group. The boys started to throw the ball to each other and over the short boy's head. Ted grabbed the ball and told them to stop. He said, "Bounce it on the floor, give him a chance." When the small boy finally finished and came back to the circle, Ted roughed up the boy's hair. He grinned at Ted and took his place. For the rest of the period, Ted played fairly and unaggressively. He is clearly in command of the group.

A seventh-grade history class, taught by the only black teacher at Lincoln, involved a great deal of "give-and-take" between the teacher and her class. The observer captures the flavor of this particular class in the following report:

There are twenty-five students in this class, including two new black pupils and seven new white pupils. The room was filled when I walked in. Miss T told the class that the principal and Mr. N would be in the room but they were not to be afraid of them. The students all laughed when she suggested they think of the visitors as "people," for a change. Miss T explained that the students were giving papers on immigrant and minority groups and their contributions to U.S. culture and society. At the end of the presentations, members of the class would ask questions, discuss the relative merits of the papers, and suggest what grade each student who made a presentation should receive. The basis for the grades was a judgment on the voice projection of the student, the material in the paper, and how well the student used his personal opinion and defended what he said. The first paper was given by Thomas, a new black pupil. It was entitled "The Contributions of the Negro." Thomas dealt with Civil Rights, Science, Education, Music, Law, and International Relations. Part of this student's discussion was a detailed description on "how the white man could let the black alone when he is engaging in any endeavor." (I speculated that perhaps Tom would like this philosophy to be effected in Lincoln.) Members of the class, including five new white students, discussed and then evaluated Tom's paper, which was given an "A." Many of the white students stated that his presentation was "informative."

During the period, other papers were given on "Jewish Contributions to American Society" and "Irish Contributions to American Culture." Throughout the presentations, Miss T gently led the class and prompted voluntary student evaluations.

In summary, the new students at Lincoln became familiar with the principal's policy ("get tough with them and they'll come around") and the teachers' preaching ("good behavior is good citizenship"). Several of the new students did not become well acquainted with students who had been at Lincoln the previous year. However, many transfer and other new students, both black and white, coped with the system and related to the old students both in and out of the classroom.

Monroe Junior High School, which is predominantly black, became a host school for fifty-two students transferred from Plymouth School, which was predominantly white. Plymouth, which had had students of both junior high and elementary levels, became an elementary school only. The reassignment was made in connection with the Board of Education's plan to desegregate the city's public schools; however, only thirty-one of the students transferred to Monroe were white.

The transfer of the new children caused no change in the racial composition of the student population at Monroe. The ratio of black to white students remained at about seventy-seven to twenty-three.

Plymouth Junior High School, like Monroe, was not considered to have a high academic rating. A majority of the Plymouth students lived in the neighborhood surrounding the school, and this neighborhood, like the Monroe district, was low in socioeconomic status. Many of the children who attended Plymouth came from families of Italian ancestry. In general, the residents of the Plymouth School District, like those of the Monroe School District, have a lower median family income and lower educational level than residents of most other areas in the city.

When the Plymouth parents were told of the board's plan to transfer their children to Monroe, they were not enthusiastic although they did not vigorously oppose it. Monroe's principal described the situation as he saw it:

> If the Plymouth parents had any real concerns, they were never voiced. At the same time, they never said they were for integration. Their grievance against the School Board for this policy of closing up Plymouth and shifting the students to Monroe lay in the fact that they were upset that their children would have to walk farther to school. I did talk with some parents on an individual basis, however, and found that there was concern on their part in having their youngsters go to a school where the majority of students was black. They were afraid that fights would occur and their kids would be socially "left out" of activities. I told them that Plymouth had too few students (at the junior high level) to get a good educational program there, they did not have the facilities which junior high schools should have as mandated by the state, and there were no lunch facilities available, so the youngsters could not stay in school all day. It was my personal belief that the Plymouth children would have been transferred in any case, be it racial balance or for the fact that Plymouth could not survive due to its lack of necessary equipment.

During the first few weeks of school, the observer noticed that teachers in Monroe constantly issued warnings against "wrong behavior." The former Plymouth students, like the youngsters who had attended Monroe the previous year, were not exempt from such admonishment:

> This is a seventh-grade English class. It consists of fifteen children—twelve blacks, and two white boys, formerly from Plymouth, and one white girl from outside. The teacher, Miss W was reading to the class from a book. The children reacted appropriately to various parts of the story and were listening attentively. Charles, one of the Plymouth boys, sat in the row of seats by the windows between two other students. As he listened to the story, he walked his fingers down the desk of the boy in back of him. As Charles' hand came near the boy, this boy made a playful pass at Charles. Both boys watched the teacher to guard against getting caught. The story being read was a mystery story whose moral was that "wrong-doers sow the seeds of their own destruction due to the fact that they feel guilt over their crime and therefore slip up in some

way which later betrays them." Miss W commented that she does not allow any of the children in her class to get into trouble. She asked the class if any of them had ever received a "blue ticket." Charles raised his hand. Miss W said, "Well, I'm sure it was not for some serious crime. And besides, that is all in the past. That is all wiped off the record and forgotten. Now you are in my home-room and you are not to get into any more trouble. I know you will have good records while you are with me." The other Plymouth boy, John, said, "Since he already has one blue ticket, does that mean that the rest of us can all get one to get even with him?" "No, indeed," answered Miss W. "Charles received that ticket before he came into my homeroom. As of right now is what counts." Miss W then told the class that she expected them to be at school every day and those days they were not there she would call to check with their mothers to find out why. Any child who misbehaved in class would have to stay after school. She stated that if she discovered one of "her children" staying after school for another teacher, they could expect to stay for her too.

In the beginning of the year, the white students from Plymouth seemed not to participate in the activities of the class. They generally withdrew:

It is the second week of school. In this ninth-grade class two white boys, former-ly from Plymouth, were sitting together by the windows. Both looked sleepy and were positioned generously in the seat and across the table. They were not taking notes, books were piled up on top of each other unopened, and one boy had to struggle to keep his eyes open at all. His feet were widely spaced be-neath the table, one straight out in front, one to the side. His head was resting on his books, his head facing the teacher, and one arm was under his head while the other arm lay across the table. The other boy was sitting low in the chair with his head resting against the back of it. Mr. C finally said to them, "All right, you boys, sit up in your chairs." The two black boys sitting closest to them exchanged smiles. Not once did the two Plymouth boys answer ques-tions or in any way relate to what was going on in the room.

While the transfer students were not taking part in academic activities they were mildly disruptive in class. Again, this kind of behavior was exhibited in the early months of school. Since these students did not know many of the Monroe youngsters, they seemed to feel the need to draw attention to them-selves in class so as to make the other children and the teacher recognize their existence. The observer recorded the following incident as typical of the former Plymouth students' activity:

This is an eighth-grade social studies class. There are twenty-four children in the room. Sixteen are boys, four of them white, from Plymouth. There are eight girls, one of them white, from Plymouth.
The child who made his presence known most was John, a transfer from Plymouth. His manner was disruptive in that he constantly spoke out without waiting to be called upon and several times got out of his chair and roamed about the room. He and two other white boys sat in a row together. The other two were quiet, not participating in the recitation but aware of what was

happening in class. They followed directions from the teacher. The remaining white boy played around with the black boys on either side of him in their row. He moved the desk of the boy in front of him, and that boy turned about and socked the white boy, not hard, and smiling as he did it. The two black boys and the white boy often exchanged remarks and seemed to be on friendly terms with each other.

The lone white girl in the class sat quietly, did not talk to any of her neighbors, and did not volunteer during the class work. The last part of the class was occupied by reading aloud from a book dealing with courage. John, the new white student, jumped to his feet, walked to the front of the room, and spoke to the teacher, loudly complaining about not having been chosen to read from the book. Mr. N sent him back to his seat and said he would have an opportunity to do so. When Mr. N called on Jackie next, a black student from Monroe, John again walked up to Mr. N's desk and announced that it was now his turn. Mr. N let Jackie finish reading and then called upon John, who read well until the class ended. As this class broke up into various reading groups, I followed one bunch of children into another room where I noticed seven black girls, five black boys, and one white student from Plymouth about to take their seats. The white boy was a tall, gangling youngster. He and two short little black boys worked together fashioning a noose of the window cord, taking turns trying to hang each other. The objective in this room seemed to be, "Have as much fun as possible before the teacher arrives!"

Most teachers at Monroe did not ignore the former Plymouth students or separate them from the ongoing process of classroom activity. Some teachers, however, tended to bypass the new transfer students:

There are six boys in the class—four white Plymouth children and two black students who have previously attended Monroe. There are also fifteen girls— thirteen black and two white (one from Plymouth). The tables are arranged in a large U shape. The four white boys sat beside three black children at one table, and the two white girls sat together at the other end. They whispered, laughed, and in general paid not the slightest attention to the class activities.

One of the white boys was asleep. Another white boy moved to a table by himself and stretched out across two chairs in full length. He looked comfortable, but was not interested in the business at hand. Two black boys in the back of the room were laughing, but stopped when the rest of the class did not respond. The class discussion was on gravity. Mr. B was asking questions and the group inside the U portion of the table were eagerly raising their hands. This group was composed of black girls from Monroe. They seemed interested in the subject and in getting the correct answers. Because of their behavior, Mr. B kept feeding them information and questions very rapidly. Occasionally, they would not get quite the right answer or not the complete answer and he would take time to show them why another answer would be better. These students really knew what was going on and showed it. They contributed much to the class, were quick and bright, and were rewarded by the teacher as he constantly challenged them. The girls expressed themselves clearly and concisely. With this group, there was no need for the teacher to establish order first and teach second.

Mr. B, who usually does not permit sleeping in class, was caught up in the excitement of the Monroe students' response and consequently let the boys from Plymouth sleep. At the same time, he seemed to forget their presence.

During the course of the year, there was an increasing tendency on the part of the white students from Plymouth to mix with the black students at Monroe. In the early weeks and months, the observer noted that white students tended to group with each other in some classrooms and in the lunchroom. Toward the end of the first semester of the school year, the separation of racial groups seemed to disappear as the students came to know one another. The observer describes this tendency in the following report of three seventh-grade classes that were watching a movie in the lunchroom:

Four white girls, three from Plymouth and one from outside, were flanked on each side by a black student. They were obviously enjoying each other's company and were quietly talking so as not to attract the attention of the teachers. At times, they whispered in each other's ears, and at other times exchanged written notes on the movie. The white boys were dispersed throughout the room; among the boys of course; seventh-grade boys do not sit with seventh-grade girls! No two white boys sat together. I have noticed since the year began that the boys formerly from Plymouth are more inclined to mix in with all the boys, and white girls tend to stay more together. Today, however, I am not aware of the girls "sticking together."

It was the observer's opinion that as time wore on and the "settling down" process took hold, the Monroe youngsters showed increased evidences of acceptance of the new students and, in turn, the transferees became more relaxed and accepting of the old students. Some of the white students from Plymouth, particularly the girls, were increasingly included where before they had been excluded.

When the school year began, the "in" group of Monroe students ostracized the new children. In the observer's words, it was as if the old students were saying, "You see, we are friends and we don't know you but we want you to be aware of how close and friendly we all are." The barriers began to break down from day to day as the once strange environment became familiar, and by the end of the year these barriers had disappeared. One example of the kind of exclusion prevalent at the start of school is reported by the observer:

This is a seventh-grade homeroom. There are twenty-five children present. The only white girl is Nancy, formerly from outside. She has hair that is never combed, her clothes are not cleaned or pressed, and she looks unkept in comparison to the other children. Nancy tried to get in with some of the black girls from Monroe who are area students. They were "doing bad things" like opening the door, stepping out into the hall, and laughing and talking. They were enjoying every moment of flirting with potential danger! When Nancy attempted to join them in such sinful activity, they cut her dead, turning their backs on her and whispering together to make the exclusion more final. Nancy walked back to her desk. She leaned forward and began to touch the hair of the girl ahead of her. The girl did not like this at all and shook her head impatiently. Finally, Nancy drew her into conversation and the girl did not shut her off unkindly but chatted with her. Nancy wants to be a part of the group, any group. She tried in four different ways in a few minutes to do the things the group did and in the group's way. The Monroe children were not having any part of her. However, there seemed to be no racial overtones in the girls' rejection of Nancy. Rather, she was not "in" and when she tried to copy the "in" behavior she was ludicrous.

There was no overt evidence that the lack of acceptance of any child by any other was based on race. There was no fighting or name-calling either inside or outside the class. If racial feelings did exist they took subtle forms. It was rather that preexisting friendship patterns were the basis of student groupings at Monroe. Children who had been friends before, either at Monroe or Plymouth, determined who could interact with them, at least in the beginning of the year. The white children from Plymouth, although they might not have known one another in their old school, were drawn together by having come from the same school and by being members of a minority group in a new setting. Furthermore, a majority of the former Plymouth students lived in a different neighborhood from most of the Monroe students and had a long walk home. When the children left school for the day, it was more common to see a white boy with a group of black boys than a white girl with a group of black girls. White girls who were transferred to Monroe seemed to be the most isolated group in the school. Black girls, however, according to the observer, interacted freely with all of the other children—white or black, girls or boys—particularly in the latter half of the year. As the classes progressed, some of the former Plymouth students became more involved in their work and the various learning experiences.

A few of the new transferred students were disruptive and engaged in attention-getting behavior; others were withdrawn, and some were quiet, studious, and attentive:

This is a ninth-grade Spanish class. There are ten children in the room. Seven are black, three are white. Two of the white children are neighborhood students who have previously been at Monroe; the other white student is a Plymouth transfer. Vertise, a black girl from Monroe, answered most of the questions put forth. She had an excellent grasp of what was being taught. Running a close second were Leo, a black boy from Monroe, and Ethel, a black girl who moved to the area from Mississippi. The teacher, Miss M, informed me later that Ethel was the best student in her class but that all of them were good. Dennis, the white boy from Plymouth, was quiet most of the period but answered questions when he was called upon. He seemed to be totally absorbed in the work, took notes during the class, and responded to Miss M's questions with knowledgeable ease. He did not, however, raise his hand or initiate any participation. Dennis did not appear to be shy, but waited for the teacher to provoke a response from him. His face reflected delight when he answered correctly.

Many of the classes at Monroe are geared to the children's various levels of ability, capability, and productivity. There is a special education class for students who cannot keep up with the work handled in regular classes. It is a small class of only four students and is unique not only in terms of the material presented but also in terms of the behavior exhibited in it. The observer related the experiences of this class:

Mrs. R tailors the work to suit her students' abilities. There are two boys and two girls in the class. One of the boys is a white transfer student from Plymouth. One of the girls is a black student who moved here this year from Florida. The atmosphere in this class is friendly. The children came in chatting and happy. Mrs. R had them come to her desk one at a time while she checked to see what they had worked on the day before and what their assignment was for the day. Ray, the white Plymouth youngster, is cocky with a smart remark always in readiness. He wears built-up shoes which clicked noisily as he walked around the room. He listened while he was given instructions, nodding his head to indicate he understood. He proceeded to go to his desk where he placed books on the floor, picked them up, put them back down, and generally wasted time. He began to work and a few seconds later spoke out loud to Mrs. R. "What am I supposed to be doing with these things?" "What do I do with adjectives and adverbs?" Mrs. R got up and went to his desk. "Is this the page I told you to work on?" "This is what you *told* me." "Ray, do you know what an adjective is? Define it for me, you had it just yesterday. What does an adjective do?" Ray could not answer but leafed through his book and found it. He then looked away, fingered some pages, and flipped them randomly.

Martha, the black girl from Florida, is quiet. She looks downcast and is withdrawn. Her job was to reduce fractions. Mrs. R had to go to her and help her correct them. Martha did not talk with any other student, nor they with her. Toward the end of the class, Ray took his work up to Mrs. R to be checked. She sent him back to complete it. Ray was unhappy about this, and said, "I'm not going to do it. I don't know how and I'm tired of working on it." Mrs. R replied, "Ray, this assignment is already two days old. You have two zeros already and this will make a third." Ray looked at her and stated, "Oh, I could almost care," and walked over to another part of the room to gaze at something. He did not do his work and spent the rest of the time at his desk sitting with his feet stretched out as he loudly drummed on the desk.

This class is a basic class but is not labeled as one. It is a study in contrasts. It typifies not merely the defiant or withdrawn behaviors associated with some children who have many problems but, moreover, suggests the nature of a conflict that the teacher must confront—the teacher is caught between the attempt to reinforce the lessons of formal grammar and the opportunity to encourage thought and investigation. Happy is the teacher who has discovered ways of combining instruction in grammatical form and methods of thinking. Too often they are taught as separate phenomena.

Some of the former Plymouth children, even toward the end of the school year, were still on the fringes. They did not relate well with the established children in Monroe, the new school to which they were assigned. Isolated incidents in the classrooms reflected this notion of them as outsiders. The observer frequently remarked, for example, that when the students were allowed to choose their own seats, the transfer pupils would always sit in a front seat, a back seat, at the end of a row, but rarely in the center. It was as if these youngsters were quite literally placed "on the fringes" of the class.

There seems to be little administrative concern about children who are able to fit into the learning system but are unable to fit in with other students. The life experiences of some of the former Plymouth youngsters differed from those of some of the Monroe students. No school program to bridge these differences was initiated. It was left to the individual pupil to become absorbed in the climate at Monroe.

The observer recalled a guidance class held at the end of the year in which the teacher asked several black students from Monroe how they would like being in a class with mostly white children. Their answers reflected a certain fear of moving into an unknown situation that would be dominated by white students: "It would be okay with a gun." "I'd take my knife with me." "I wouldn't like it but I guess I could get used to it." The teacher asked them why they would need a knife or a gun. "Well, you don't know when they'd gang up on you," came the response.

The Plymouth students did not express this kind of fear. Most of them began to feel comfortable at Monroe by the second semester. One boy who had transferred to Monroe in the fall wrote an essay in the school newspaper, and the opinions he presented seemed to be shared by a large number of other students who were formerly at Plymouth.

I like it here as much as I did at Plymouth. The teachers are understanding and the kids are friendly. The work isn't easy but when you do it it helps you get along with the teachers. The books and other materials are more plentiful than at Plymouth. The principal is nice and I like to take his advice. The vice-principal and counselors are fair in solving problems. The rules are a bit tough but I guess you need rules to run a good school.

In spite of the hostile climate of Lincoln or the laissez-faire setting at Monroe, the reassigned white and black children began to become a part of their new schools during the latter half of the school year. This indicates that there may be a development process to integration, moving at its own pace once white and black or poor and affluent youngsters are brought together; therefore, any assessment of the success or failure of integration in the schools would need to indicate the time in which the assessment is made and the length of the period of observation. The racially homogeneous groups during the first semester transformed into racially heterogeneous groups the second semester. All this points toward the need for more information on the different phases of the integration process and the conditions under which they are shortened or lengthened.

It is sometimes asserted that the process of racial integration is more difficult when the persons involved are also of different socioeconomic status levels.
A qualitative analysis indicates that lower-class youth who were transferred to a
middle-class school were treated as strangers during the first semester and not
admitted to the fellowship of the many different groups in that school. Likewise, the lower-class youth who were transferred to another lower-class school
were shut out of the informal groups and they too were treated as strangers.
Thus, it would appear that the newness of the students to each other is a more
important variable limiting interaction than differences or similarities in their
social class. This principle is stated in a tentative way because of the limited
social class levels available for analysis.

Finally, we see that the reassignment of students to improve racial balance
is only the beginning of the integration process, and that probably as much
attention needs to be given to preparing the schools as to preparing the children.
Neither Lincoln nor Monroe were prepared to foster the integration of new
children into the existing student population. The school year was basically
a trial-and-error experience with some teachers trying harder and others erring
greatly. And the children were blamed for the staff's mistakes; they were
blamed for being what they were and for coming from where they came; they
were blamed for not being like the rest of the children; they were blamed for
being new.

# 11

## The Role of Teacher and Principal in Integration

The attitudes of the principals and teachers of the four schools in our study (Highland, Simpson, Monroe, and Lincoln) are important factors to consider in our understanding of school integration. In the previous chapters we stressed the students' reactions to integration. In examining the teachers' and principals' reactions, the differences and simularities in the schools again become apparent. It will be important to seek explanations of the kinds of adjustments made and to identify the factors that facilitate or interfere with the process of integration. All principals of the four schools studied are white.

Two of the schools, Simpson and Lincoln, displayed similarities as to context. There was great resistance to the presence of inner-city students. These schools were oriented toward high achievement, and the students were constantly reminded of this orientation. Many faculty and parents thought that the reassignment of inner-city students to these schools was unnecessary. It was as if they were saying, "Why spread the problem of underachievement around? It is not my problem; it does not fall within my jurisdiction. Let somebody else take care of it." Thus the similar responses at Simpson and at Lincoln to the transferred students were based on similar orientations. There was fear that the students from the inner city would lower the schools' achievement ratings. There was constant reiteration of the achievement goals in these schools. In summary, many believed that the images of these schools would be tarnished, the academic standards hampered, and the teacher-student relationship upset by the school desegregation plan.

Monroe and Highland, on the other hand, had different kinds of environments that were associated with different responses to the desegregation plan. These schools were not strictly achievement-oriented, although Highland had a reputation as a fine institution. Essentially, Monroe and Highland were more flexible. While Highland was administered in a democratic way, Monroe seemed to operate on a rather laissez-faire philosophy. There were academic expectations but they were not stressed as much as at Lincoln and Simpson.

In particular, the principal and faculty at Highland were not concerned with image-building but with helping the students. Highland's experience with integrating physically handicapped and nonhandicapped students also probably accounted for the ease with which it responded to the proposal to achieve racial integration.

As becomes apparent in the case of these four schools, we can better understand a school climate by examining the various influences exerted by the principal, faculty, students, and parents.

Administrators in each of the four schools exhibited definite patterns of leadership, and each pattern produced its effect upon the integration experience. Simpson's principal maintained formal control of the policies and procedures that were carried out in the school. There were many rules, and they were strictly enforced. The principal was not hostile to reassigned inner-city children but she handled them in a firm way. The students and staff at Simpson knew what was expected of them, and the principal indicated to the new transfer students that they too must fit into the Simpson system. Thus some of the new students were given private lectures in addition to public scoldings and chidings when they got "out of line." The new children were made aware of the normative pattern in the school as quickly as possible. In the beginning of the year the principal's response toward the new black youngsters was "tense" and "stern"; she did not know the youngsters, their brothers and sisters, or their parents; she did not know what to expect and was therefore uneasy in her relations with them. In the latter part of the year the principal began to relax, urging and cajoling the students to fulfill her expectations rather than admonishing them. The transfer children began to know the principal and to respond favorably to her expectations and to the normative pattern of the school. Their adjustment was made less difficult as the principal began to respond to each child individually rather than as "one of those Corliss children." During the second semester she began to address them by name, joke with them, and talk with many about their academic progress. The principal who had attempted to direct the new youngsters' adjustment by continually checking on their behavior finally relaxed and began to accept the new children; they, in turn, began to follow the rules.

Highland's principal gave leadership in deliberately planning for further integration. He emphasized a flexible rather than a rigid approach. The principal's style of administering the school and relating to the students did not change with the arrival of a greater number of black students. His administrative orientation had always been one of participating with faculty and students in the operation of the school. He constantly urged the staff to guide and encourage the new children. He did not look upon the black students as potential behavior problems. He tailored discipline to the individual. What was perhaps most crucial for the new children's adjustment was the principal's awareness of what was actually happening in his school and his own recognition that as principal he was in a position to support the deliberate move toward integration by fostering an atmosphere of acceptance.

Lincoln Junior High School's principal was anxious about the desegregation plan. His style of leadership became more authoritarian as the year progressed. The Lincoln principal maintained a kind of militaristic stance against the new children. He was on guard and gave no quarter to the inner-city black children transferred to his school. Emphasis was upon quick compliance with the administration's regulations. The students were controlled by threats and punishments which some of them believed to be unjust. The principal reiterated his views and policies throughout the year, saying, "These transfers obey the rules or else!" There was an uneasy feeling among the new students.

The Monroe Junior High School principal generated an entirely different kind of atmosphere. He led from afar in a laissez-faire fashion. The principal was seldom seen talking with students in the halls or classes. Even discipline was not handled by the principal. Faculty members or the vice-principal handled most of the behavior problems. The transfer students, most of whom were white, were left alone. In general, they were on their own with little, if any, deliberate help in adjusting to Monroe. At times the school appeared to be without visible leadership. There was no observable planning on the principal's part to use his power and authority to make the integration process at Monroe either more or less difficult.

From the above analysis, it is clear that the most favorable school environment—that which contributed most to good education, racial integration, and pleasant working conditions for the teaching staff—was to be found at the Highland Elementary School. This environment was due, in part, to the school's history of caring for physically handicapped children. But more than this, it was due to the principal's attitude of acceptance and his leadership skill. This suggests that the principal's role is most important in establishing a school climate favorable to integration.

As we now see, the principal plays an important leadership role in helping to establish an educational environment that is favorable to learning and that fosters positive social relationships among students. Neither a threatening nor a laissez-faire approach seems to be helpful. In Monroe, where the principal was aloof from the daily happenings in the school, neither he nor the faculty knew what students actually experienced at the school and how they really felt about the school. The extra services provided in a magnet school or a "higher horizons" school like Monroe are of limited value, if the principal and faculty are not dedicated to education and desegregation.

An important factor in the variation in school adjustment in a desegregated setting is whether or not the student is new. When all four schools were combined, the adjustment self-ratings of students who were new neighborhood residents and those of reassigned or bused children from the inner city were similar. The reassigned inner-city children, in general, felt assimilated into the new school about as much as new neighborhood residents. This is an important finding that resulted from the comparative analysis. In many studies of desegregation and integration, investigators focus only upon the black or poor children and have no information on whether white or affluent children have similar experiences. This, of course, is one of the weaknesses of noncomparative studies.

Teacher expectation is a factor that fosters or impedes integration. Some teachers complained during the year that the transfer students, in particular the black children were disruptive in class and a burden to both the other pupils and the faculty. These complaints were most frequently heard at Lincoln Junior High School and Simpson Elementary, the two schools with high academic reputations. Some faculty members at these schools tended to generalize from the behavior of a few students; if one black transfer student was troublesome then he or she began to symbolize for some teachers all of the transfer students. The data revealed that black and white children were among the troublemakers, but that most students of both races adjusted well.

Several teachers responded differentially to disruptive behavior in students of different races. Thus, as one observer reported, a black transfer student at Lincoln was suspended for exactly the same behavior that had previously gone unpunished in a white neighborhood student.

On the other hand, several teachers used ingenious methods and techniques to involve new students in classroom activities. In many instances they avoided activities that involved one student choosing another to assist him. New students were usually left out of such activities since their names were not known to the old students. Some teachers singled out new students because of their disruptive behavior while other teachers singled out new students as models of good behavior.

In general, one might say that teachers of diversified student populations must be more sensitive to the implications of their actions if they are to be successful. In one school children were given morning milk if they paid a modest fee. The job of passing out the milk was assigned to a youngster from a low-income family whose parents could not pay for the milk. The teacher assigned the student this job as a way of involving him, but did not recognize the irony of having a milk attendant who could not drink the milk he passed out to others. This is an example of insensitivity, a problem frequently observed among teachers. A diversified student population cannot be successfully taught if the teachers have an attitude of "business as usual." Extraordinary planning and effort must be made to deal with the extraordinary circumstances and disparate experiences.

Teachers tend to feel that new white neighborhood residents made better adjustments to school than new black inner-city bused students. The teachers persist in expressing this position, but we obtained similar self-ratings of adjustment from these two categories of pupils. This indicates that teachers are rating the white or affluent student in terms of an expectation that may differ from the student's own experience. We conjectured that the distortion of the adjustment of white children as always favorable could cause resentment among black children and even be harmful to whites in need of help. Poor adjustment behavior of blacks might be singled out because of their high visibility, while whites exhibiting similar behavior could be ignored because they were not expected to adjust poorly. Thus, the black youngsters would experience differential treatment not so much because the teacher misjudged their behavior, as is sometimes claimed, but because the teachers misjudged the behavior of their white or affluent classmates who may in fact have exhibited the same good or bad behavior as the black or low-income children.

In light of the above, we may conclude that people tend to react to situations in which they find themselves in terms of their system of beliefs. If teachers believe that white middle-income children assimilate better than black or low-income children, then these teachers tend not to notice the poorly adjusted behavior of some white children. The same teachers also tend not to notice the well-adjusted behavior of some black children. The disprepancy in teachers' ratings of new-neighborhood white and reassigned black students would appear to be a function of the stereotype.

We discovered that in addition to the school environment, which is created mainly by the attitudes and actions of the school professional personnel, the students had to deal with the new interpersonal experiences resulting from the coming together of children of disparate backgrounds in a single school.

At the two junior high schools, the student's sex seemed to influence the integration process. Social isolation in a new school appeared to be less frequently experienced by boys than by girls. In Monroe Junior High, for example, the white boys who had been transferred tended to follow the example set by the black boys who were the majority and had attended Monroe the previous year. There was much interaction between the old students and the new white boys at Lincoln Junior High. They walked together to and from school and engaged in the usual hit-and-run play activities. However, the white girls at Monroe, which was predominantly black, were somewhat isolated. At the two elementary schools, which were predominantly white, both black boys and black girls tended to be "in the swing of things" by the end of the first semester.

**Part IV:**
**Integrating Colleges and Universities**

# 12

## The Social Life of Black Students at White Colleges

The black experience at a white college is a story of hope, frustration, and disillusionment, of individual and institutional racism, and of racial separatism.

Consider the experience of Catherine (her name is fictitious, as are the others in this chapter), a black woman on a white campus. Her feelings are representative of those expressed by many other black students. She has chosen separatism in reaction to the stresses of a white environment. Catherine was a third-year student from a middle-class family in a middle-sized industrial city. She said this about her three years on a white college campus:

> . . . [I was] in a hall with 500 girls, all white except me. My roommate was from [the South]. It just so happens I did get along with my roommate. You could call her a liberal . . . . Isolated, I began to get into the system of having mainly white friends as my good friends. . . . To a certain extent I was getting involved in a lot of white activities . . . . [Then] little incidents started happening. My white friends would make some mistakes in what they'd say and do. They would hurt my feelings. But I would take into account that they were really my friends and sometimes they do make errors.
>
> We used to always study together for exams in one course. The content for one exam was about prejudice and poverty. They didn't call me in when they were studying. When I found out they had already studied and did not include me, I asked why and was told that one of the girls said blacks were inferior and the other girls said they thought it wouldn't be right to include *me* in the study session after that type of attitude had been aired . . . .
>
> The Union of Black Collegians got to be more active. I began to make a break there and began to look at myself and these so-called friendships . . . .
>
> When you are put into a situation like I was where you're the only one out of 500 and every day you're exposed to some kind of racism, whether subtle or blatant, it begins to work on you.
>
> Most of my friends now are black.

We surveyed approximately 150 black and 200 white students on the campuses of four predominantly white colleges. The random sample represented 40 percent of all blacks and 1 percent of all whites enrolled in these schools. For the black students, we obtained in-depth case material in unstructured and semistructured interviews and tape-recorded student rap sessions.

Like Catherine, many other black students told us of uncomfortable racial experiences and said that they find it hard to make white friends when initial encounters involve whites' staring at them and asking questions like: "What is your hair made of?" and "How can you tell when you have the measles?"

As interactions between the races increase, because of increased enrollment of black students at white colleges, trust and confidence between the races appear to decrease. Since blacks feel that support from whites is not dependable, they increasingly turn to each other. They are reluctant to risk white friendships that may turn out to be fragile and unstable.

We found that the social life of most blacks on white college campuses tends to be limited to interaction with other blacks. Almost half (43 percent) reported not having been in a racially mixed social group in the six months preceding the survey. Further, three-fourths reported that their participation in interracial parties was rare or only occasional. Nearly three-fourths of the black students (73 percent) reported that almost all of their closest friends were black.

The actual experience of racial exclusivity tends to exceed the students' expectations. For example, only 28 percent of the blacks believed that they should live apart from whites; yet two-thirds had lived with other black students all or most of their college careers. Two-thirds of the black students expected to have parties only with other blacks; in reality, three-fourths said the parties they attended were all black.

As blacks turn to each other more and more, we find that the quality of the black student's social life on white college campuses is conditioned by the number of black students enrolled. The black-student population on one of the four campuses in our study was about 200 out of a total student enrollment of 15,000. On three of the campuses, however, there were fewer than seventy-five black students in each student body.

It appears to us that the size of the black-student population is related to the quality of the campus social life for minorities. Further research is needed to determine the degree of association, if any, between the size of the black-student population and the tendency toward self-conscious separatism, and the extent of interracial dating.

Our findings indicate that very small black populations on white campuses merely appear to be cohesive. Stand-off relationships between men and women, complaints about dating, and concern over compatibility were less often issues or topics for discussion on the one campus where black enrollment was relatively large. There also was much more off-campus activity in the colleges with small black-student populations; instead of spending their weekends in the college community, the students returned home or went to the black communities in metropolitan areas for social activity. There is less cohesion and more tension among black students at white colleges where the black-student population is relatively small.

The chance of a black person's finding another black person with whom he or she is compatible is limited on a white campus. Any extraordinary personal characteristic may compound an already difficult situation. For example, a black woman in her thirtys, who attends a college with a black-student population of fewer than seventy-five, calls the campus social life "a living hell."

"I am an old lady compared to the guys in school," she said. "They don't want no part of me and I don't want anything to do with any baby."

Even when there are no extraordinary circumstances, encounters between black males and black females are tense and uncertain when there are few black students on the campus. When two black students find they are compatible and have much in common it is a joyous thing. However, the joy is tempered by anxiety that the small black population on campus may not yield another compatible relationship if the existing one should end. Thus, one partner may press another prematurely for an exclusive relationship. Black men, especially, place a high value on maintaining their freedom; they put a premium on not getting "trapped."

The complex problem of achieving a satisfactory social life when the number of blacks on campus is small is summarized in this series of statements by students.

There aren't enough blacks . . . .
  I'll be glad to get out . . . .
  A little social life would be best. I don't know many of the girls, only a couple. The rest are conceited and stuck up and act like they are Miss Black America. I dated Betty once; she was nice. But she kept calling me up. I don't want a girl like that. I date a girl [off campus in a nearby town now] . . . .
I see her pretty often; she keeps me satisfied so I don't get too uptight.

Marjorie said more simply: "We don't have much of a social life here at school. We just don't have dates." Jackie summarizes another consequence of too few blacks on campus: "Socially I don't like it at all because there are so few black people here. You are used to seeing the same bunch and after a while you get tired of seeing the same people." Essentially, Jackie described a small black-student population as "a dull scene."

A small black-student population on a white campus eliminates anonymity— the old small-town syndrome. The dating process is easier if all partners do not always know all other partners. A reputation has a way of traveling ahead of one in a small, closed society, and it can interfere with new dating opportunities.

By the time you're a sophomore, you're old blood. Everyone knows you, whom you went with, what you're like, what you're doing, what you're not doing, whether it's worth their time or not.

In our study, an increase in the black-student population from seventy-five to 200 or so seemed to be associated with an increase in freedom, flexibility, and anonymity. Harvey Cox has called anonymity a liberating phenomenon that ". . . helps preserve the privacy which is essential to human life."[1] It is one device that protects one from excessive personal claims by others.

On campuses where black populations are relatively small and the social life of their members are limited to interaction with other black students, the black-student groups take on the character of extended families. When this occurs, all relationships, including those that might otherwise be secondary, become intensely personal. The black students who make unlimited claims upon each other find such relationship sometimes supportive, but they also find them sometimes stultifying and confining.

This suggests that white colleges that deliberately recruit black students must enroll a substantial number; otherwise, the few who are enrolled are condemned to inadequate social lives and discord with other blacks as well as whites.

Despite frustration and disillusionment, black students are likely to increase in numbers at predominantly white institutions. Although they may say unkind things about white colleges, black students nevertheless will encourage other blacks to enroll so that they may benefit socially and otherwise from an enlarged black-student population. One of the best ways to recruit black students at white colleges is to enlist the aid of blacks already enrolled.

While nearly all blacks on white campuses sometimes feel isolated and confined, it is the black women who feel it most heavily. We tried to compare the quality of campus social life for black men and black women. Our study offered a modest opportunity to inquire whether black women find it harder to adapt to white-college social life than black men do, or vice versa.

We found that black women do less interracial dating than members of any other group in our study. Black men do more interracial dating than any other group. Thus, the forces that inhibit or restrain interracial dating are stronger for black women and white men than for black men and white women. Sixty-four percent of the black men say that they date black and white women; 64 percent of the white men say that they date white women only. These data have important implications regarding freedom and control of men in the two racial populations.

Table 12-1
**Black and White Students Who Date Interracially, at Four Colleges**

| Race/Sex | Percent Who Date Interracially |
|----------|:---:|
| Black women | 29 |
| White men | 36 |
| White women | 45 |
| Black men | 64 |

The combined responses of black men and women revealed that only about one-fifth (22 percent) think that black dating should be black-only; the proportion of black women (31 percent) who hold this belief is more than double the proportion of black men (13 percent). Based on these data, it is clear that a substantial majority of black men and black women accept interracial dating.

In this respect, black men and women have similar attitudes and beliefs. In actual dating activity, however, they are almost opposite. While 78 percent of the combined population in this study believe that blacks should be free to date persons of any race, only 29 percent of the black women had acted in accordance with the belief, while 64 percent of the black men had done so.

White men are at least partly responsible for this disparity. The usual practice in our sexist society is for men to initiate dating situations. It need not be this way and may change. For the nonce, however, most females respond to the initiative of males. Black females report that white males tend not to ask them out on dates. Interracial dating is often discussed as a triangular affair involving black and white women and black men. Seldom are white men implicated. However, our study suggests that they may be the key to opening the blocked social life of black women on white college campuses.

According to their responses, only 10 percent of the white men believe that blacks should date black-only. Presumably they have accepted interracial dating. Yet their actions are different from their attitudes. They practice racial separatism in dating and in their choice of friends. The closest friends for 71

**Table 12-2**
**Social Expectations for Black Students, at Four Colleges**

| Statement of Expectation | Percent Who Believe that Blacks Should Act in Accordance with the Statement | | | |
| --- | --- | --- | --- | --- |
| | Black Men | Black Women | White Men | White Women |
| Black students should have exclusive recreational activities | 60 | 73 | 9 | 9 |
| Black students should date only other black students | 13 | 31 | 10 | 2 |
| Black students should have separate dormitory facilities | 24 | 30 | 3 | 1 |
| Black students should have social affairs with other groups on campus | 57 | 56 | 90 | 91 |

percent of the white men in our study are white, and 64 percent say that they
have limited their dating to whites.

Part of the variance in interracial dating behavior may be due to white-male
aspirations for the future and the desire to be successful and in control. Among
white males who have rejected the traditional status aspiration of success and
upward mobility, other inhibitions are at work. When we presented a preliminary
draft of this paper to two sociology classes, white-male inhibitions about interracial dating came out. In the long discussions that followed, white males spoke
of guilt feelings about past exploitation of black women, and some were afraid
that black women students would misinterpret their motives. There was also
a fear of being rejected by the black woman, a humiliating experience for one
who expects always to be in charge in interracial matters.

A few black women say that they have refused to date white males who
asked them because, as one woman put it, "They just don't appeal to me."
However, others who dated white men found the dates pleasant. In the main,
black women, like white men, are racially exclusive in their dating in spite of
their stated openness to interracial association.

Our data then indicate that the dating situation for black women may be a
function of the absence of opportunities.

Janet, a nineteen-year-old sophomore, said: "Black girls on campus do not
have access to making it with the white guys. This is why they get mad and
uptight when the brothers fence jump."

Most black girls who reported that they would date whites say that they
seldom are asked for dates. "The white boys are afraid of us," observes Mitzi.

Mary Lou, at a school where the black enrollment is less than seventy-five,
summarized the attitude of many of the other black women:

There just has to be more people so that when you wake up in the morning—
particularly for girls—you can think that "maybe I'll meet my special someone
today." But when you know everyone who's on campus [you say to yourself],
"Why put on makeup? Who am I trying to impress? I know everyone who's
here."
It wouldn't make any difference [going out with someone white] but
they're not asking us out. There are one or two black girls here who go out
with white boys and quite a few black boys who go out with white girls.

Another black woman, Celeste, said, "Interracial dating makes my jaws
tight." She is embittered when she sees interracial dating because, in her words:

White chicks have an advantage over the sisters. Sisters must compete for the
black guys; white chicks don't have to. She has her man and whenever she wants
to, she comes over and raids the black women's territory, something not freely
available to black women.

In addition, there appear to be social sanctions from the black community
that affect a black woman's freedom to date interracially.

While black men offer all kinds of justifications for their interracial involvement—including exploitation, an expression of freedom, and a bridge for racial
reconciliation—they tend to be stern against interracial dating for black women.
Because of the historical exploitation of black women by white men, especially
in the time of slavery, some blacks believe that any black woman-white man
relationship is a continuation of this.

John, a nineteen-year-old second-year student from New York City, said:
"The only time I see a black girl with a white guy is when she is a prostitute.
White guys don't formally ask black girls out."

Another black student, Emmett, said: "Black male-white female dating
is more common, [but] if a white man goes out with a black woman, the man
only has sex on his mind."

Emmett does not make a value judgment about the motivations of black
males who date whites as he does for white males who date blacks. This accusa-
tion is an interesting reversal of the myth of the sexuality of black males. Some
blacks now accuse whites who date blacks of being interested only in sex, a
charge that whites used to level at blacks.

Sylvia, a black woman, admits that some whites have this single-minded
interest in dating, but she insists that this interest is not restricted to white men.
She said: "I go with black guys once in a while and I go out with white guys
once in a while. They're basically the same, all after sex . . . ."

Interracial dating for black males continues, despite some pressure for
unity and solidarity from the black community on campus, which most black
males acknowledge.

A twenty-year-old black-male sophomore student from a large metropolitan
community explains that interracial dating at his college is done "a little under
the cuff, a clandestine thing." He continues:

I go out with white girls and black girls. And you can't ask anybody not to do
it. Of course, you don't take a white girl to a black party. I go with an Italian
girl myself. But she is a little dark, so I slide by. Actually, there is quite a bit of
black-white dating. I think it should be up to the individual person. If you
don't try to bridge the gap, you just add to the troubles you already have, like
prejudice, hate and war . . . . Actually there is no difference between going
to bed with a white girl and going to bed with a black girl. But still there is a
lot of ostracism among the blacks for going out with whites. But anybody who
tells me anything about it, I just tell them to kiss my ass.

Such determination is hard to restrain. Thus, two-thirds of the black-male
students in our study state that they date interracially.

The behavior of college black men at white schools illustrates the relative
influence of attitudes against interracial association versus opportunities for
interracial contact. One-fourth of these men said that blacks should have
separate housing on campus. Of the separatists, about half restricted their dating
to black women; the other half did not.

This means that about half of the black separatists also dated interracially. Thus, attitudes against interracial dating have an effect. But opportunities for black-white interaction appear to be importantly related to interracial dating, too, as our analysis of high-school racial composition will indicate.

There is an orientation toward freedom of choice within the black campus community, and it would support dignified and respectful new interracial arrangements. Thus, some of the stated values appear to be contradictory. Blacks insist that one should be free to do his or her own thing but they also believe that black group demands should take precedence over personal desire. On balance, the push for individual freedom usually transcends the call for racial solidarity whenever there is conflict between the two.

Social sanctions from the black-student community, opportunities for interracial dating, and aspirations for the future are variables that condition inter-racial social life. But past experiences seem also to help explain interracial social activity, most particularly the extent of integration in the students' primary- and secondary-school years.

Although most of the students in this study lived in the Northeast (87 per-cent of the whites and 74 percent of the blacks), their experience of integrated education varied greatly. Most black college students attended elementary and high schools that were predominantly white or that had student bodies equally divided between the races. Only about one in ten whites attended schools where the proportion of black students was half or greater. In fact, the number of whites who had experienced significantly integrated education before college was so small as to be statistically insignificant.

We analyzed variations in interracial dating of black and white college-age students by the types of high schools that the students attended. For black students we analyzed these variations for three types of high schools: all black, predominantly black, and racially balanced. Fifty-five percent of the black students in this study had attended these three types of schools. More than 90 percent of the white college students had attended two types of high schools— all white and predominantly white.

Few whites had attended racially balanced or predominantly black high schools. There were so few whites who had attended racially balanced or predominantly black schools that we could not justify an analysis.

Variation in interracial dating in college is associated with the racial com-position of the high school one attended. Black men who attended predomi-nantly black high schools, where there also were some whites, were more inclined to date interracially in college than were black men who had attended all-black high schools.

Interracial dating activities of black women also are a function of past experience. However, the critical mass of whites with whom they interact in high-school situations must be considerably larger for black women than for black men, if there is to be a carry-over effect on future dating behavior in

**Table 12-3**

**Interracial Dating Experience of Black and White College Students by Racial Composition of High School Attended, at Four Colleges**

| Dating experience | Black Men | | | Black Women | | | White Men | | | White Women | | |
|---|---|---|---|---|---|---|---|---|---|---|---|---|
| | *All Black School* | *Predominantly Black School* | *Half Black and Half White School* | *All Black School* | *Predominantly Black School* | *Half Black and Half White School* | *All White School* | *Predominantly White School* | *Half Black and Half White School-* | *All White School* | *Predominantly White School* | *Half Black and Half White School* |
| Never have dated interracially | 50 | 33 | 27 | 91 | 92 | 55 | 67 | 63 | – | 58 | 58 | – |
| Have dated interracially | 50 | 67 | 73 | 9 | 8 | 45 | 33 | 37 | – | 42 | 42 | – |
| Total | 100% | 100% | 100% | 100% | 100% | 100% | 100% | 100% | – | 100% | 100% | – |

[a]So few white students attended racially balanced high schools that reliable analysis was not possible.

college. Fewer than 10 percent of the black women who attended predominantly black or all-black high schools have dated interracially in college. However, 45 percent of the black women who attended racially balanced high schools have dated whites in college.

Our data clearly show that college-age black students who had opportunities to interact with whites in integrated high-school settings are more apt to date interracially. The same principle may apply to whites. However, there were so few white students in this study who had attended high schools with significant numbers of blacks that it was not possible to analyze the effect, if any, of this variable. There is a hint in the data that white men who attended predominantly white schools (where a few blacks also were enrolled) are slightly more inclined to date interracially in college than are white men who attended all-white high schools.

Thus, opportunity for interracial encounter in the past influences interracial dating activities in the present for blacks and also may influence such dating for whites.

Our main conclusion is that the *idea* of interracial dating is generally accepted by the black and white students. However, there are variations between the race and sex groups in the extent to which they act on their beliefs. The discrepancy was particularly pronounced for white men and for black women. Persons in each of these groups tended to do less interracial dating than the others.

There are, to be sure, negative social sanctions against interracial dating among blacks and whites. However, our findings indicate that the sanctions have little effect unless they are acknowledged by individuals. The striving for success among white men and the desire for unity among blacks are psychological conditions that acknowledge and facilitate the application of these sanctions. Even when the sanctions are acknowledged, our findings indicate that an interacial context tends to dull their effect. Indeed, we conclude that the situational factor of *interracial contact* is more significantly related to variations in interracial dating than are psychological orientations or social sanctions against it. The full report of this study has been published as a book entitled *Black Students at White Colleges*.[2]

## Notes

1. Harvey Cox, *The Secular City* (New York: Macmillan, 1965), p. 40.

2. Charles V. Willie, and Arlene McCord, *Black Students at White Colleges* (New York: Praeger, 1972).

# 13 Styles of Adaptation of Black College Students: Cooperation, Withdrawal, Aggression

In the past, analyses of racism experienced by blacks and members of other minority groups have focused on the negative consequences of life for a person in a racist society. Little attention has been given to the multitude of possible responses to racism. Fortunately, James Comer has begun to bring these alternative responses into focus. His professional experience taught him that the "constant daily reminders that it's tough to be black caused many youngsters enough discomfort to turn off or turn away." Then he remembered his personal experience in a family where the parents always said, "You never let race stop you from doing what you want to do." Comer concludes that the formula worked. He went to school—"hurt feelings or no hurt feelings"—got an education, and got ahead. When his self-esteem was battered, his parents patched it up and sent him back into the battle.[1] Today he is a psychiatrist and a member of the faculty at the Yale University Medical School. The professional and personal experiences of Comer illustrate that adversity can turn one off and turn one on.

Alexander Leighton also called attention to the multiple responses which individuals may make to similar situations in his study of Japanese-Americans in relocation camps in the United States during World War II. He wrote that cooperation, withdrawal, and aggressiveness are three basic adaptations which persons may make to forces causing disturbed emotions and thoughts; and according to the person and the circumstances, each form of adaptation may do either of three things: free the individual from the disturbed feelings and thoughts, permit their continuance, or lead to new pathological conditions.[2]

A proper approach to the understanding of the adaptations of minorities is an analysis of how they manage adversity. According to Claudewell Thomas and Comer, "The state of being mentally healthy represents possession of the ability to cope or function within society in an adaptive way"; by that they mean that "the results of everyday endeavors to cope which produce in turn a heightened capacity to cope and an increased willingness to engage the society."[3] Some blacks function effectively in predominantly white colleges and universities while others do not. The purpose of this chapter is to identify some factors associated with successful and unsuccessful coping experiences.

Clarification of the concept "adaptation" is needed. It does not refer to adjustment to and acceptance of a racist environment in a passive and fatalistic way. Indeed a successful response could be the attempt to transform a racist society or transcend it if transformation is impossible at a particular point in

153

history. This, of course, may result in a struggle. But René Dubos tells us that
"to live is to struggle." Moreover, he states that "a successful life is not one
without ordeal, failures, and tragedies, but one during which the person has
made an adequate number of effective responses to the constant challenge of his
physical and social environment."[4] It was an outlook like this one which
caused the distinguished black educator Benjamin Elijah Mays, President
Emeritus of Morehouse College, to title his autobiography *Born to Rebel.*[5] Being
a rebel in a racist society is one way of coping and therefore should be classified
as a successful form of adaptation, if rebellion is designed to achieve a double
victory: a beneficial result for the victim and the victimizer.

Martin Buber has characterized Jewish creativity as the ". . . striving to evolve
unity out of the divisions of the human community."[6] Dubos calls the rebel
"the standard-bearer of the visionaries who gradually increase our ethical stature."
He promised that "as long as there are rebels in our midst, there is reason to
hope that our societies can be saved."[7] Racism is an endemic experience at most
predominantly white colleges and universities. Yet there is reason to hope that
they too may be saved as long as there are rebels in their midst.

A few years ago, the athletes were rebels. Paul Hoch reports that "during
the 1970 college football season at least seventy-nine black athletes boycotted or
were suspended from their teams over charges of racism."[8] At Syracuse University, probably the most celebrated case involved eight black athletes who were
suspended from the football team because they boycotted spring training due to
the failure of the university to hire a black as a member of the nine- or ten-person
football coaching staff. I was a member of the Trustee-Faculty-Student Committee which investigated the charges of the black athletes. After receiving
testimony from black and white football players, members of the coaching staff,
and administrators of the university, our committee unanimously concluded
"that racism in the Syracuse University Athletic Department is real, chronic,
largely unintentional, and sustained and complicated unwittingly by many
modes of behavior common in American athletics and long-standing at Syracuse
University . . . ." Then the committee branded the sanctions against the black
athletes (their suspension from the football team) as a form of institutional
racism unworthy of a great university because the university had not taken into
consideration the racist condition of an all-white coaching staff which gave rise
to the boycott. Indeed, the university had hired a black assistant football coach
following the boycott and thereby legitimized the issue raised by the black
athletes. Following publication of the committee's report, the black football
players were reinstated. Here, then, was a racist experience at a predominantly
white university to which the black students adapted by withdrawing. Their
method of adapting or responding resulted in effective action—integration of
the football coaching staff. The rebellious action of withdrawal induced an
ultimate response that benefited the university and the minority athletes.

At the same university two years later, a fistfight broke out between black and white students during a student assembly meeting. The assembly is the legislative unit of the Syracuse University Student Association and approves the allocation of funds derived from the student activity fee to various student groups. Up until that time, the Student Afro-American Society had no financial relationship to the Student Association largely because a few years earlier the administration of the university had made a special grant to the organizations of black students and Puerto Rican students. The black-student population had grown considerably since the time of the initial special grant. Moreover, administrative officials increasingly were of the opinion that the special financial arrangement with organizations of minority groups which enabled them to bypass direct involvement with the Student Association was paternalistic. The black students needed more funds to underwrite the costs of their expanded programs due mainly to the enlarged black population on campus. The student assembly initially indicated a willingness to allocate only enough funds to cover about one-fifth of the $10,000 requested by the blacks. In rejecting the request of the blacks, some student assembly representatives made remarks which some of the blacks felt were insulting. The fight which ensued was stimulated by these remarks. Later the student assembly acquiesced and allocated the Student Afro-American Society a sum of money which was about four-fifths of the initial request. Peace and calm returned to deliberations of the student assembly, which at that time had only two black members in it. Here, then, was a racist response—the failure of the student assembly to make adequate financial provision for the program needs of blacks—which was met by aggressiveness on the part of the oppressed. Apparently their aggressiveness was effective. The fistfight, of course, was not a necessary component of the aggressive stance. Violence is degrading to the victim and the victimizer. The aggressiveness of the black students was manifested in their massive presence at the student assembly in which their demands were presented, in their evening demonstrations on the campus quadrangle, in their insistence that their demands be treated seriously, and in their rejection of the first proposed allocation as a token and, thus, no solution at all.

A third style of adaptation, that of cooperation, was seen in 1973 in the democratic elections held by Syracuse University undergraduate and graduate students. The governing body for undergraduates is the Student Association and, for persons pursuing post-baccalaureate degrees, the Graduate Student Organization. Black students were elected as presidents of both groups for the academic year. They accepted the high honor and responsibility of the office of president. Here, then, was a situation in which the blacks spoke for all students and were student leaders of the campus establishment at a predominantly white university. They worked in behalf of minority and majority students who cooperated with them for their mutual benefit. One might say that these black leaders were cooperating with the system of organized student life on campus and therefore had an effect through the power of the organization that they led.

As indicated by Leighton, either cooperation, withdrawal, or aggressiveness may or may not be a successful strategy, depending upon the person and the circumstances. We have described three situations, all of which were trying and difficult and each of which required different adaptations for effective participation in the university community. It is important to point out that use of one mode of adaptation in a situation that requires another could result in failure. Despite the presence of racism in the environment as a constant experience, no single approach is always effective in countering it. Flexibility is needed.

We come now to an examination of the effect of these modes of adaptation upon the black students. Evidence from our study of black students at white colleges indicates that some black students are tending to cope with the situations with which they are confronted in a way that increases their willingness to engage the university community while others are falling back from their encounters with whites and using a stereotyped, inflexible, and unimaginative strategy. We found the "black students moving through a series of adaptation [–] some . . . in the cooperative stage, others in the withdrawal stage, and still others in the aggressive stage."[9] We point out that "it is well to view these stages as a series or as a continuum of which [black] students may move back and forth according to their experiences."[10] One student with whom our interviewer had an extensive conversation had moved "from cooperation with whites to withdrawal and toward aggressiveness" because "the stress of white racism did not abate during the first and second stages of adaptation. She is tending toward aggressive radicalism now because other kinds of adaptations did not work."[11]

It should be repeated that any form of adaptation is mentally healthy if it relieves the stress which contributes to troubled emotions and thoughts and enables the student to cope with the university community of which he or she is a part in a way that enhances both the student and the community. Thus the black football players in 1970 who withdrew, the black members of the Student Afro-American Society in 1972 who were aggressive, and the black presidents of the Student Association and the Graduate Student Organization in 1973 who led and therefore cooperated with the established student power groups exercised adaptive methods which were situationally appropriate and effective for these students, at the specific school, during those particular times.

Our research on black students and blacks in general reveals that most adapt according to the requirements of the situation and therefore survive. In *Racism and Mental Health,* the editors make this observation:

What has not been recognized by professionals and the public is the extraordinary way in which many blacks and members of other racial minorities have coped with adversity. How they have strengthened themselves to overcome the obstacles of racism is worthy of careful studies. Such investigations would make significant contributions to the accumulated body of knowledge and clinical practice in mental health. Well-documented life styles of effectively coping individuals and families could serve as models for dealing with danger and difficulty.[12]

A problem for black students on predominantly white college and university campuses is that administrators, faculty members, and white-student colleagues often do not realize that the multitude of adaptive responses which blacks exhibit have survival value.

Pathology tends to develop when blacks are encouraged or forced to ignore their existential history of racial oppression, which is unlike the existential history of whites in the United States. Arthur Jensen, for example, makes this statement that was mentioned in an earlier chapter about precollege school-age students: "The remedy deemed logical for children who would do poorly in school is to boost their IQ up to where they can perform like the majority. . . ."[13] While intellectual activity is important in elementary school, high school, and college, blacks have other concerns that are as important to survival as intellectual performance. Mentioned in an earlier chapter were such concerns as learning how to endure, how to develop a positive self-concept, and how to gain some control over the social environment within which one must operate. Indeed, if their adaptive activity is successful in these other areas, there is a high probability they also will do well academically. Already we have mentioned our study of black students at four predominantly-white colleges that revealed that the proportion of black seniors with good grades at the A and B levels was higher than the proportion of white seniors with similar grades.[14] A report on college seniors in a study conducted by the Educational Testing Service revealed that more black seniors than white seniors said they intended to earn doctorates.[15] It could be that the black seniors finally have "put it all together." Thus, the boosting of the IQ may not be the point at which to start for disadvantaged students as suggested by Jensen. Other coping concerns and adaptations might take precedence for blacks.

It could be that premature focus on the intellectual performance of blacks when they should be assisted in achieving other adaptive behavior could have negative consequences. Adaptation should be understood as a function of the contemporary situation as well as the historical context of the individual and the group with which he or she is affiliated. A set of adaptive responses appropriate for one person or group in a specific setting at a particular point in time may not be appropriate for another. Thus, the adaptive responses appropriate for whites in predominantly white colleges and universities may not be appropriate for blacks in predominantly white colleges and universities. This fact is the reason for suggesting that the Jensen prescription could be appropriate for a majority of the population but inappropriate for members of the minority.

Despite the rhetoric which calls for black separatism (which is a form of withdrawal), we found most blacks on the white college campus utilizing a range of adaptive responses (including withdrawal, cooperation, and aggressive-ness) to cope with racism and other campus problems. This flexibility in adap-tive responses we consider to be mentally healthy.

Blacks do what they have to do according to the requirements of the situation. We have noticed, however, a tendency for withdrawal as an adaptive response to be used more frequently in recent years than in the past. The black students say that they withdraw from active participation with whites as a way of avoiding insults and insensitivity. Thus, "Black separatism on the predominantly white college campus cannot be understood, apart from the circumstances and conditions of life created by whites for blacks."[16] Thus far the separatist response on the part of blacks has been a direct response to racist stimuli by whites. It is interesting to note that on the predominantly white university campus where the undergraduate and graduate student bodies were presided over by black presidents, a proposal failed which recommended that blacks change the name of their organization from the Student Afro-American Society to the Student Association for Black Unity. Presumably, black unity is important but not of sufficient symbolic value to change the historic name of a black campus organization in a setting where blacks are participating in the mainstream of campus student affairs as leaders. This dis-inclination to emphasize black unity which thrives under conditions of with-drawal from participation in the mainstream, which indirectly is a way of excluding whites was situational.

The tendency toward separatism could accelerate on college campuses and elsewhere if the racist experiences of rejection occur more frequently than those of acceptance. Indeed it is quite possible, as we point out in *Black Students at White Colleges*, that "an adaptation such as withdrawal, though originally a response to racism, may take on a life of its own and seek to per-petuate the special arrangement of a community of likeminded and look alike people."[17] If this kind of adaptation becomes institutionalized and takes on a life of its own apart from the stimuli which gave rise to it, such would con-stitute a pathological adaptation with the loss of freedom to change according to requirements of the situation. From what we have observed on the pre-dominantly white college campus, the National Advisory Commission on Civil Disorder had sufficient reason to warn that if the stress of white racism is not eliminated, soon this nation would divide permanently into two societies — one black and one white.[18] This is not the campus scene at this time. But there is a lessening in the creative urge by blacks to evolve unity out of the divisions of the college community. There is more of an inclination to let each group do its own things and merely to demand freedom for black self-determination, without regard for what others on campus are doing. In some respects this inclination could further contribute to a weakened sense of community on campus and consequently less safety and security for blacks as well as whites. Such a situation, of course, would increase self-preservation anxiety for all. As the authors of the *Book of Common Prayer* probably would say, there is no health in the absence of community.

## Notes

1. James Comer, *Beyond Black and White* (New York: Quadrangle Books, 1972), p. 23.
2. Alexander H. Leighton, *The Governing of Men* (Princeton: Princeton University Press, 1954), pp. 256-66.
3. Claudewell S. Thomas and James P. Comer, in Charles V. Willie, Bernard M. Kramer, Bertram S. Brown, eds., *Racism and Mental Health* (Pittsburgh: University of Pittsburgh Press, 1973), p. 166.
4. Rene Dubos, *So Human an Animal* (New York: Charles Scribners' Sons, 1968), p. 162.
5. Benjamin E. Mays, *Born to Rebel* (New York: Charles Scribner's Sons, 1971).
6. Martin Buber, *On Judaism* (New York: Schocken Books, 1967), p. 28.
7. Dubos, pp. 5-6.
8. Paul Hoch, *Rip Off the Big Game* (Garden City: Doubleday, 1972), p. 184.
9. Charles V. Willie and Arline Sarkuma McCord, *Black Students at White Colleges* (New York: Praeger, 1972) p. 12.
10. Ibid., p. 13.
11. Ibid.
12. Charles A. Pinderhughes, "Racism and Psychotherapy," in Willie et al., *Racism . . .*, p. 582.
13. Arthur Jensen, "How Much Can We Boost IQ and Scholastic Achievement?" *Environment, Heredity, and Intelligence* (Cambridge: Harvard Educational Review, 1969), Reprint Series No. 2, p. 3.
14. Willie and McCord, pp. 86-87.
15. Gene I. Maeroff, "Academic Goals Differ for Sexes," *New York Times*, September 10, 1973, p. 16.
16. Willie and McCord, pp. 73-13.
17. Ibid.
18. National Advisory Commission on Civil Disorders, *Report* (New York: Bantam, 1968).

# 14 Affirmative Action Practice: Desegregating the Faculty and Staff

I have been a faculty member of a university more than a quarter of a century. Presently, I have a tenured appointment at Harvard University where I serve as Professor of Education and Urban Studies in the Graduate School of Education. Earlier I was affiliated with Syracuse University, where I was appointed as an Instructor of Sociology in 1952. At Syracuse University, I served in every rank from Instructor to Professor. Moreover, I did my stint as Chairman of the Department of Sociology for four years and became a full-time administrator in 1972 as Vice President of the University.

I share with you this brief biographical sketch of my career to indicate the extent of my experience in institutions of higher education. One could say that I was present at the creation of Affirmative Action in higher education. Affirmative action is designed to increase the number of women and minorities on faculties and staffs of colleges and universities and to guarantee equality in employment opportunities. Affirmative action in higher education is analyzed from a perspective that includes my personal experiences.

Federal Executive Order #11246 issued in 1965 required that ". . . all contractors, including universities with research contracts, sign an agreement not to 'discriminate against any employee or applicant for employment because of race, color, religion, or national origin.' Sex was added to that list by Executive Order #11375, effective October 1968. . . ."[1] Later, in 1972, the President signed into law Title IX, which amended the Civil Rights Act of 1964. It stated explicitly that sex discrimination is prohibited as a matter of public law and that the prohibition against discrimination in Title VI of the Civil Rights Act which exempted educational institutions originally now applies to all of them, whether or not they have federal assistance. Moreover, the Higher Education Amendments of 1972 extended the provisions of the Equal Pay Act to cover executive, administrative, and professional employees in colleges and universities.[2] The effective dates for federal action, then, which rendered race and sex discrimination in higher education illegal and which provided procedures for granting relief to aggrieved parties were 1965, 1968, and 1972. It was during these years that affirmative action came of age. Thus the federal laws and Executive Orders prohibiting discrimination because of race or sex came approximately 100 years after the Fourteenth Amendment to the Constitution, which guaranteed "equal protection of the laws" for all citizens born or naturalized in the United States.

The Carnegie Council on Policy Studies in Higher Education issued a report containing twenty-seven recommendations. The full report, "Making Affirmative

161

Action Work," was published by Jossey-Bass, Inc., of San Francisco, California. *The Chronicle of Higher Education*[3] is the source of the information about the recommendations which I shall discuss. The most troublesome recommendations of the report were buried as recommendations 10, 11, 12, 13, and 15. My purpose is to unearth these and to expose them to the sunlight of cross-examination. These recommendations will be analyzed in relation to my personal experiences in the past with affirmative action.

Recommendation 10 of the Carnegie Council on Policy Studies seems to be of little consequence, but on closer analysis is a passive way that the higher education system can cop out. It states that "institutions of higher education should emphasize policies and procedures that will provide opportunities for women and minorities to serve in administrative positions." The sentiment of this recommendation is laudable but the language is lamentable. It is too mild and permissive. In a recent speech at the seventieth annual meeting of the American Sociological Association in San Francisco, Benjamin Payton, a program officer of the Ford Foundation, called for more minorities and women in management positions in foundations and other organizations. He said that their presence in these organizations at the management level probably is more important than serving as trustees or as members of the board of directors. The management level is where the action is in most organizations, he said. Although administrators operate within the guidelines provided by higher authority, their recommendations for action are accepted more frequently than they are rejected. For this reason, they occupy a strategic position as initiators of action.

Not only for the benefit of the college or university as a whole but also for the benefit of newly recruited minority and women students, persons other than white males *must* be added to the management staff of colleges and universities. My study of *Black Students at White Colleges* indicates that black administrators frequently provide the only link of trust between predominantly white institutions and their minority students.[4] "Must" is a stronger word than the indecisive phrase "higher education *should emphasize* policies and procedures . . . ," which was contained in the report of the Carnegie Council (emphasis added). Minority students will not trust a college or university that excludes minorities from the faculty and staff.

The President and Fellows at Harvard, in a statement of *Reaffirmation of the University's Policy Concerning Nondiscrimination and Equal Employment Opportunity*, said, "It is not sufficient merely to have a policy." How well they spoke! The university's Affirmative Action Officer said, "We have . . . had a great deal of trouble and have been forced into confrontation with department heads on listing of high level administrative positions with the Personnel Office."[5] This statement by the Affirmative Action Officer demonstrates that it is not sufficient merely to have a policy of equal opportunity employment. Harvard has a policy, but the Affirmative Action Officer found a lack of commitment to implementing it. In fact, he found this to be the prevailing attitude among some administrators with reference to affirmative action policies and procedures: "How little can I do to fulfill the requirements of the policy . . . since I already have a candidate?" In most cases, said Harvard's Affirmative Action Officer, the preferred candidate was white and male; the recruitment *practice* made the affirmative action *policy* a sham, he said.[6]

Hence, the Carnegie Council's recommendation is timid and too limited. Placing a new emphasis on an old policy is not enough if more women and minorities are to be employed as faculty and administrators in predominantly white colleges and universities. Institutions of higher education tended to act and to act affirmatively with reference to the employment of women and minorities when internal and external pressures work in concert. Walter Leonard said, "It is clear . . . that educational institutions moved one step closer to the practice of the principles of equal employment opportunity and affirmative action only at a time that the federal government was functioning as a reviewer of Civil Rights practices of these various institutions."[7] The Carnegie Council, therefore, should have called for new enforcement initiatives by the federal government and the escalation of activities by women and racial minority groups against discrimination in college and university, as a way of implementing public law that already exists. A basic principle of social change is that those who suffer oppression, rejection, and exclusion will continue to be oppressed until they decide to cease cooperating in their own oppression. Thus colleges and universities are not likely to take new affirmative action initiatives voluntarily. They usually respond to pressure.

The report of the Carnegie Council on Policy Studies in Higher Education is filled with notions of what colleges and universities as corporate authorities should do in behalf of women and minorities. The report is silent on what these groups must do themselves. Yet the major institutions of our society, including the government, did nothing to get blacks off the back of the bus, for example—despite the presence of the Thirteenth and Fourteenth Amendments to the Constitution, which eliminated slavery and involuntary servitude and guaranteed all equal protection of the laws. Until blacks, through Rosa Parks, decided to cease cooperating in their own oppression, segregated seating continued. She refused to give up her seat to a white person and move to the back of the bus. Her act of personal resistance was the beginning of the movement in Montgomery, Alabama, that finally ended officially sanctioned segregation in the area of public accommodations.

Indeed the practice of excluding blacks from matriculating as graduate students with full rights and privileges to participate in all aspects of the learning environment at professional schools in the South was not ended because of a new policy-emphasis by these schools. It ended because of a challenge by members of the minority population, a favorable decision by the Supreme Court, and enforcement of the law by the government. Texas created a separate law school for Heman Sweatt in response to his effort to enroll in the University of Texas

Law School. In *Sweatt* v. *Painter*, the Court ruled that this arrangement was inadequate in that the segregated school for blacks further contributed to "isolation" and did not facilitate "the interplay of ideas and the exchange of views" with the dominant majority. The University of Oklahoma admitted G.W. McLaurin to its graduate school and eventually let him use "the same classroom, library and cafeteria . . ." but insisted on assigning him to a seat or a table designated for colored students. The Supreme Court ruled in *McLaurin* v. *Oklahoma State Regents* that seating McLaurin apart from the other students "would impair and inhibit his ability to study, to engage in discussions and exchange views with other students," and hence was unconstitutional.[8]

I digress to elaborate upon these happenings at midcentury to demonstrate the dual contribution of *challenge* and *response* to social change. Policies and procedures are of value, but they are not enough. They do not displace challenge in the scheme of social change. In fact, they probably develop only as part of an appropriate response to an effective challenge. The mild and permissive language of the Carnegie Council about emphasizing policies and procedures that will provide opportunities for women and minorities to serve in administrative positions appears to be the plaintive call by those who want rain without thunder and lightning and who want new crops without plowing and tilling the soil. Years ago, Frederick Douglass, ex-slave and great black statesman, reminded us this could not be. Desegregating faculties and student bodies in schools, colleges, and universities can be a turbulent and disrupting experience. It is well that colleges and universities prepare to endure the difficulties by realizing that they are not fully in control of the process of challenge and response as much as the Carnegie Council's recommendation suggests that they are.

Recommendation 11 of the Carnegie Council on Policy Studies in Higher Education calls for goals and timetables, as well as strictly nondiscriminatory policies for each department, with reference to the appointment of instructors and assistant professors. This recommendation commits the sin of omission by exempting departments from a requirement of developing goals and timetables for tenured appointments. By eliminating tenured or senior faculty appointments from the promises which departments make, regarding their intention to diversify the faculty, the Carnegie Council, in effect, is promoting selective justice. Selective justice, of course, is no justice at all.

Decisions about the promotion and retention of junior faculty (instructors and assistant professors) usually are reserved for action by the tenured senior faculty. In effect, the senior faculty at most colleges and universities operates as a jury before which the accomplishments of younger members in the profession are paraded. Junior faculty members are weighed and considered and a thoughtful decision eventually is rendered concerning their accomplishments and their potential for scholarly activity. Because judgment is a subjective factor, different perspectives are necessary and essential if a just decision is to be rendered. Without appropriate diversity, a tenured senior faculty that is homogeneously male and white is likely to extend invitations only to those members of the junior faculty who are fashioned in its own image. If the senior faculty is not diversified in terms of race, sex, and other characteristics of its members, it should be as a matter of policy, as the court requires such diversity in juries for the sake of justice. To accomplish appropriate diversity, the setting of attainable goals and a commitment to their fulfillment are necessary, for the senior tenured faculty as well as the junior faculty.

At Harvard University, the Affirmative Action Officer described the employment of minorities as a bleak and discouraging picture. He asked, rhetorically, why there had not been a better performance in recruiting and retaining racial minorities on the junior faculty. As if answering himself, he observed that the senior faculty of tenured professors at Harvard in the mid-1970s consisted of 766, twenty of whom were women and thirty-six minority males. Women and minorities were less than eight percent of the tenured faculty. These figures, in part, contained the answer. Senior faculty have a great deal to say about who become junior faculty and who among junior faculty receive tenure. There must be a change in the kinds of people who are senior faculty if there is to be a corresponding change in the kinds of people who are invited to join the junior faculty. Also women and racial minorities who are few in number as junior faculty members are not likely to be promoted to the ranks of senior faculty if their seniors are exclusively male and white. All of this is to say that the senior faculty cannot be exempted from affirmative action requirements if the junior faculty is to be diversified.

Recommendation 11 of the Carnegie Council does have a positive thrust in stating that "a search for outside candidates for tenure appointments will be appropriate . . . ." This search will be initiated and continued only if there is a firmly stated goal and a timetable for the implementation of the goal. For example, the Graduate School of Education at Harvard identified in 1969 the appointment of a tenured professor proficient in the area of Education and Urban Studies as a goal to be fulfilled. It carried on a continuous search for five years before making an appointment and would have despaired had the goal not been publicly stated. As late as 1975. no women and no blacks held tenured faculty appointments in the Department of History and the Department of English at Harvard.[9] One wonders if these departments would have been without such diversity at that period in their history if a publicly stated goal to achieve diversity had been established earlier.

My experience at Syracuse University as one of the original members of the Affirmative Action Committee was similar to the Harvard experience. Departments which set goals tended to fulfill them. Departments that did not, tended to drag their feet. For example, in the early years of the 1970 decade, when affirmative action first appeared on the Syracuse University campus, some members of the Religion Department seemed to resent inquiries into why women or minorities were not among senior faculty members. As a contrast, the

Sociology Department, at that time, welcomed the requirements of affirmative
action, chose diversity as a goal, had a black chairperson, two other blacks, and
a woman of Japanese-American ancestry on the faculty. The experience of the
Department of Sociology at Syracuse University is no different from that of the
Department of Sociology of the University of Massachusetts in Boston during
the middle years of the 1970 decade, when there was a black chairperson, other
minorities, and women on the faculty in all ranks. The same may be said of the
University of Pennsylvania's Department of Sociology, which celebrated the
Bicentennial year with a woman scholar in charge as chairperson. Where there
are minorities and women in positions of power on the senior faculty, sometimes
it makes a difference in the faculty profile of a department. These selected examples indicate why it is important to have women and minorities as members
of the tenured faculty. This cannot be accomplished without goals and an appropriate timetable. Without such, most departments will follow their customary
procedures and recruit  conventional candidates.

By setting goals for diversifying the tenured faculty and deliberately searching for candidates, the faculty is forced to reflect upon its definition of excellence
and to determine if it is too narrow. By exempting tenured faculty appointments
from the full affirmative action process, the Carnegie Council's recommendation
would open the door to further abuses in the area of institutional racism, sexism,
and elitism, the three major forms of institutional discrimination that are alive
and well on college campuses and that are enemies to diversification.

Thomas Pettigrew has stated that "institutional racism is extremely difficult
to combat effectively . . . ." He goes on to say:


Many of these arrangements, perhaps even most of them, were originally designed
and established to serve positive functions for the institution without thought
of their racial implications. They have been used precisely because they do in
fact accomplish these positive functions. Thus, Harvard University in the 1930's
set up a variety of meaningful criteria, including publication of scholarly works,
to select their tenured faculty of high quality. Yet the publishing requirements
effectively acted to restrict the recruitment of Black professors, for most of them
carried heavy teaching loads in predominantly Black Colleges, which limited their
time to write. Not surprisingly, then, Harvard University in the 1960's found
itself with only a handful of Black faculty members. Yet the university is understandably loath to give up a selection procedure that has served its intended
function well, though its unintended racist consequences are a matter of record.
This example can be repeated almost endlessly in American society. The problem, then, is not simply to eliminate racist arrangements, difficult as that alone
would be, but to replace these arrangements with others that serve the same
positive functions equally well without the racist consequences.[10]


Pettigrew, a Harvard professor, said that he used the Harvard example because it is close to his experience. He said, "It . . . illustrates how each of us can
find prime examples of institutional racism in our immediate lives," and he urged

individuals who ask what can be done to combat racism "to work for structural change in the very institutions of which they are participants." For instance, as a transitional device to encourage intransigent departments to seek minority candidates, he states that the university could set aside a certain portion of faculty funds which would be made available only to those units that find competent minority faculty members. This way, Pettigrew believes, the competitive system within the university for funds would be inverted and departments would have a financial incentive to find new kinds of faculty members. Some may disagree with this approach, but it or other creative devices may be necessary in the interim before there is full-scale commitment to affirmative action by all departments for all faculty ranks. The exemption of tenured appointments from affirmative action goal-setting and timetable requirements as recommended by the Carnegie Council would indirectly sanction the institutional racism and sexism that presently exists in higher education and would delay the search for new and ingenious ways of overcoming these unjust forms of exclusion and oppression. In effect, the recommended exemption of tenured faculty appointments not only would perpetuate institutional discrimination but would slow down and, in some instances, cancel the beginnings of institutional change now in evidence. The tenured faculty sit at the top of the academic power hierarchy and tend to call the shots. They, therefore, need to be diversified, consisting of members with multiple perspectives based on different existential histories. There is an increased probability that the decisions of such an academic power structure will be just and equitable.

Recommendation 12 of the Carnegie Council on Policy Studies in Higher Education states that "timetables should be set for periods not exceeding five to ten years. The institutions should make good-faith effort to achieve its goals for additions of women and minorities to the faculty during that period." A simple response to this recommendation is a long-standing legal principle that justice delayed is justice denied. If segregated public education (including a segregated faculty) is inherently unequal education and, therefore, unconstitutional as determined by the Supreme Court, now is the time for the United States to abide by its Constitution. This is what law and order are all about.

Some who call for a gradual approach do so not as a way of evading change. They know that opportunity for planning before implementation of decrees, for example, such as those governing desegregation, can cushion the impact of the new behavior required; in the planning process some of the shock of the requirements can be absorbed before the events actually occur.[11] The planning process also can lead to an opposite outcome. Such a period before implementation of a decree governing desegregation of the faculty and staff may provide sufficient time for opposition to crystalize and for cleavages among adversaries in the organization to develop.[12] There is no inherent advantage in slowing down or speeding up conformance with affirmative action requirements. A five-to-ten-year period could be an asset or a liability depending on the setting and the circumstances.

In view of the charges by some white males that deliberate efforts to create opportunities for members of black and brown minority groups is reverse discrimination (despite the fact that there were proportionately fewer blacks as university teachers in 1970 than in 1960), my best guess is that further delay in the implementation of affirmative action—say, five to ten years—would provide the time for further development and crystalization of opposition and would contribute to greater cleavages among groups that formerly stood together against oppression.

If the kind of reaction persists which has been given in the testimony before the House of Representative's Special Subcommittee on Education, and which has been reported in *The Chronicle of Higher Education*[13], we are in for tough sledding. The opposition mounting already is severe but is often disguised as efforts to maintain excellence. What would such opposition be like after five to ten years of indecisive action, as recommended by the Carnegie Council?

Based on this analysis, I am inclined to be guided by two other principles set forth by Williams and Ryan in their study of community decision-making and desegregation. First, they state that "a clear definition of law and policy by legitimate . . . authorities may reinforce willingness to conform to the requirements of new situations." Hence, the great importance of clarity and decisiveness in the policy articulated and in the practices engaged in during the early months and years of a desegregation program such as affirmative action cannot be overemphasized. Second, Williams and Ryan point out that "long-drawn-out efforts and fluctuating policies appear to maximize confusion and resistance." If one were to base affirmative action policy on the Williams and Ryan finding pertaining to desegregation, one would have to opt for a "clearcut policy, administered with understanding but also with resolution . . . ."[14]

To permit colleges and universities five to ten years to fulfill the requirements of affirmative action as recommended by the Carnegie Council would diminish the "moral capital" and reveal them to be self-centered agencies concerned with justice and decency only to the extent that these are required in the operations of systems other than higher education. Richard Lester said university personnel would be "on the defensive" morally for favoring federal action against race and sex discrimination in employment for industry but not for universities.

Their image would be tarnished no less than that of some religious organizations in the United States which are embroiled in controversy pertaining to an affirmative action matter of whether or not women can seek work as priests in the church. The learned leaders of the church may rationalize discrimination against women. Nevertheless, they look pretty silly trying to seal off the pulpit to professional priests who are female and barring them from the communion table as celebrants. The approach of some sexist religious organizations symbolically is not unlike that of standing in the schoolhouse doorway to prevent blacks from entering. Male religious leaders look especially silly doing this when one recognizes that the members of religious organizations were some of the most ardent advocates for the 1964 Civil Rights Act, which made it unlawful for business to discriminate in employment.

The public response will be negative to a discriminating system of higher education, if it should default on its search for truth by excluding women and minorities from full participation in the learning environment.

The time for justice and equity is now. The stretch-out form of the cop-out will not work. Colleges and universities do not need five to ten years to fulfill their affirmative action plans. An interesting finding of the Annual Audit of Departments of Sociology authorized by the American Sociological Association shows the progress of affirmative action to date in sensitizing that profession to ways of recruiting minorities and women. During a three-year period the percentage of departments that reported difficulty in locating women and minority scholars was significantly reduced. In 1972-73, 80 to 85 percent of the sociology departments said they had difficulty in locating minorities—male or female; but this percentage dropped in three years to a figure of 50 to 55 percent. With reference to women the percent who had difficulty in locating them dropped from 32 to 15 percent during the same three-year period.[15] The locating of minorities, which looked like an impossible job once upon a time, now is becoming easier so far as sociology is concerned. And the ease with which departments are able to find minorities and women has occurred within a period of three years, not five to ten years.

Recommendation 13 of the Carnegie Council on Policy Studies in Higher Education states that "the Department of Labor—in consultation with the Department of Health, Education, and Welfare—should develop a special supplement or set of interpretations to [the Department of Labor's] Revised Order Number 4 that will be especially appropriate for higher education . . . . Data requirements should be revised to reflect the modified provisions . . . . [For example,] separate data should not be required on . . . tenure [and] transfer [reassignment] . . . ." I already have spoken about the need to keep tabs on the affirmative action process with reference to the appointment of tenured professors. Without records on transfers, it could become the venerable "clerical error" which is a way that grades can be changed on the official transcript in most schools without further justification. To bypass equal opportunity requirements, new appointments for white males already on the faculty or staff could be called transfers, if transfers were exempted from the affirmative action process.

Recommendation 15 of the Carnegie Council on Policy Studies is the final one that I will comment upon. It recommends that an institution which demonstrates that its proportion of women and minorities among faculty members and other academic employees is similar to the pool of such qualified persons, and that minorities and women are well distributed throughout the institution should be exempted from requirements calling for continuous reassessment of goals and timetables; also it is recommended that institutions with a demonstrated good record of recruitment and employment of women and minorities should be exempted from detailed reporting requirements relating to academic employment. One observation against this recommendation is that few problems are solved once and for all times by individuals or institutions. All should be anxious about keeping honest. The periodic audit is one method of keeping that way.

In his report to the annual meeting of the Associated Harvard Alumni on Commencement Day 1975, Derek Bok, President of Harvard, set forth the best case for affirmative action monitoring that I have heard. While he counseled against "ill-advised government restraint," at the same time he acknowledged that "private universities will not necessarily meet their obligations to society if they are left entirely to their own devices." For example, he said that "universities did not provide adequate opportunities for women or minority groups until the Congress required them to do so."[16] A reporter asked Kingman Brewster, when he was president of Yale, if universities would have hired and admitted more women and minorities if the government hadn't pushed. His reply was succinct and straightforward: "No, not as effectively." Then he said: ". . . In terms of getting cracking with adequate search procedures and adequate administrative surveillance . . . the affirmative action thing has not been a wasted effort."[17]

Finally, Bok said, "It would be folly to assume that the government will not continue to intervene, or to content ourselves with last-minute efforts to block legislation and preserve the status quo." Bok called upon colleges and universities "to seize the initiative and help to devise new mechanisms that will enable higher education to work with the government to insure that universities respond to public needs without being subject to restrictions that ignore [their] special circumstances and impair [their] ability to be of continuing use to society."[18]

These remarks seem to me to be a more sensible approach than continuing to lobby for the exemption of higher education from affirmative action requirements. The pressure for suspension of continuous reporting is a call for return to the status quo. Remember that in the past higher education did not provide adequate opportunities for women or minorities until the federal government required it to do so. It is too soon to talk about eliminating governmental surveillance of an unjust condition. To return to the status quo is to return to race and sex discrimination, a record of which colleges and universities should be ashamed.

The story of affirmative action in higher education in the United States is a unique development of the final trimester of the twentieth century. It is too soon to fully assess its benefits. But leading voices in education are increasingly supporting it despite some obvious defects. Affirmative action guarantees the presence of all sorts and conditions of people on the college campus, necessary ingredients for truth-seeking institutions.

## Notes

1. Richard A Lester, *Antibias Regulation of Universities* (New York: McGraw-Hill Book Company, 1974), pp. 3, 133.

2. Committee on Education and Labor, *Hearings before the Special Subcommittee on Education*, Part 2B, Appendix, Civil Rights Obligations (Washington, D.C.: U.S. Government Printing Office, 1975), pp. 805, 1014, 1016.

3. *Chronicle of Higher Education*, "Carnegie Council's Affirmative-Action Recommendations," August 18, 1975, pp. 3, 4.

4. Charles V. Willie and Arline Sakuma McCord, *Black Students at White Colleges* (New York: Praeger, 1972), p. 59.

5. Walter J. Leonard, "Walter Leonard Finds Few Gains Have Been Made in Affirmative Action Here," *Harvard Gazette*, March 14, 1975, pp. 8, 9.

6. Ibid., pp. 8, 9.

7. Ibid., pp. 8, 9.

8. Notre Dame Center for Civil Rights, *The Continuing Challenge: The Past and the Future of Brown vs. Board of Education* (Evanston: Integrated Education Associates, 1975), p. 3.

9. Leonard, pp. 8, 9.

10. Thomas F. Pettigrew, "Racism and the Mental Health of White Americans: A Social Psychological View," in Charles V. Willie, Bernard M. Kramer, and Bertram S. Brown, eds., *Racism and Mental Health* (Pittsburgh: University of Pittsburgh Press, 1973), pp. 275, 276.

11. Robin M. Williams and Margaret W. Ryan, *Schools in Transition* (Chapel Hill: University of North Carolina Press, 1954), pp. 239, 242, 247.

12. Ibid., p. 239.

13. Cheryl M. Fields, "Affirmative Action: Changes in Offing," *Chronicle of Higher Education*, August 18, 1975, pp. 3, 4.

14. Williams and Ryan, p. 242.

15. Joan R. Harris, "Women and Minorities in Sociology: Findings from Annual ASA Audit," *ASA Footnotes*, January 1975, p. 4.

16. Derek C. Bok, "Harvard: Then, Now and the Future," *Harvard Today* Vol. 18, No. 3 (1975), p. 4.

17. *Boston Globe*, "Kingman Brewster, Jr.," March 20, 1977, p. 2.

18. Bok, p. 4.

# 15 Conclusion: The American Dream and the Dreamers

We conclude this book with a chapter that focuses on the contribution of minorities to stability and change in human society. They are the creative dissenters who increase our ethical stature and keep alive the vision of justice for all. Minorities are the people most likely to do this in any society because their well-being depends on how well the total society accommodates deviations from the norm. The maintenance of an equilibrium in social organization contributes to social stability. Yet, a stable society will rigidify an eventually will decay without continuous movement that results in renewal and social change. From the beginning of this society, the minorites have been the dreamers. They have alternatively focused on new social arrangements or fulfillment of the professed values of the society. Their concepts of new social arrangements in due time have been adopted by the society at large as the norm. Eventually they become the venerated practices of the majority. It is appropriate, then, to classify minorities as the dreamers in society who initiate social change.

Dreams are filled with . . . symbolic representations of repressed desires," said psychologist Calvin Hall. "We dream about what we want." For example, "A hungry person who has a mental representation of food is in a better position to satisfy his hunger than is a person who does not know what to look for. [Otherwise] . . . a person could satisfy his [or her] needs only through trial-and-error behavior."[1]

When Martin Luther King, Jr., said, "I have a dream," he was not engaged in aimless rhetoric. He was stating his mental representation of how he would like the United States to be. According to Freudian pscyhology, it is necessary to have an image of what one needs before one can set about getting it. We dream about what we want. Martin Luther King, Jr., said his dream—his image of America as a nation—was that one day it would "rise up and live out the true meaning of its creed: 'We hold these truths to be self-evident; that all . . . are created equal.' "[2]

In this respect, a dream is a phase of reality. It is the run before the jump, the identification of that which one wants or needs and enables one to go about getting it. It is not an illusion.

King said his dream was "deeply rooted in the American dream." It is fair to classify the Preamble to the Constitution as the American dream. The Preamble does not have the force of law. It identifies what the American people want. The Constitution attempts to fulfill these images and wishes that are expressed in its Preamble.

It might be helpful to review the guiding images for a nation governed by a Constitution based on the consent of the people. These are the images for our government which were held by the members of the Constitutional Convention in 1787. They believed that the Constitution they recommended would enable the people of the United States to:

1.  form a more perfect union,
2.  establish justice,
3.  insure domestic tranquility,
4.  provide for the common defense,
5.  promote the general welfare,
6.  secure the blessing of liberty for [persons] living then [and] their posterity.

This was the dream of what could be. The actual experience of government in America in 1787 was quite different.

Then, the holding of property was a qualification for suffrage. And "the cruel and barbarous system of imprisonment for debt . . . continued in several of the states long after the Revolution."[3]

Philosopher John Rawls has defined justice as fairness.[4]  Since the power to vote was limited to men who owned property, there was majority rule by those who could vote. But the voters were limited to the minority of affluent men of property. There was no protection for the poor or those not permitted to vote even though the poor at that time were the majority. Such a system was unfair; which is to say, such a government was unjust. It is only because members of the Constitutional Convention were idealists who had a dream, an image, a mental representation of what could be, that they were able to transcend their experience of what was, at that time. They, of course, were acting in their self-interest as well as in the interest of the majority of the people. We fast were approaching a breakdown in social organization toward the close of the eighteenth century which would have erased the gains of the revolution, without significant changes in our society.

Today we tend to idolize the pragmatists—the no-nonsense persons who have a good understanding and a firm grasp on public affairs. We esteem the realists, not the idealists. Yet we celebrated the Bicentennial of this nation because the members of the Constitutional Convention had a dream that the people of this nation could establish justice, promote the general welfare, and secure the blessings of liberty for all—and not just for the affluent people of property. Had they been realists or pragmatists, they would have settled for what was and never dreamed of what could be. Had they done this, your life and my life would be different today.

The dream then and now has had the same function. It is a mental representation of what could be rather than an actual indication of what is. Moreover, the dream is still necessary if we are to transform what we are into what we could become.

The main difference with the present compared with the past is that the dreamers have changed. During the latter half of the twentieth century, the dreamers are black or brown, they are preachers or professors, female or youthful. They dream dreams, too; and these are not less significant for our way of life now than were those dreams of the past by the founders of this nation. Then, the dreamers were male and white, merchants and manufacturers, property and plantation owners. Most of the delegates to the Constitutional Convention were lawyers by profession,[5] not farmers, artisans, black and brown people, or women. Dreamers are not limited to any category of people. They may be rich. They may be poor. They may be lawyers. They may be laborers. Sometimes they are students.

Our Bicentennial was celebrated while the United States was at peace with the world. What a glorious celebration it was—because of our 200 years of freedom and because of our timely experience with peace.

The dreamers called for peace long before the decision-makers would respond. In the 1960s, Martin Luther King, Jr., reminded us of the admonition in the Scriptures to love our enemies. Then he asked the question: "Have we not come to such an impasse in the modern world that we *must* love our enemies—or else?" (emphasis added). The answer he gave was this: "The chain reaction of hate begetting hate, wars producing more wars must be broken, or we shall be plunged into the . . . abyss of annihilation."

Because of his opposition to the Vietnam War, King was criticized severely by some black as well as white members of the Establishment. They said he was an idealist; they called themselves realists.

Toward the close of the 1960 decade, young people began to oppose the war too. They dreamed dreams of peace. And because of their dreams, they were called idealists. The youth of those years resisted the name-calling of their elders. Said one young worker in a national campaign for the election of the President, "This college generation is very patriotic. If we don't do something now for this country, it's going to blow. It's up to us." The university youth at the close of the 1960s were characterized as a group most worthy of consideration. They were the dreamers of that period.

It was not until the 1970s that the politicians really began to respond. At a Yale University lecture in 1971, Senator J. William Fulbright foresaw the decline of constitutional democracy in the United States if this nation did not reverse its foreign policy based on what he called "great-power militarism." Then, in measured speech, he said, "Neither constitutional government nor democratic freedom can survive indefinitely in a country chronically at war . . . ."[6]

Earlier, the dreamers—some black and others young—tried to tell us this to save our society. But we would not listen. Eventually the war that none could win came to an inglorious but realistic end, as the idealists had predicted years before.

Herein lies our difficulty. The American dream is not an illusion. But our response is often disillusioning. We want to maintain what is and to deny what could be. The merchants and manufacturers, the people of property—the dominant people of power—no longer dream dreams as they did during the Constitutional Convention. Today, they are the realists, not the idealists. They refer to dreams as illusions.

But I declare unto you that dreams are still necessary if this society is to renew itself. Without dreams, images, and mental representations of what could be, our society would spend itself in endless routine behavior, focusing on being rather than on becoming.

Today the dreamers are black or brown, female or young. And they insist that we deal with the possibilities of the future as well as the problems of the present and the realities of the past.

The maintenance of a system of justice is of high priority, according to the dreamers. Not only justice, but honesty and truthfulness should be significant goals for America. Our recent history has demonstrated this. We have just experienced the double tragedies in less than two decades of two Presidents deposed from their office by assassination and resignation. Our nation ignored the dreamers and was caught up in perpetuating its power and what is. The United States fell prey to a great evil and forgot about what it could and should be. Government agents, using public funds, conspired to murder some leaders of other nations. Meanwhile, the leader of our own country was killed, demonstrating that no one is invincible and all-powerful.

We are paying a fearsome price for not honoring the ideals of our contemporary dreamers. James Russel Lowell, a nineteenth-century dreamer, observed that "the real will never find an irremovable basis till it rests on the ideal."[7] Our nation needs to learn this lesson, and learn it well.

A study by Marie Peters, that was submitted as a dissertation to the Harvard Graduate School of Education in 1976, revealed that black parents rank honesty and truthfulness in their children as very important. The idealists continue to speak. It is well that we listen. Failure to do so could be tragic.

Veracity is something of value. Where there is not truth, there is not freedom. When there is not freedom, there is not justice. When there is not justice, there is oppression. And this I believe: the oppressors, whether they be individuals or institutions, will receive their just reward.

The trouble is not with the American dream. The problem is how we respond to the American dreamers. We too often will not listen to the dreamers who are minorities, young people, and women. Indeed, our public policy is to remake them in the image of men or the majority, without recognizing their unique function as dreamers, the creative dissidents.

The creative dissidents saved this nation from the brutality of slavery, the political tyranny of minority rule by a male aristocracy, and recently from the continuous erosion of personal freedom of three decades of war. We would not have the kind of constitution we now have if the dreamers of the past had been ignored then as we attempt to ignore them now. Then, as now, they were a minority who saw things a bit differently. The dreamers are the iconoclasts. They break with the old and make way for the new.

We would not be experiencing the disorganization associated with school desegregation in our communities today if we had followed the letter and spirit of the Constitution, prepared by our dreamers of the past. And failing that, we still might have been spared our difficulties of this day had we listened to the forecast of our contemporary dreamer. In 1963, in Washington, D.C., Martin Luther King, Jr., said, "The whirlwind of revolt will continue to shake the foundations of our nation until the bright day of justice emerges."[8]

We killed our dreamer. What do you think happened to his dreams? They have been resurrected in legislation, administrative regulations, and judicial determinations that promote affirmative action, proclaim equality of opportunity, and prohibit discrimination.

There is nothing wrong with the American dream. The problem is our response to the American dreamers. Yet, there is hope. We may kill our dreamers, but not their dreams.

The creative dissidents are called upon to save our society from its institutional sins of sexism, racism, and elitism that can slowly undermine our historical belief in liberty, equality, and justice for all. They have saved us before and they can do it again.

## Notes

1. Calvin Hall, *A Primer of Freudian Psychology* (New York: Mentor Books, 1954), pp. 101, 25, 26.

2. Martin Luther King, Jr., "I Have a Dream," speech delivered at the March on Washington, Lincoln Memorial, Washington, D.C., August 28, 1963.

3. J. Allen Smith, "The American Government of the Revolutionary Period," in A.N. Christiansen and E.M. Kirkpatrick, eds., *The People, Politics, and the Politician* (New York: Henry Holt and Co., 1941), pp. 34-36.

4. John Rawls, *A Theory of Justice* (Cambridge: Harvard University Press, 1971), pp. 12-17.

5. J. Mark Jacobson, "Writing the National Constitution," in A.N. Christiansen and E.M. Kirkpatrick, eds., *The People, Politics, and the Politician* (New York: Henry Holt and Co., 1941), p. 39.

6. *New York Times,* April 4, 1971, p. 27.

7. James Russell Lowell, "Democracy," in Charles W. Elliot, ed., *Essays*

*English and American* (New York: P.F. Collier and Son, 1938), p. 451.

8. Lotte Haskins, *"I Have a Dream," The Quotations of Martin Luther King, Jr.* (New York: Grosset and Dunlop, 1968), p. 63.

# Index

# Index

## About the Author

**Charles Vert Willie**, a sociologist, is Professor of Education and Urban Studies at the Graduate School of Education of Harvard University. He was awarded the Bachelor of Arts, Master of Arts, and Doctor of Philosophy degrees by Morehouse College, Atlanta University, and Syracuse University, respectively. At Syracuse, he was Chairman of the Department of Sociology and Vice President for Student Affairs.

Dr. Willie has served as a court-appointed Master in the Boston school-desegregation case, an expert witness in the Dallas school-desegregation case, a consultant to the Illinois Department of Education to evaluate the Chicago desegregation plan, and a member of the President's Commission on Mental Health.

His articles on education and desegregation have appeared in *School Review, Integrated Education, Educational Record,* the *Journal of Negro Education, Psychology Today,* and *Ebony.* His books include *Black Students at White Colleges; Oreo, A Perspective on Race and Marginal Men and Women;* and *Black Colleges in America.*